# PRAISE FOR *DOWSING BEYO*

M000199924

"Dave Cowan attended my class several years ago and was remembered because of his intelligent comments. Meeting him again recently, he impressed me with his knowledge and abilities. I believe you will find this book interesting and helpful."
    —Raymon Grace, author of *The Future Is Yours*

"The healing wisdom of Spiritual Dowsing is a practical way to bring us to the state of peace, love and joy that is a natural result of communication between our conscious and superconscious mind. In that state, all answers are available to us through accessing One Consciousness. This is the most incredible experience of Love and Blessings that Spiritual Dowsing brings to our lives. *Dowsing Beyond Duality* not only reflects the philosophy of Oneness but also presents the way to live it. In my experience as a Spiritual Dowser and Healer, this book offers the most practical, complete, and effective processes for transformation into Oneness, Consciousness, and Spiritual Healing."
    —Miriam Divinsky, M.A., Ph.D., *www.LivingByIntent.com*, founder of
    Center for Wellness, New Jersey

# PRAISE FOR *NAVIGATING THE COLLAPSE OF TIME*

"I am a shamanic practitioner who has been both a scholarly and experiential student of the extraordinary period of change and transformation we're experiencing prophesied by indigenous shamans from the Q'ero, to the Hopi, Huichol and Mayan. *Navigating the Collapse of Time* has codified a tremendous amount of information and insight with a clarity that is also extraordinary. Dave is a tremendous teacher, a weaver of the mysterious threads of consciousness that frequently escape capture. I highly recommend this unifying piece of work."
    —Kevin Johnson, Shamanic Teacher

"*Navigating the Collapse of Time* stands apart from other metaphysical works about this timeframe transition. Simply put: David Cowan lives from a dimensional place of synergizing all theories and academics around this galactic transition. A treat awaits the reader. While experiencing the beauty of David's word pictures that warmly download the reader with energy, it's as if a catapulting occurs into self discovery as it relates to past, present and future time and planetary evolution with humor and fun."

   —Carol Calvert, Share the Light Community

"With David Cowan's book, *Navigating the Collapse of Time*, we get a fascinating picture of the transition period that is approaching for the human race. What kind of a transition it will be, and what nature and direction the illusory dream of time and space will take, is up to us, depending on how we choose our thoughts. I highly recommend this enjoyable page turner."

   —Gary Renard, the bestselling author of *The Disappearance of the Universe*

"I have known Dave for many years, and think highly of his work, both as an educator and an author. *Navigating the Collapse of Time* is no exception. Dave provides an educated and insightful look at what is transpiring in the world at this time. He has done a masterful job of pulling together so many possibilities and making sense of them all, helping us to navigate an uncertain but exciting future. Solid information coupled with wit and humor makes this book a 'must read.'"

   —Bonnie Bogner, Spiritual Teacher and Facilitator

"David Cowan has brought the question of extra dimensional contact down to earth, with a style that cuts straight through to the heart – like a metaphorical sword of truth. It is refreshing to find an author who can create new perspectives on the question of this age of transition, when the wisdom from higher dimensional beings speaks to our souls of all that lies before us."

   —Patricia Cori, author/channel of the Sirian Revelations

# DOWSING BEYOND DUALITY

## Access Your Power to Create Positive Change

David Ian Cowan and
Erina Carey Cowan

WEISER BOOKS
San Francisco, CA / Newburyport, MA

First published in 2012 by Weiser books, an imprint of
Red Wheel/Weiser, LLC
With offices at:
665 Third Street, Suite 400
San Francisco, CA 94107
*www.redwheelweiser.com*

ISBN: 978-1-57863-522-1

Library of Congress Cataloging-in-Publication Data available upon request

Cover design by Jim Warner
Cover photograph © Exactostock/SuperStock
Interior by Maureen Forys, Happenstance Type-O-Rama

Printed in the United States of America
MAL
10 9 8 7 6 5 4 3 2 1

# TABLE OF CONTENTS

# AUTHORS' NOTE

THANK YOU FOR PURCHASING THIS BOOK and taking this leap into a whole new realm of possibilities. This book represents over two decades of our combined dowsing experiences, many years of traveling a joined spiritual path together, and the remembrances of lifetimes of adventure and mastery in the Art of Dowsing.

By the time David and I met, we were both proficient dowsers and it was one of our earliest communication tools. "You show me yours, and I'll show you mine!" Both of us had seen amazing results in so many areas of our lives through the use of a pendulum as a tool to "shift energy." Over the last several years, we have cultivated this art together and have developed distinctly different styles in our approaches. David began to introduce biofeedback practitioners to the benefits of dowsing in classes he taught. I shared this technique with clients, friends and family members, and professional colleagues. We both appreciated the openness of this method and realized that there were no apparent boundaries to the use of this tool. Together we have offered this teaching to students worldwide.

We have witnessed an exponential growth in interest in dowsing over the last five years, with confidence in and creative exploration of this skill increasing as the practices of many of our students blossomed. During this time, David wrote two comprehensive dowsing manuals, which became big hits. These books transformed folks from neophytes to competent dowsing practitioners in a short period of time.

In our early days together, we were introduced to and embraced the teachings of *A Course in Miracles*. This is a self-taught course that corrects students' perceptions with the purpose of revealing what has always been true—that we are and always have been integral parts of One Creative Pulse in the Mind of God. This teaching has served us well and its principles are foundational to our understanding of spiritual healing. We realize that our spirits need no healing. Rather our minds, corrupt in the erroneous belief that we are somehow separate from our Source, need correction. We need only correct the misperceptions that have obscured love's presence from our vision to be healed and whole. I was inspired to create a third dowsing book to integrate our growing understanding of Truth with the practical applications of dowsing. We evolved our dowsing method to become a spiritual healing technique. More accurately, the focus of our dowsing method is to heal the mind of what conceals awareness of ourselves as Spirit. It is the purpose behind any action that determines whether it is brought into the realm of a spiritual practice.

We are grateful and honored to merge our manuals into one comprehensive guide to Spiritual Dowsing. The purpose of this book is to offer a practical method that anyone can master that has the potential to empower individuals, inspire life transformations, and contribute to the creation of a new world paradigm. We will expound more on the idea and practice of spiritual healing throughout this book. We invite you to dive in with total abandon, immersing yourself in this combined treasure of ours. Let us teach you the Art of Dowsing through spinning a pendulum—for the greater purpose of making room for miracles.

With gratitude,
ERINA CAREY COWAN, B.S.
*Licensed Spiritual Health Coach*
*Certified Spiritual Dowser*

# DISCLAIMER

THE INFORMATION IN THIS PUBLICATION is for educational purposes only. It is not intended to diagnose, prevent, cure, or treat any disease or illness, mental or physical. For the diagnosis or treatment of any disease, please consult a licensed practitioner.

# INTRODUCTION

AS DOWSING IS, IN ONE SENSE, AN AMPLIFICATION or focusing of a human potential to interact with Nature on many different levels or dimensions, its scope is potentially limitless. One of the challenges in putting together a volume like this one lies in deciding on the limits of what will be presented. Hopefully, readers and students of our method will grasp this open-ended potential and freely explore their own possibilities, discovering new horizons of insight and empowerment along the way.

The general theme here is that we are all much more powerful than we may have been led to believe, particularly in the power of our minds. Many today speak of "awakening." I believe the True Awakening lies in simply coming to realize what we already are as Divine and creative beings. The accumulated research into quantum physics has begun to explain how the mind, or consciousness, has always played a major role in determining our particular experience of reality. We have been making our reality all along, simply without being consciously aware of it. Our method will give you a tool to help you take control of your own mind and begin to steer your life in the direction you want to go.

As we grow in our power to affect ourselves, others, and the world positively, a heightened sense of responsibility must guide our behavior. Dowsing must only be used for "the highest good of all." If it is used for selfish gain or to inflict harm, the karmic backlash will be inevitable and, in some cases, immediate. The world and others are our mirrors. They show us, without exception, the exact content of our minds. If our motivation is for the uplifting, betterment, and healing of ourselves, others, and the planet, the results can only be positive for everyone.

Sometimes, you may not notice an immediate result from your efforts. Rest assured that you have been "heard." Often, there are circumstances and other players involved in a situation that need to move into the optimal position before your intention manifests. In this case, make your request and let it go.

This book can be read as simply a study or overview of an interesting topic to satisfy curiosity. However, unless you actually "dive in" and "play along," you may never truly appreciate the ideas presented. I heartily invite all readers to climb the learning curve. Do the work, and you will be rewarded beyond measure.

Why "Dowsing Beyond Duality"?

Duality simply means the apparent co-existence of opposites. It is rooted in a deeper assumption of the "reality" of the separation of objects and events in space and time. Although duality is a seemingly pervasive condition in our world, it is only a perceptual "sleight of hand" we play on a continual basis through our conditioned dependence on mental perception, language, and the unspoken agreements among us. We can say all thought is dualistic in that we select one discrete object or subject to observe to the exclusion of all else. And this chosen perception will always have an opposite among all of the unobserved and excluded phenomena.

Duality is neither good nor bad, but it is a condition that needs recognition. Once recognized, we can perceive the inherent limitations in the dualistic view, along with the broader possibilities in a non-dual perspective. All conflict is rooted in duality—opposite opinions, positions, moral judgments, and beliefs are only possible within a dualistic framework. The upside of duality—and duality demands that there be an upside—is that being in such a state forces you to exercise your will in navigating all of the choices you must continuously make. In so doing, you may ultimately become empowered to the point of consciously directing every thought and activity toward an altruistic goal and higher purpose, or to evolve as a conscious being. We can thus overcome the limitations of victimhood, blame, and projection; all mental habits that threaten the very survival of the human race at this point in our history.

The risk inherent in any healing modality, including dowsing, is that we may fall into the trap of making essentially artificial or illusory dualistic perceptions true or real simply by giving them attention. This tendency is known as reification—making real what is in truth only a perceptual symbol of a deeper reality. It is the trap of a diagnosis becoming a self-fulfilling prophesy.

This ego trap leads to endless attempts to heal (literally, to "become whole") by emphasizing separation. Hence the limited scope of reductionism in modern science, particularly in the health sciences.

We have thus chosen to look at dowsing in a more expanded or non-dual manner. When we dowse to correct or remove an energetic blockage for example, we do so not to emphasize the power of the blockage so much as to clear the mind of its belief or attachment to it. By clearing the mind of its belief in a condition established in duality, we not only address the fundamental level of the cause of all phenomena (the mind), but we open a clear space, as it were, to experience wholeness, peace, and "now awareness"—all states of mind pointing to the non-dual reality waiting beyond the battlefield of dualistic conflict and confusion.

The goal, then, of *Dowsing Beyond Duality* is not to offer just another means to stay mired in suffering, but to free the mind of all deeply conditioned attachments and return with full awareness to our original self—the One Self we share with all beings and the Source of creation.

DAVID IAN COWAN
*Licensed Spiritual Health Coach*
*Certified Spiritual Dowser*

# PART I

# A Comprehensive Mini-Course in Spiritual Dowsing

# CHAPTER 1

# Some Basic Principles

IN THIS BOOK, WE WILL EXPLORE THE ART OF DOWSING "from the ground up." I appreciate that many of you may already be dowsers, and I applaud you for that. In order for this work to move forward as the basis for certification in Spiritual Dowsing, however, we aim at establishing a standardized approach—at least for the preliminaries (please see our website at *www.bluesunenergetics.net*). I therefore encourage all readers to adopt a "beginner's mind" as the Zen Buddhists suggest, so that we may all stand together on the same foundation and help bring dowsing out of the historical closet and into the light where it belongs as a complementary healing modality and valid spiritual healing system.

Dowsing is an ancient art that can be understood in terms of modern science. Dowsing can be used as a way to access subtle information via changes in the human energy field through changes in the autonomic nerves and micro-muscles of the body, much like muscle testing or kinesiology. It is a form of biofeedback. It can also be thought of as a form of intentional prayer.

For many years, the practice of dowsing was somewhat limited to seeking water, oil, or minerals on a property. Many mineral and oil exploration companies still employ dowsers today, although they may not admit it at shareholders' meetings. Traditional dowsing of this type can be considered a "read-only" application, as the dowser simply asks for information about a place, person, or thing and gets yes or no responses to questions, as well as quantitative or qualitative data like the percentage of probability that water is available or an estimate of gallons per minute. This data can be read on a numerical chart, a map, or simply off the digits of your spare hand. The quality of the data you receive depends on the purity of intent, mental clarity, and questioning skill of the dowser, as well as the dowser's ability to "get out of the way" mentally and emotionally once the question has been put forth.

In other words, with classic as well as active dowsing—the differences will be explained shortly—there is a required detachment from the results. The dowser becomes the neutral observer of the movement of energy, and thus exerts minimal influence over the process. Just as with trance channelers and mediums, the degree of ego-less detachment has everything to do with the accuracy of the data received.

A basic principle here is that everything on the most fundamental level is pure vibrating energy, the basis of which is light. What differentiates things one from another is their rate of vibration. Your brain is a powerful energetic broadcaster and receiver of electromagnetic and other subtle energies, even if you are not consciously aware of it. Our emerging understanding of quantum physics and the neurobiology of the brain can help to explain all this, but that would merit at least another chapter. We do know from cutting-edge research that the power of the mind has been vastly underappreciated in the Age of Materialism largely due to our unquestioned loyalty to the concept of the separation of the individual and the world, and to the concurrent belief that thoughts are purely private phenomena. This is "old-paradigm" thinking.

Suffice it to say that, at one time or another, we have all experienced a strong "hunch" or intuitive knowing that later turned out to be true. This is especially noticeable between mothers and children, as well as among animals who run on pure instinct. This intuitive ability is partly due to the strong biological link between mother and child and the survival "hardwiring" of the mother. It is also due to the fact that female brains are generally constructed in a manner more conducive to whole-brain or alpha brain-wave states and modes of operation. This is one reason why intuition is just as likely to be called "women's intuition." It is also why you usually won't find as many men at Spiritual Dowsing classes, although that is changing. Some men are beginning to come around and pull themselves out of the mind-set of extreme male polarity that has, historically, been predominant on the planet for eons. They are seeing that this limited pattern and role just isn't working for them or allowing them to be whole persons.

Many people have learned through their own experience to trust this inner knowing, or intuition, despite the lack of a rational explanation for it. A rational explanation for intuition exists, but eludes many people, as it is furnished by the proven principles of quantum physics—not a topic of everyday conversation or part of standard education. Let us just say, at this point, that it is well understood that mind, or consciousness, is a non-local phenomenon—that is, not limited by ordinary time or space. Thus, although we appear to be separate beings on the physical level, on the level of mind—or spirit, if you prefer—we literally fill the universe. Mind does not require a body. The body requires the power of mind to animate it. Mind is the "supreme cause" of our universe. All else is effect. This puts you in the driver's seat, doesn't it?

Recently, dowsing has taken on a more active form, in which the focused intent of the dowser can create a change in the selected target or issue regardless of the physical distance involved. The dowser does not do the work; the "dowsing system," for lack of a better term, does. The dowsing system consists of a planetary healing grid, or energetic connective network, and all of the extra-dimensional beings and Guides who are here for the same purpose—the healing of humanity and the planet.

When you place yourself in an alpha brain state, you greatly increase your intuitive powers and access to the dowsing system. You could say that cultivating an alpha brain-wave state is a *mandatory pre-requisite* to becoming an effective and powerful dowser—or becoming a balanced individual, for that matter. Being at a 10-hertz brain state (alpha) connects you to the dowsing system, or planetary intelligence grid. This grid corresponds to Edgar Cayce's prediction of a new energy coming to Earth at this time in history. Some have called this the Christ Consciousness Grid. This is where the healing originates. The grid responds instantly to sincere requests for help and, being also non-local, instantly manifests positive healing intent anywhere on the planet or in the universe. You can also think of this energy grid as a template for the Global Brain, or an emerging manifestation of the coalescing Unified Consciousness Field on the planet.

By the way, in Native American culture, the alpha state is equated with what they call the Land of the Spirit. Beta brain waves—where we are in our everyday busyness with business—relate to the Land of the Living Dead. You may think you are being active and instrumental, but what are you really accomplishing by solving endless problems from a limited, linear perspective? We merely become chained to endless problems when operating only from the beta state.

Classic dowsing refers to what most think of when they use the term "dowsing." Either that or they confuse it with putting out—or dousing—a fire. Classic dowsing has been around a long time, particularly among those who work the land. It has been an indispensible tool for locating good sources of safe drinking water, finding lost objects or animals, discovering negative energy sources in the land (or geopathic stress), and other very practical applications. Classic dowsing was apparently practiced as far back as the Egyptian civilization and likely much further back than that. It is a natural extension of an intuitive body connection with the forces of nature: geo-magnetism, emission fields of specific minerals or elements, and the movements of the energies of water underground.

Today, classic dowsing often takes the form of simple yes or no responses to questions—finding out if an infant in the womb is a boy or a girl, or asking about foods and supplements. Even at this rudimentary level, this form of dowsing is an invaluable tool that can take the guesswork, and thus the stress, out of the many taxing decisions we need to make every day.

Historically, dowsing in any form got a "bad rap" when the male-dominated Church hierarchy did everything they could to eliminate competition in any form for people's faith and allegiance. This occurred not so long ago in historical terms. Some say as many as three million people, mostly women, were murdered outright for using non-sanctioned methods of healing or "divination." Along with dowsing, herbalism was also outlawed as "Satanic" by those with a greater agenda to degrade the feminine in favor of a male-dominated system, both religious and economic. We are still pulling ourselves out of the remnants of this insane imbalance.

Active dowsing involves a non-local transfer of energy operating on a quantum level. It takes dowsing to the "next level," where, after we receive information on a subject or condition, we decide that we are not going to settle for the situation, and instead take a more active role in changing the conditions or probable outcomes. By doing so, we take the reins of our own powers as "co-creators of realities," which is our divine birthright. Interestingly, this also describes the new paradigm in planetary awareness that is foretold in the predictions of the ancient Mayan calendar. (Please refer to my first book, *Navigating the Collapse of Time: a Peaceful Path Through the End of Illusions*, Weiser Books, 2011).

Active dowsing not only opens up new vistas of empowerment and self-realization; it also implies a greater level of responsibility and thus accountability to your clients, society, and the planet. One way of describing the many problems we have is that the world is a "mis-creation"—that is, the motives behind our making of this world were skewed from the start. This is the basic "split" in the mind that was the result of our mutual desire to experience separation, rather than the endless bliss of Oneness with the Creator and each other. I have just given you a thumbnail sketch of the metaphysics offered in *A Course in Miracles*, which is an amazing document based on the principles of non-duality. Again, I refer you to that work if this topic interests you.

Grasping non duality is essential to a full understanding of "why we dowse" at all. Duality is an artificial condition. Duality, however, only arose from a previous state of non-duality, or Oneness. Duality is the only the *perception* of opposites created by our own decision at one point to experience separation instead of Oneness. This was the fundamental cause of the Big Bang and the subsequent creation of a universe of seemingly separate forms. As (somewhat) intelligent humans, we look out on a world of our own making, which can only reflect back to us the state of mind that made or is projecting it. Although perception seems to give us an accurate picture of "reality," I ask you—where does perception take place? In the mind, right? So where is the world taking place? And what is the world but a projection of a mind that is currently inwardly divided, or in a state of believing itself to be separate from its Source, and from all other "selves" as well.

Duality thus sets up a world of endless separate forms. Everything that you can conceive of in this world is accompanied by its "opposite"—hot and cold, up and down, left and right, rich and poor, happy and sad, war and peace, good and evil. You get the picture.

So, if duality is only an entrenched belief, you can also say that our belief in duality as "reality" is illusion. We "fell" for our own misperceptions. The reason I am even going into this discussion is that, within duality, we run the risk of making things either good or bad in our own perception, not truly understanding the non-dual reality that everything here is neutral until we give it meaning. In other words, we take our own fantasized perceptions for "real" and run the risk of continuing the spell of duality and perpetuating the conflict and suffering that duality eventually produces.

For example, when I dowse to remove an attachment of some kind—a demon or entity—the dualistic view is that something outside has attacked a person, making him or her a vulnerable victim of something outside of themselves. Thus the person should rightfully live in fear of the next "attack." This, by the way, is the logic of the ego, that made-up self we settled for to help explain the mystery of our separate existence. The ego is only an idea, and nothing more.

The same scenario from a non-dual perspective sees the "attacker" as simply a disowned and projected thought or thought form coming back to the mind of the person who denied it in order to be received, healed, corrected, and brought back "home." It is simply an exercise in self-love, acceptance, and forgiveness. This approach elevates dowsing to the level of spiritual healing, which is why we refer to this technique as Spiritual or Soulful Dowsing. It is only by taking the non-dual view that we can diffuse the fear and victimization that so often keeps problems and issues, including illness, present in our lives.

I admit this view is counter-intuitive for many in what I call the "mirror world." The consensus reality here is almost exclusively dualistic. This is what keeps the conflicts, wars, and inequality that have plagued mankind and the planet in place. For now, don't worry about solving the world's problems. Just consider the possibilities of being able to look at every situation presented to you as existing simply on the level of the mind. That is all we need to heal. The outer picture will shift to conform to the inner picture we choose. People may think that what you are dowsing for is "out there," but you know what you are changing is the thought patterns that made and projected that situation in the first place. You just need to *know* that this is the level you are working on.

With active dowsing, we now have a means to make things right and undo many of the deeper causes of suffering, which inevitably leads back to the healing of the mind. In the non-dual perspective, the material universe is simply a projection on the screen of consciousness of the desire and purpose that we give the universe from our present state of mind or awareness. Quantum physics gives credence to these ideas.

There are some other scientific principles that can help you to understand this—at least at a basic level. One is the idea that matter and energy are made of the same stuff (light) and are interchangeable as noted. This was the idea behind Einstein's famous equation $E=MC^2$. Because consciousness, or thought, is a form of energy, your thoughts can affect both energy and matter. This is why we can say confidently that all thought produces form on some level and that energy follows thought. Thought empowered by feeling, or emotion, is all the more powerful. Thought, as a function of the mind, is not subject to physical laws, but rather operates in a quantum dimension—the fourth dimension or astral plane, which is simply the range of energy vibration that holds all of our thoughts in a unified field from which our brains attune and "pull" thoughts. Thus the brain is more like a two-way radio than a "maker" of thoughts.

The observer effect noted in quantum physics states that observation or focused mind-power is always linked to, and thus will always affect on some level, what is being observed. In other words, everything is connected, and the mind is what connects everything. So even without dowsing, wherever you place your attention you create change, however subtle. Sometimes, according to the principles of homeopathy, a subtle change can have much more significant effects than an overt or obvious energy exchange.

And finally, we have the quantum principle of indeterminacy, which states that the more accurately you can measure or predict one quality of an event—like an event's location—the less accurate the measuring of the other qualities becomes—like knowing when the event will occur. We live in an indeterminate universe, which means that it is wide open to change and novelty. This means that the universe of light vibration is at your command. Now this is powerful stuff, and consistent with the non-dual metaphysical ideas we discussed earlier on the origin of the universe and our central place in it.

With this in mind, I encourage you to take the information in this book both playfully and seriously. Play with the ideas and try the practical applications out for yourself. At the same time, realize the awesomeness of your power to create change and affect your world and others for the good, and honor that power with the respect and reverence it deserves.

## WAYS TO ACHIEVE ALPHA

Achieving an alpha brain-wave state is a skill that is fundamental to effective dowsing. You may need to work with these techniques for a while before you notice any direct changes in yourself, although results are often tangible right away. Generally, we are more relaxed, open, and intuitive in an alpha state. An alpha state is evidence that you are harmonizing both hemispheres of your brain into a more ideal balance, thus tapping into the potential of your "whole brain." You are typically in a faster beta brain-wave state when you are awake and navigating the decisions and responsibilities of day-to-day life in the world. This level of functioning draws primarily on the resources of the left hemisphere of the brain.

Although you may be working harder in this state, you do not have the balancing power of the more intuitive and holistic right hemisphere to give a broader perspective. The simple techniques below will help to bring both sides of your brain into equal play, thus increasing overall mental efficiency and effectiveness, while decreasing the amount of total energy expended. Getting into an alpha state will also connect you to the planetary healing grid mentioned above. In and of itself, this creates a peaceful atmosphere around you that is inherently supportive of others and conducive to healing.

Try not to be interrupted or distracted by day-to-day concerns when doing these exercises. Give yourself the time it takes to become relaxed.

1. With your eyes closed, gaze upward about 20 degrees from the imaginary horizon. Breathe deeply and evenly, and create or remember a multi-sensory visualization. Describe it to yourself in as many sensory domains as you can—sight, smell, sound, tactile feeling, etc. A landscape works well for this. I like to use a beach scene. Once you are relaxed and simply enjoying the peace of the scenario, create a physical trigger for yourself with the intent to bring you back to this state spontaneously—placing the tip of your tongue behind your top teeth or tugging an ear lobe, for example. Tell yourself that whenever you create this physical connection, you will automatically be returned to this relaxed state.

---

TIP: Placing a written affirmation on the wall about 20 degrees up in your field of vision and repeating it aloud as you view it helps to imprint the suggestion more completely. We are more open to positive suggestion in the alpha state.

---

2. Imagine or draw in the air a figure 8, moving horizontally across your field of vision, like a big pair of glasses. This brings your attention to your peripheral vision on both sides and unites and balances the

activation level of your brain hemispheres. Or simply become aware in the moment of what you can see in your peripheral vision, but are not usually paying attention to. You can do this without anyone knowing this is what you are doing. Just look at the person, and "go peripheral."

3. Do a simple "cross-crawl" exercise, tapping your knees rhythmically with the opposite hand as you march in a standing position. (This is an exercise from the Brain Gym educational kinesiology system.)

4. Listening to relaxing music, Nature sounds, or drumming are other ways to go into an alpha state. You know you are there because you feel more physically relaxed, your breathing is slow and deep, and disturbing thoughts and concerns seem to fade into the background of your awareness. There's a sense that everything is okay, that you are being supported and valued just by being. It is much like being in a mild meditative state, or the pensive relaxation we experience when we contemplate beautiful music or art. No analysis, just appreciation.

## BELIEFS

You may find some of the concepts in chapter 4 (The Clearings) unfamiliar, uncomfortable, or challenging to your view of reality. If so, simply pass over these items and go on to things with which you are comfortable. A rule of thumb is never to go further than what your mind can accept without fear. This is true when working with others as well as for yourself. On this note, however, bear in mind that, in the modern materialist Western world, the predominant institutionalized spiritual or "religious" view has been very contrary to the idea of personal empowerment and directly accessing the Divine without going through the supposed official representatives of God on Earth. This view has historically been all about control.

The first politicians were, in fact, the first priests. Funny how these two topics—politics and religion—are considered taboo in polite conversation. One particular group even purposely removed from their scriptures all references to reincarnation or personal spiritual empowerment in a deliberate attempt to consolidate the Truth under one authority. This led to the Dark Ages in Europe. Those who still insisted on side-stepping the official version of Truth often found themselves burned at the stake. Fear of our personal power still permeates many of our social institutions and is part of our cultural heritage. Why let it be part of yours?

Power is not inherently evil, especially if it is balanced with an equal measure of love and wisdom. Cultivate these three and you will begin to appreciate that all that has been assumed and taught to be outside of us, including "God," is actually within each of us without exclusion or exception.

Thus, most of our limiting beliefs are not truly our own. They are adopted—ideas we absorbed without question from seemingly sincere authority figures and elders. The historical "chain of dysfunctional belief," however, is an integral part of the human enslavement to illusion, and so needs to be examined closely by any serious student of life. When a belief is found wanting or based on fictitious assumptions, simply toss it out!

It is true that most beliefs operate below our conscious awareness. We may not even be aware of our limiting beliefs until we are presented with an opportunity to expand our personal power. Then an insidious little voice says: "Who do you think you are? You can't do that! Get real!" This is where many sincere dowsers get knocked off the path. When this happens, you know you have stirred up a limiting belief that you have every right to examine and dismiss, if you so choose.

Unconscious limiting beliefs often coalesce into attitudes—a general approach to life and circumstance. The ego's beliefs in littleness and limitation usually contribute to attitudes of victimization, finding enemies or problems outside ourselves onto which we project our inner conflicts, and a deep inner sense of sadness and disconnect. Never believe that this voice is telling you the Truth! Your Truth, which is the same as mine and everyone else's, is that you are a divine, perfect creation who, as Spirit, can never die. Moreover, you are destined to awaken fully to the Truth of your Self at the appointed time.

Finally, I must mention that the methods outlined in this book work just as well at a distance as they do face to face. This is because we are dealing with the superconscious mind, which communicates according to quantum principles in the great ocean of consciousness underlying all matter in the universe. Having a body confuses us, because, on that level, we are clearly separate. But our minds don't play by those rules. They are much freer than we can currently imagine—but we are getting there!

# WATER

Ensuring proper hydration has a definite impact on your dowsing. How so? When we dowse, at least on one level, we send a thought form or intent through the non-local field of intelligence underlying all material reality. Our brains and bodies are capable of subspace communication. We actually receive quantum information all the time, but usually call these experiences as they reach the conscious mind "hunches," or "instincts," or "gut feelings."

Throughout your body, which is mostly water, you have a network of special protein structures made mostly of collagen, which, along with clustered or ideally organized water molecules, provide the basis of an entire electromagnetic and subtle energy—a sending-and-receiving web that acts like a body-wide antenna. This system is known as the "extra-cellular matrix" or ECM, a largely unrecognized aspect of biology. (See Dr. James Oschman's book, *Energy Medicine: The Scientific Basis*, Churchill Livingstone, 2001.)

Another way to think of your body is as a battery, with all your activities, including thinking and intending, requiring and producing some electrical activity. This activity accounts for the EEG and ECG readings in biofeedback. As a battery, your body needs plenty of water and electrolytes in the form of minerals. Otherwise, your battery will run down quickly and you may not have much endurance. The minerals needed for proper electrical functioning include magnesium, plant-based calcium, true sodium, and potassium. Eating foods rich in these nutrients will make you a better dowser. A good suggestion is to take alfalfa or kelp tablets daily. Drinking a tall glass of water before doing any kind of energy work is also a good habit to get into. If you are feeling energetically depleted and in need of rest, please honor that need before attempting to dowse.

## CHOOSING A PENDULUM

The material or energy of a pendulum essentially does not matter. I know this may come as a shock to some of you who are attached to a special pendulum. My question to you is this: Why give your power away to a rock? Although minerals and crystals definitely have a specific frequency and application in crystal therapy, a rock or a piece of gum and a string work as well when it comes to providing simple kinetic feedback, as does a paperclip and dental floss, or a needle and thread. The magic is in *you*, not the tool!

That said, most dowsers find a pendulum that appeals to them esthetically, and that is fine. Most important is the weight and therefore the spin speed of the pendulum. It should not be too heavy for you, as this will lead to a slow response and very long sessions; and it should not be too light, as it will be super-sensitive to every subtle movement and may be hard to control. Find a reasonable weight for you, keeping the string or chain on the short side. Three to five inches of chain or string works fine. A shorter string length saves time and allows you to move through the clearing more efficiently. I suggest that you work with what is available and, when you can, try out a few different sizes, weights, and materials until you find something just right for you.

There are, of course, a variety of other dowsing instruments available. Classic dowsers often rely on dowsing rods or "L Rods"—two L-shaped (usually copper) rods held out in front of you with the short parts as the handle. I've made these out of metal coat hangers. You may also want to check out "bobbers," which are made of some kind of flexible material like wire that acts like a large pendulum, but is held horizontally rather than vertically. This works well when teaching classes, as it's easier for more folks to see what's going on. I have found that the most compact, versatile, and least threatening (to the uninitiated, that is) of dowsing instruments is still the simple hand-held pendulum. As a right-handed person, I naturally tend to dowse with my right hand. I can dowse with my left, but it's a little awkward, as are most things I try to do with my left hand.

## SPIRIT GUIDES

We've discussed the global consciousness grid as one of the actual means for active dowsing, but that's not all that's involved. We all have Spirit Guides—some experts say between three and five of them, although some people may have as many as nine once they request an "upgrade." A lot of this understanding comes from researchers into near-death experiences, in which people who die get a little tour of the other side. In most cases, they are told that they don't have a reservation and aren't expected yet, and end up back in their bodies! The Munroe Institute has done a lot of this research. (See *The Destiny of Souls*, Llewellyn, 2001 by Michael Newton, PhD for some fascinating case studies of life between lives.)

Spirit Guides are fourth-dimensional beings with whom we are well acquainted on the spiritual planes. We often stay with the same team through various incarnations. We may be their Guides when they are incarnated down here! They are not, however, perfected beings like Ascended Masters, and so can still be working out their dualistic issues in another dimension.

Since fourth-dimensional forms can operate anywhere in the universe at the speed of thought without a body to slow them down, the quality of your Spirit Guides is a major factor in the quality of your dowsing. It seems that, until we are aware of them, they pretty much have *carte blanche* about how helpful they want to be or can be. Spirit Guides are a lot like people (I guess they would say they are!)—some are helpful, some are neutral, and some can be a real pain in the . . . astral! The following represents a "fast forward" utilizing some of the skills we will cover together in more detail in later sections. This upgrade is an indispensible factor in supporting your success as a dowser, and so is very appropriate to address at the outset of your learning. If need be, mark this page and come back to the exercise when you feel more confident with the basics of dowsing.

Assuming you are already dowsing on some level, ask if you have permission or need to do a Spirit Guide upgrade for yourself or for others. I have never been told "no" when I asked this.

First dowse to see how many Spirit Guides are working with you now and ask if they are all of 100 percent pure Light. With a left spin, declare:

*I now request that all aspects of my Spirit Guides that are not of 100 percent pure Light be raised to the 100 percent pure Light of Truth and divine love.*

If any Guides are not willing or compliant with this request, I ask that they be replaced immediately with Spirit Guides of 100 percent pure Light, and that this upgrade be irreversible and irrevocable until no longer necessary or beneficial.

Say "Thank You" and ask the same questions you started with. How many Guides do you have now?

# CHAPTER 2

# Working with Yes and No

IF YOU ARE BRAND-NEW TO DOWSING, you will want to work at this level for a while to build confidence before moving into the active type of dowsing. Yes and no answers can be invaluable, and can be applied to any question you can conceive. Your success with classic dowsing will be determined by your ability to ask the right questions. To establish your yes and no responses, you must program your nervous system, including your brain and muscles, with your intent. We will use a vertical movement of the pendulum for our yes response and a horizontal motion for no. It's okay if you are currently using other movements for yes and no. You can simply reprogram your body/mind at will. The reason we want to use these movements for yes and no responses is that we will be using "spin" movements later for the active form of dowsing.

## A NEURO-QUANTUM EXPLANATION

There is a way to understand how this kind of dowsing works physiologically and how it is we can program our response signals. First, we need to acknowledge that what we usually call consciousness really only represents a very small part of our brain's potential. With linear linguistic-based intelligence informing most of our waking hours, we are, in fact, using a very limited roadmap based entirely on past conditioning. No wonder we feel lost and confused as often as we do! Broca's Region in the brain, where our language-based cognition is processed, accounts for about 7 percent of our total neural capacity. This is perhaps why many are plagued with feelings of endless days of the "same old, same old," for, as far as what we think daily, this is mostly true! We'll call this limited mode of operation the conscious mind.

The conscious mind expresses primarily via the motor nerves, an aspect of the central nervous system involved in using the larger muscles of the body. For example, my conscious mind decides I'm thirsty. My brain then activates my major muscles and gets me off the couch and over to the tap or refrigerator. Simple.

However, the vast majority of my mental power lies below the surface of my conscious mind, like the bulk of an iceberg. In traditional psychology, this has been called the "unconscious." I suspect it was referred to in negative terms ("un"-conscious) because no one knew what was in it, and we tend to suspect the unknown. This is a fear-based assumption. Freud was convinced that the unconscious was like a dark basement full of ugly secrets and suppressed desires. It sounds more as if he were projecting the repression typical among males in Victorian-era European society.

Just as the conscious mind expresses through the motor nerves and major muscles of the body, the unconscious mind—or what I prefer to dignify as the superconscious mind (let's give ourselves a little credit!)—expresses primarily through the autonomic nervous system, a vast network of nerves wired into every system of the body. It is the superconscious mind via the autonomic nervous system that literally runs all of life's bodily processes—of which we are largely oblivious, yet which are crucial to our physical survival. Take breathing or the beating of the heart, for example. If you had to remember to breathe or make your heart beat consciously, you would fall over dead the moment you got distracted from your task! But thankfully, all of this is hardwired into our physiology, and we can be happily distracted as much as we like.

A clear example of the superconscious mind expressing through the autonomic nervous system is the classic fight-or-flight response. This is an automatic physical reaction or reflex to the perception of physical threat. Most of the muscles involved in these reactions—vascular constriction, shortness of breath, tunnel vision, etc.—involve the micro-muscles of the body. Now, the superconscious mind, being the vast bulk of intelligence that lies below the surface of our conscious minds (as in the iceberg analogy), is also in touch with the much broader ocean of intelligence. It is on this level that we are all connected to what Carl Jung first called the "collective unconscious." Here we have a means to grasp the metaphysical precept that all minds are joined and that we are truly One with each other and our Source—not on the level of bodies or conscious minds, but on this deeper level, which is subject to quantum reality and is not limited to the realm of linear and Newtonian logic.

If you rely solely on your verbal mind to navigate your life, you will be like the explorer in the cave with only one box of matches to see your way. However, when you tap into the vast field of intelligence available to you through your superconscious mind, you have a huge searchlight at your disposal. Because of your connection with all minds, you literally hold the library card to all the knowledge ever formulated in the One Mind from all times and dimensions. While we are here in our bodies, however, this information is generally filtered through our limited left-brain processing, our social conditioning, and our beliefs, assumptions, prejudices, and fears—you get the picture.

In classic dowsing, we have a way to bypass the logical filters of our own limited verbal minds and go straight to the source of all information—what Deepak Chopra at one time called "the cosmic computer." By accessing this computer with our own superconscious minds, we can receive intelligent responses to well-framed questions through pre-programmed movements of the micro-muscles in the body—in this case, in your hand, wrist, and forearm. Please re-read this last sentence until you have thoroughly chewed and digested it. This is really all that is happening when we dowse, along with some help from our Spirit Guides and a few other helpers, as needed.

## INSTRUCTIONS FOR SELF-PROGRAMMING YES AND NO RESPONSES

First, get into an alpha state. Do this at a quiet time of day when you will not be disturbed.

1. With your pendulum in your right hand (for the right-handed), make a firm and steady vertical movement with the pendulum in the air and repeat to yourself *aloud:* "This is my Yes."

2. Say it a few times. Seven repetitions will get the information from your short-term to your long-term memory. I usually suggest nine repetitions, as nine is the number of completion in numerology.

3. Now stop the movement and check the results. With the pendulum stationary, say: "Show me Yes" and wait.

4. Let go of any need to control the outcome. Be still, but not stiff. Stay in your alpha state and don't forget to breathe! It may take time at first, and the movement may be small and tentative.

5. Continue to ask about things you know are true: "My name is _____" or "Today is Tuesday" (when it is) or "Hot dogs are toxic."

6. In a similar manner, produce a steady horizontal movement and program yourself with nine repetitions of "This is my No." Keep the movement strong and intentional.

7. Affirm the response with some obviously false statements or questions that you know require a no to be true: "Rain always falls up" or "Lawyers are underpaid."

Get in the habit of dowsing for simple decisions like food or supplement choices by simply asking, "Is this food good for me?" or "Does my body want this supplement?". Once your confidence builds, you can begin to ask about more abstract things like people and situations.

## WHEN IT DOESN'T WORK

Our experience has been that the above programming exercise works about 90 percent of the time. Typically, in a class of twenty students, there may be one or two where nothing at all happens. I am the first to admit that dowsing is not for everyone, and that it is clearly not the only way to access information or do healing work. So I am hesitant to insist that it *must* work for everyone.

However, there does seem to be two issues that have come up repeatedly for folks who get stuck at this stage. By investigating these issues here, we will be jumping ahead somewhat, but for those few readers out there who may be stumped at this point, this is for you.

The first issue is a simple reversal in the polarity or direction of the bio-electric flow in a part of the nervous system. This is often the result of a former trauma or shock to a given organ at some time. For example, let's say you have a toxic issue with your kidneys due to some heavy-metal poisoning. Your body, in its survival intelligence, says to your kidneys: "You can take a break and put your energy into detoxifying and recovering. We'll take you offline and reverse your electrical flow temporarily to give you a break." This works well, as long as the organ in question gets a chance to recuperate. But in a case where the toxin or stressor of any kind becomes chronic, that organ may never go back online, but will remain in a semi-permanent energetically disabled or compromised state. This is the organ that then becomes susceptible to degenerative disease, infection, or other mishaps, because it is already in a weakened state.

If you are stuck at yes and no, you can't really ask the question for yourself: "Do I have an issue with reversed polarity? Is this blocking my dowsing ability?" But someone else can ask this on your behalf. Or (jumping ahead again) you can simply go ahead and, with a left spin started by you, say:

*I now ask my Spirit Guides and helpers to please go to the time of the original trauma that is behind my blockage with dowsing, and reduce at the point of origin all ill effects, blockages, memories, and energies associated with that trauma now. Transmute this energy into the most favorable energy to correct the polarity in my body and fully support me in expressing my spiritual gifts. Thank you.*

Wait for the left spin to naturally slow and stop when it wants. The second possibility here is a bit more esoteric. This is the not-too-uncommon memory of being punished or persecuted in the past—either in what we call a past life or in our lineage held as DNA memory—for dowsing or for any other "taboo" practice in the fairly recent era known as the Dark Ages. This was a time when religion and superstition were one, and when the (male) authority of the day felt it was their divine duty to murder anyone who practiced healing arts or any other Nature-based practice outside of the approved modalities. Hmm—some things haven't changed much, have they? Just claim you have found a cure for cancer outside the drugs-and-surgery monopoly and you'll see close to the same results today!

It is not unusual for many of us to have these fears lurking just below our conscious awareness. They can come out in the form of a "don't rock the boat" mentality, still a common mind-set among the world's population today.

If you suspect that this may apply to you—and even if it doesn't—there is certainly no harm in doing this anyway. Then, with a left spin started by you, say:

*I now ask my Spirit Guides and helpers to time travel to the point of any persecution or punishment I may have suffered in any time frame or dimension where I was punished for dowsing or expressing my natural spiritual and healing gifts. Transmute the energy, emotions, feelings, and frequency of this memory into pure joy, and bring this joy now into my present-life timeline, thus liberating me from all limiting memories in this area now and forever. Thank You.*

Wait for the spin to stop. With these two clearings, you should be able to get at least a tentative yes or no movement when you simply ask: "Show me yes" and "Show me no." Release any stress or anxiety you may have about doing it correctly, and breathe! Even if you get just a slight quivering movement in the right direction, go with it! It will strengthen as you relax into and accept your natural powers.

## RESISTANCE FROM OTHERS

It is not necessary that others appreciate or understand what you are doing when you dowse. Generally, a wise position is: "What you think of me is none of my business." However, it's usually not wise to dowse publically unless teaching a class. There's no reason to raise the anxieties of others who may believe, like many, that what you are doing is some kind of witchcraft. Is this still the Dark Ages? I guess it is for some!

You may also hear from well-meaning skeptics: "Oh, I see your hand moving. You're just doing that on your own!" At first, I had no response to this observation. I could see that, from where they were sitting, this appeared absolutely true! Yet I know that, in my own practice of dowsing, I start out with a conscious intent and decision to dowse, but then I step back mentally and detach from the process so as not to interfere with or limit what is actually going on. I start out from the conscious mind, but then shift over to the superconscious mind.

So now my favorite snappy reply to the skeptic's challenge is: "Yes I am, but it's not the me you think I am."

## PERMISSION

I strongly recommend that, before any personal dowsing session, you ask permission: "May I, can I, and should I dowse for myself (or whomever) at this time?" This is a courtesy and acknowledgment to the dowsing system, but also may alert you to any inappropriateness of your dowsing at this time, or any form of interference or lack of willingness on the subject's part. The questions actually cover a lot of ground:

*May I?* asks: "Do I have permission of all involved or affected?"

*Can I?* asks: "Do I have the ability and support of the dowsing system?"

*Should I?* asks: "Is this an appropriate time or issue about which to dowse?"

You may also want to ask if it is in the highest good of all involved to dowse for the issue at this time. If you get a no, which is admittedly rare, simply choose another subject or topic. Ask if you can check in later.

Sometimes, it is not possible to get a person's direct permission to dowse for them and yet you know that they would benefit from your intent. In these cases, I am comfortable with asking the person's Higher Self. It's funny how I have never been denied by anyone's Higher Self! It seems to be only the lower self, with its tendency toward fearing the unseen and unknown, that recoils when being offered healing. The prime criteria for appropriateness is the dowser's motivation. Are you motivated by a sincere desire to help and reduce suffering, and for outcomes that are for the highest good of all? Then, go for it! There are some experienced professional dowsers who work with law-enforcement agencies to disable serious criminals. I don't think they need to ask permission to stop a chain of crimes or suspected energies behind the behavior of a criminal, as disempowering them is clearly in interests of the highest good of all. The criminals would very likely say no anyway!

Again, you may want to work with yes-and-no dowsing for a while before moving forward to build your confidence. As noted, a good and valuable area to work with is food. With your pendulum over an item of food or meal, ask questions like: "Is this food nourishing for me? Does this food enhance my energy? Am I allergic to this food? Is this food toxic for me? Was this food prepared with Love?"

## ANSWERS OF QUANTITY AND QUALITY

The next step in basic classic dowsing is to begin to get answers regarding quantity or quality. This adds a whole new dimension and depth to your dowsing. There is nothing that can be measured that you cannot quantify or qualify. You just need to know what questions to ask. To do this, all you need is a scale of 0 to 10. You can draw one out like this:

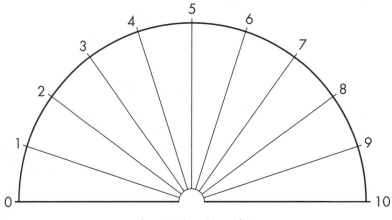

*Chart 1. The Chart of Ten*

This chart, which we will call the Chart of Ten, can be used in a number of ways. It is your mental intent that determines how to use and read it. You can see 10 as representing 100 percent, for example. Sometimes 10 can represent a positive value, like the degree of happiness. On the other hand, sometimes 0 will be desirable, as when measuring the probability of getting a parking ticket on any given day. Your intent establishes the purpose and how you interpret the chart.

To start, ask if you have the full permission and support of your Spirit Guides. I assume you do. Then hold the pendulum still over the central pivot point, and simply ask to be shown certain readings—"Show me 9"; "Show me 2"—until you see that, whatever you ask, you get. The dowsing system is telling you: "Your wish is my command!"

By the way, I use the term dowsing system—a term I learned from Raymon Grace—to mean all of the Guides, angels, helpers, supports, and systems that work with us in this field of spiritual healing. We may not even be aware of most of these. But, even if we don't know them, the dowsing system knows who they are and they will respond.

To use the Chart of Ten as a percentage chart, assume that each number represents 10 percent, with 10 meaning 100 percent. Hold the pendulum loosely and center it over the hub point. In each case, specify what 10—the optimal or best outcome—means. Here are some examples of language to use when reading percentages:

> With 10 being 100 percent, or ideal, please show me the percentage of my overall energy level.

> With 10 being ideal, what is the percentage of my hydration at this point?

> With 10 being 100 percent, what percentage of my income is ideal for me to put in a savings account?

> With 10 being 100 percent, to what percentage does this (food, person, place) energize (or deplete) me?

And, with a different intent:

> With 0 being ideal, what is my stress level today on a scale of 1 to 10?

You can see that it is important to set the parameters of your question. Always clarify what you are looking for by saying "with 10 as ideal" or something similar. Sometimes 0 may be your ideal, as in asking: "With 0 as ideal, how many times will I have to date my best friend's cousin?"

To use the scale to determine numerical values like weights, distance, or time (days, weeks, months, years, a specific year), first determine your measurement criteria by asking if you can receive information in pounds, ounces, gallons, days, months, years, etc. Next, ask *how many digits* are in the final answer. Let's say you're asking about a specific lost object. Here's a typical dialogue:

> Can I, may I, and should I get information on Bob's missing Rolex watch? Answer: yes.

> In establishing the location of this missing object, is it most appropriate to measure the distance to its location from here in miles? Answer: no.

> In kilometers? Answer: no.

> In yards? Answer: yes.

> How many digits are in the correct number of yards from this point where we stand to find Bob's watch? Answer: 2.

> The first digit is _____ . Answer: 1.

> The second digit is _____ . Answer: 2.

So the lost Rolex is within 12 yards of where we stand? Answer: yes.

Sometimes I like to test this by saying: "Is the watch 13 yards from here?" I will always get a no, until I ask the right question based on the information already given. You can then point in different directions and ask if it is the proper direction to search until you get a yes.

Your only limit to this chart's application is your imagination. As you will see in the Clearings section, quantifying any issue you are dealing with is an important part of tracking and validating results, thus building confidence.

## USING THE CHART OF TEN AS A PROBABILITY CHART

This application vastly expands the Chart of Ten's usefulness, particularly around future outcomes. At this point, however, I must make clear that the future is not fixed, and that outcomes are subject to change by the free wills of all those involved. So future predictions, or "fortune telling," is risky as far as reliability is concerned. I would not bet the farm on a racehorse that I dowsed would win at 100 percent probability because too much can happen before the race is over. I always qualify dowsing for future probabilities by stating: " . . . *under current conditions*," recognizing that conditions can and will likely change. If the issue you are dowsing is particularly important to you, monitor it carefully and dowse around the peripheral issues, always making the statement "for the highest good of all" in your wording. You may also want to invoke the Rule of Inevitable Outcome in your requests, recognizing that, in the grand scheme of things, everything is moving ultimately toward a state of perfect Oneness. In other words, you may say: "In recognizing the inevitable outcome of peace, what is the probability on a scale of 1 to 10 that I will get the job I want tomorrow?"

Nonetheless, the chart above is useful for probabilities and can help guide present choices, as in the following examples:

With 10 as 100 percent, what is the current probability that I will pass the (math, driver's, final) exam tomorrow? (answer: 50%)

If I study an extra hour a day, what does the probability become that I will pass? (answer: 90%)

With 10 as ideal, under the current conditions, what is the probability that my new business will prosper?

If I add (Mary) to the staff, what does this probability become? If I lay off (Susan), what does the probability become?

With 10 as ideal, at my current rate of skill acquisition, what is the probability that I will be an expert dowser in one week? In one month? In one year?"

You can easily sketch a Chart of Ten on a napkin, notepad, or any scrap paper and you're in business! Don't, however, get a Chart of Ten tattoo! In fact, we all have a built-in scale of ten in our hands if you use the digits and spaces as illustrated in the diagram below. This picture shows how you can use the left hand as a Chart of Ten. Obviously, this is how a right-handed dowser would work. You may flip your hand over and look at the front of it if you like. How you see it is how it will work for you. For the sake of consistency, however, we suggest that you look at the back of your hand as shown and use the suggested number spacing designations.

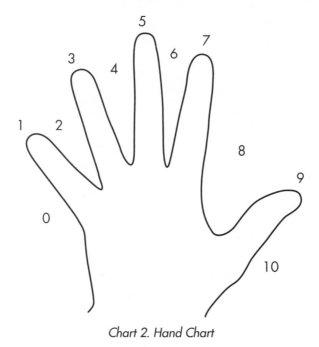

*Chart 2. Hand Chart*

Again, in order to dowse for numbers over 10, ask how many digits there are in the answer. Or you can ask if the answer is in tens, or hundreds, or thousands.

Let's say that the pendulum swings to 4 in response to the first question above. You then know that your answer is in the thousands. Then ask for each digit in order. The hand chart can save time and lots of paper. Practice often and use this chart as much as you can. It will be an important part of the clearings that follow in chapter 4.

## THE BALANCE CHART

Another useful chart is one that allows you to assess both sides of a question. Here's a good example: "What is the overall effect on my energy of this (person, place, thing, or event), with plus 10 being incredibly wonderful and minus 10 being really terrible?" This chart is for questions whose answer can go either way—that is, either positive or negative effects or results. Some appropriate uses would be for measuring yin or yang energies, for determining advantage vs. disadvantage, for finding the outcome of certain decisions, or to predict the effect of foods on your body or your moods. Be sure to qualify for your question exactly what plus 10 and minus 10 mean.

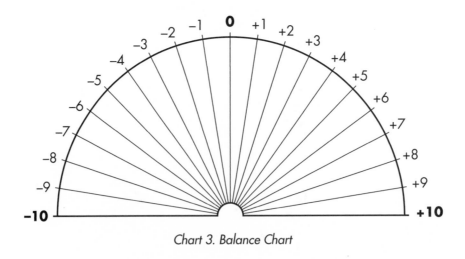

*Chart 3. Balance Chart*

The zero reading on this chart will always mean "balanced" or "neutral." For example, with the center line (or middle finger if you are using your hand chart) being the neutral point, anything to the right may be in a yang state, while anything to the left may be yin. Thus: "With '0' as energetically balanced, what is the effect of this (person, food, place, or event) on my meridians? On my _____(specific) meridian?"

More fundamentally, you can ask to measure the current energy state of any meridian or organ. Yang (the plus side) usually means some kind of inflammation, injury, infection, or general agitation. Yin (the minus side) usually means weakness, often from some more chronic condition or imbalance. You can use this chart to measure integrity, love and truth indices, and spiritual quality or condition as well. Always do this before doing business, purchasing, or entering into a contract with anyone. Measure the person's intent, honesty, and integrity.

Later, when we discuss shifting energies with active dowsing, you'll see how, if something is deficient (minus side), you can right spin it up to the balance point of zero. Or if it's in excess (plus side), you can left spin it down to zero.

These charts are simply tools to help you form questions and learn more by creating measurable data, always for the highest good of all. Please practice with them as much as you can, noting positive changes, perhaps with your own graphs of improvements as you make changes in certain areas. For example, measuring daily improvement with bodily and cellular hydration is a good project for all of us, as we are all more or less dehydrated, especially as we age.

## CUSTOM CHARTS

Actually, anything you can imagine can be made into a chart of different choices for you to dowse. Just draw a pie chart, (blanks are provided at the end of the book for you to copy for your own use) and list the choices along the outer edge, drawing a line from each choice back down to the focus point. Colors, ice cream flavors, remedies, business decisions, people—the list is endless. I sometimes like to make a chart to prioritize my day when there are too many tasks and too little time. It's always a pleasant surprise to find out that you really only need to do one or two things today, and can let the rest go for another day.

Another general rule is always to include "other" as one of your choices, as it is impossible to know or see all the possibilities in any situation. I line up the choices across the top arc of the chart and first ask how many of the tasks I can realistically expect to complete in a day (Answer: 2). Then I ask to be shown the priority number for each task. If you start making and collecting charts, you will eventually end up with a custom set of charts that are uniquely your own. This is how I created the charts in chapter 6, which are simply my personal collection of charts for things as they came up in my life, studies, and practice.

With these measuring tools, you can now learn about any number of events, effects, quantities, etc. from any time frame and for issues at any distance. Remember, your superconscious mind operates outside the usual boundaries of time and space. It is working in the quantum realm, which is stranger than fiction yet entirely real! This practice can provide excellent guidance for you, your family, your friends, and your clients. Keep these charts and questioning techniques in mind when we explore the clearings in chapter 4. You are only limited by your imagination as to what you can learn with clear intent and access to the cosmic library via your own superconscious mind and the quantum energy field.

## WHAT IS THE SUPERCONSCIOUS MIND?

You may well be asking this question at this juncture. Although we have discussed this to a degree, let's go deeper. We are operating under many limiting assumptions here on Earth at this time. Let's look at a couple of ideas to help us grow in understanding and an appreciation of a "bigger picture."

### Mind over Matter

In the 20th century, mainstream science gravitated toward the assumption that anything that can be measured is "real," while anything unseen is not. This simplistic notion fit very well with a sensory orientation to the world, and has furnished us with some clear understandings of the material world. Scientists went so far as to say, however, that unseen qualities like mind or consciousness, if they exist at all, must have evolved from matter, as matter was assumed to be primary in the universe. That said, something as miraculously magical as the human mind evolving randomly from mud has a very low probability of just "happening."

Quantum physics, a 100-year-old science that still hasn't fully hit mainstream awareness (but that is changing!), has proven that consciousness, or mind, affects matter and is primary to the appearance of subatomic particles from a wave to a particle state giving rise to all matter. As all matter is made of the same "mind stuff" everywhere in the universe, your mind is a primary co-creator of realities. So mind is primary to matter, not the other way around—of course, if you don't mind, it doesn't matter!

## All Minds Are Joined

Distance and separation are illusory. On the material plane, it appears as if we are all separate beings in separate bodies. On the physical plane, this is true. But what about thoughts? They are energy as well, and can be measured with instruments like EEG devices. The question is: When you share an idea, where does it go? You still have it and so does the next person, and if it's shared enough, everybody has the same idea! An idea only grows as you give it away. It appears that, on the level of the energy of the mind, there is no separation. The appearance of separation arises only when we mistakenly think that the mind is limited to the body. The brain is simply the mind's physical processor or space-time vehicle.

This misidentification of the mind with the body, by the way, is responsible for 99 percent of the suffering in the world. Yet people who have had near-death experiences know differently; they know that the mind does not require a body to be able to see, hear, have feelings, etc. Neurobiologists are beginning to recognize that the brain is not the mind; rather it is an attractor for the mind to come into a bodily experience. The brain has equal send-and-receive functions, so it is more like a transceiver of thoughts that all emanate from the "Big Mind" or One Consciousness we all share.

This means that your thoughts and feelings are common to all, and that there really are no private thoughts. Rather, you draw or attract to yourself specific thought forms drawn from the pool of collective consciousness. The conclusion here is that you have a connection to all other seemingly separate minds now—not through the 10 percent of the conditioned mind that we call consciousness, but through the other 90 percent, your superconscious brain/mind operating under the radar of your conscious mind. Once you accept this, you can join the 10 percent to the 90 percent and become whole-minded. This is your "wholey" Self, your superconscious Self, which is your true identity—and the one you share with all of life. By approaching dowsing from this place of deeper understanding of our energetic connection to each other and all of life, it becomes easier to let go of the nagging doubts of the linear mind and its scripted conditioning. Realizing your full potential is a "letting go" process more than anything. Release your self to your Self and know your unlimited nature and power to do good.

# CHAPTER 3

# Active Dowsing

WHEN I FIRST LEARNED TO USE A PENDULUM, I was quite pleased with the level of guidance working with yes and no and the percentages and probabilities provided. I was quite amazed to learn from a friend at one point that she was using her pendulum to help broadcast homeopathic remedies at a distance to her friends and clients. This was quite a shocker to me! And yet, on another level, I understood that humans are currently operating at a very low percentage of our mental, and thereby psychic, potential. As mentioned, we typically use only around 10 percent of our brains. And I'm sure you know a few folks who are getting by on considerably less! And much of our DNA appears to be inactive as well. It seems that the human species is mostly potential at this stage.

My friend gave me a sample statement to read, or intend, as I swung the pendulum in a circle. After trying it out on a number of sensitive friends, I was convinced, as were they, that something was going on. It was shortly after this that I was privileged to attend one of Raymon Grace's seminars, where he taught the methods my friend had shown me. It turned out that she had learned them from Raymon as well. I highly recommend the experience of Raymon's classes to anyone serious about dowsing. He is a national treasure! You can track him down at these locations on the Web:

*www.raymongrace.us*

*www.raymongraceprojects.com*

*www.raymongracefoundation.org*

His books and DVDs are very inspirational, as is he. Much of what you read here, I learned first with Raymon.

One of the reasons we programmed your yes and no responses as vertical and horizontal movements was to free up your left- and right-spin circle movements for active dowsing—that is, taking out and bringing in energies respectively. This will give you a total of four movements altogether. A left spin goes counterclockwise; a right spin goes clockwise.

Just as you programmed yourself for yes and no in an alpha state, purposely produce a left, or counterclockwise, spin and tell yourself: "This is for removing energies." Repeat this nine times. Then do the same for the right, or clockwise, spin, saying: "This is for bringing in energies." Repeat this nine times.

You will always start these two movements yourself—that is, from your conscious mind. You have decided to effect a change. So just start it up! It is equally important, however, that you let go of any mental or emotional attachment to the outcome. You must become simply a neutral observer as your superconscious mind takes over the reins. I like to call it "putting in the mental clutch," as you purposely disengage your mind from the process. When you do this, you'll find that the spin takes on a life of its own, and will simply continue until the job's done. You will notice a natural slowing and then stopping of the movement. Then you can check for a yes or no response, or re-measure the issue you were focusing on to see the improvement.

Some beginners will notice the spin wants to "go" on its own. I see this as an overly enthusiastic superconscious mind that is running ahead and doing its own thing out of pure excitement! I do discourage this, however, as we don't want to give away our power to processes of which we are not consciously in control. You need to be the rider of the wild horse, not the other way around. You can rest assured that you will eventually get around to what wants to clear, but from a place of conscious knowing and power.

As with any natural healing system, we find most of our work is in removal, or left spins. This is because, as we remove the stressors, healing spontaneously results. In natural healing, this tendency toward self-balancing is referred to as "homeostasis." This is also true for physical, mental, emotional, and spiritual healing. We are self-healing, self-regulating organisms. Occasionally, you will use a right spin to "top up" an area, or make a quick improvement because you don't have time to go into deeper levels of causation. I call this quick approach to an issue "allopathic dowsing," because, just like modern materialistic medicine, it is more focused on correcting the symptom than the issue the symptom represents.

Now let's look at how the two levels of dowsing can work together. Let's say you measured your life force at 60 percent today. Now you have two options. With a right spin, you can simply ask the dowsing system to raise your life force to 100 percent. Start the spinning movement yourself, but once the spins starts, *let go of all expectation.* After the spin begins to slow naturally to a stop, and it will, measure your life force again.

Did your life force improve? I have noticed that the length of time the spin takes to resolve can be a general indicator of the depth of the problem or situation. Deeper issues take longer, which makes perfect sense. As long as the spin continues, hold the intent in your mind.

There was a time when I thought the spin served mainly as a timer, or indicator of when the request was complete. Looking into the physics of vortices and spirals in the pattern produced by the spin, however, got me thinking that the spin itself may actually be playing a more active role here.

A vortex, by nature, acts as a transformational portal to other dimensions. The spin dynamic is involved in the very appearance of matter itself, according to the pioneering scientist Walter Russell and more recently David Wilcock with his studies of torsion fields. The spinning of water in natural streams is what infuses water with the life force, something that is lost when we add chemicals to and bottle or store water in huge cisterns. The multi-dimensional aspect of spinning can be observed when a tornado passes over an area and leaves debris in "impossible" combinations—like straw embedded in metal, for example. This could only happen if the matter is temporarily transmuted into a non-physical state in which the "blending" takes place in the split second before it returns to normal three-dimensional reality.

We also see a vortex at the center of the galaxy in the form of a Black Hole. Some scientists now speculate that the matter falling into the Black Hole may be going into dimensions beyond our present limited view—the missing 90 percent of "dark matter" in the universe. So the spin you make with your pendulum may actually be taking your intent, or thought form, and facilitating an outcome in a non-physical dimension first that will later manifest in this dimension. Wild, isn't it? Reality is stranger than fiction!

But let's look at what we've actually accomplished here. Your energy was down for a reason—maybe lack of sleep, energy-draining people or environments, poor nutrition. The list of possibilities goes on and on. If you do not identify and/or balance the causes of the energy loss, you have really just given yourself an "energy band-aid" and will likely find that your energy will drop soon after. Would it not be better to take the time to investigate possible causes and remove them as influences? By the way, that's why I think it's misleading for people to call themselves "healers." All healing is of the Divine and works though us. We never "heal" another. We can help someone's healing process, but ultimately it is the *individual* who chooses to accept healing with the help of the Divine—facilitated or "nudged" by your intent.

Let's revisit the above scenario with these questions in mind:

With 10 as 100 percent, where is my life force today? Answer: 60 percent.

Are there blockages to my life force that I can dowse out now?" Answer: yes.

Are these blockages physical? Answer: no.

Are they environmental? Answer: no.

Are they mental? Answer: no.

Are they spiritual? Answer: no.

Are they emotional? Answer: yes.

Are these emotional blocks more than 10 in number? Answer: no.

How many emotional blocks are there? Answer (on your hand chart): 3.

Is it necessary or beneficial to know more about these emotional blockages in order to clear them? Answer: no.

If the answer to the last question is yes, you will need to go deeper with your questioning. For instance:

Are these blockages from a past or future life?

Is this the best time to proceed with this clearing (Should I . . . )?

To what degree (percentage) is this person willing to let go of these blockages?

If no more work is required, make the following request with a left spin:

*I now ask that these three emotional blocks to my ideal life force be completely removed and replaced by pure life energy of the highest vibration.*

You didn't really have to stop half way and right spin the energy up, because your intent was that the released energy be transformed immediately into what you wanted. This is an important concept. When you release (left spin) an energy, *you have to do something with that energy.* Either you send it somewhere or change it into something desired.

The reason for this is a law of physics called the Law of Conservation of Energy. Energy cannot be destroyed, only changed into another form. Thus, you either include the intent within the left spin, or add a right spin and bring in something to replace it. Often, I just ask to send the released energy "to the most appropriate dimension for the highest good of all." Or ask that it be transmuted into 100 percent pure life-force energy.

After this, remeasure your life force. Again, I'll not be surprised to see it naturally rise to 100 percent once you remove the identified blocks. Now the improvement is more likely to "stick." So left spinning is great for clearing, neutralizing, removing, reducing, de-activating, erasing, reversing, undoing— you get the idea. Right spinning is the choice for adding, increasing, repairing, improving, maximizing, optimizing, raising, etc. You'll probably be doing at least 80 percent left spinning, then topping up with right spins as needed.

In chapter 4, you will find that the majority of the work involves removal. And sometimes you may have to go back and repeat a removal, as some hidden aspect of the blockage may likely bring it back. When Raymon was asked if dowsing once removes an issue forever, his reply was: "Well, do you only take one bath for a lifetime?"

What may explain this need to repeat things is that we can only go as far or as deep as our minds will allow in that moment without going into fear or resistance. Sometimes, your mind has to be convinced that it's safe to proceed to deeper levels. Be patient and recognize that the healing process is under the control of your superconscious mind, which knows all, sees all, and is infinitely patient. It took lifetimes to get to "now," so it may still take some time to completely clear all our issues. *A Course in Miracles* states: "Only infinite patience yields immediate results!"

When removing, or dowsing generally, don't get stuck on a set or memorized way of speaking. Raymon uses powerful words like "scramble," "deactivate," and "neutralize" to give some emotional "oomph" to the request. Be imaginative, and *really mean* what you are asking for! See the results in your mind's eye. Accept it as being done. Faith can move mountains and does not require physical evidence. Don't worry about what you may forget to say—the details are known by the dowsing system. Your intent is more important than the wording you use. The more you learn through study and hanging out with other dowsers, the broader your approach and vocabulary will become. But for now, accept that you are in the perfect place with the perfect understanding to be very effective now!

As for the following clearings, my general advice is to use them on yourself first. Get good and cleaned up before you start helping others. You'll get better results if you do. When you're on an airplane, they always tell you to put the oxygen mask on yourself first; otherwise, in an emergency, you're no good to yourself or anyone else! The same is true of dowsing.

I have found that the first dozen or so items cover the broadest ground, so, even if you are pressed for time, you can feel a lot lighter in a few minutes by just checking these.

After you've covered the clearings all the way through, your follow-up or maintenance sessions can be made a lot shorter. You may point to an item and ask: "Is this an issue for me?" and simply go down the list. Or, you could dowse the total number of issues to clear, then dowse each item number into a master list. (Remember to ask how many digits there are in your answer.)

Please do not consider the clearings to be "gospel." If an item rubs you the wrong way, or is against your belief system, pass it by. But please don't let your adopted beliefs limit your power either! This was the reason many limiting beliefs became institutionalized centuries ago—to keep people weak and under domination. Do not be afraid of your power.

So use the clearings in chapter 4 as a foundation, and you will likely begin adding new things as you go along and learn more. There's not a subject under the Sun that cannot be dowsed. I am always cheered when I come up with a new concept for a clearing or a new chart. It makes my day!

## WHAT IS REALITY?

Before going to chapter 4, I want to dispel some illusions that folks may have about the objective "reality" of a lot of the issues we'll be clearing, especially the "spooks" in the early part of the chapter. According to the metaphysics of *A Course in Miracles*, a very profound non-dualistic thought system, the manifest world in all of its aspects is a grand projected image or illusion of the mind—not the divine Mind, however, but the divided and fearful mind that is "split" between its dim memory of Spirit and its adopted identity as ego. The egoic mind was the result of an unfortunate decision of God's creation (us) to venture from Oneness and experience "something else." This understanding, by the way, answers the question: "How could God create a world of such pain, misery, and death?" Simple: He didn't! We did—you and I and our very human "split" minds. There is nothing "out there" that is not a projection of our experiences "in here."

Quantum physics has, for over 100 years now, shot holes in the belief in a solid objective world existing outside of or separate from the observer. If a tree falls in the forest and no one is there, does it make a sound? No. As a matter of fact, there's no tree or forest either! Sorry if this upsets your applecart or your assumptions about reality. Well, no, I'm not really. The truth doesn't have to be comfortable to be true. And if a new idea can shake the foundation of our assumptions, doesn't it make sense to look again at those assumptions?

However, even uncomfortable truths ultimately lead to peace. The *Course* states:

> *Anything real cannot be threatened, anything unreal does not exist. Herein lies the Peace of God.*

If what you thought was true is subject to change, was it really true? "True" truth must be changeless. Some truths are more accurately described as "relative truths"—true in one context or dimension, but not all.

Truth, once accepted without fear, is ultimately liberating. And the truth is—envelope please—we are all One! If all these phantoms (entities, demons, etc.) that we clear with dowsing are merely projections of our own misguided consciousness, what is there to fear? The Light of Truth will, in every case, dispel all illusions. That, by the way, is the job of the Holy Spirit. Please suspend any religious connotations that term may conjure up. You could call the Holy Spirit the active aspect of the Prime Creator. It is also called the Divine Messenger in some traditions. It is the memory of Oneness buried deep within the minds of all who are currently dreaming they are separate. So active dowsing is all really an exercise in personal freedom and helping others awaken to the truth about themselves. It clears the deck of all the old baggage and misconceived ideas that cloud our reality as spirits having a human experience.

Our aim when working with others is not to give these phantoms (entities, etc.) any more reality than they deserve (which is none), but to allow others the experience of themselves as unburdened by these useless vestiges of an outmoded, obsolete, and dangerous level of consciousness—the fearful ego. When we deal with these things in their symbolic form as thoughts, images, and feelings, we unburden our minds of a limiting illusory belief that is keeping us from awakening to our natural state—the full awareness of Oneness. The mind currently operates with the language of symbols—like words and pictures—so we use a language the mind can accept to help heal the mind of what is ultimately not true or real.

Some say the conditions on the planet now are simply the collective dream we are having in a state of spiritual sleep, and that the projected world we create daily is none other than our collective nightmare. There's a big benefit to waking up from this dream! Awakening from the dream is the prerequisite for the new world of peace and harmony that we all want at the deepest levels.

Too many people are enamored by the "spiritual" simply because it is beyond their understanding—that is, "mysterious." Add to this our tendency to fob off responsibility on someone or something else for how our lives unfold. We are all already eternal spiritual beings. We have nothing to add to ourselves to become all we are—just a lot of "stuff" to remove—like beliefs, illusions, fears, imprints, and memories. And where do all these blockages exist? Out there, in the objects and events of the physical world? Nope. They exist only where you experience them—in your mind. In the Tibetan and Egyptian Books of the Dead, we see the same dynamic being played out as departed souls face a series of their worst fears, each symbolized in a personal and poignant manner, usually in the form of some horrific demon. And each image disappears as soon as it is looked at with neutrality and without fear.

So, despite the dualistic language we may use in dowsing, which cannot be avoided because language is inherently dualistic, we are actually clearing out phantoms of illusion that seem very real until they vanish in the Light of Truth driven by our intent. This idea of total responsibility (and total response-ability) can be summarized with the affirmation: "*All* I ever experience is myself."

As you go through the various clearings, the language and assumptions inherent in the words are conducive to projecting these issues outside ourselves. Bear this in mind, and feel free to dowse out any fear that an issue may bring up. And of course, always ask permission with the Can I? May I? Should I? questions before dowsing for someone else. And respect those who do not want your help at any given time. To summarize, although we deal with dualistic ideas and language, we do so from a basis or footing in non-duality. For more on this liberating view, I suggest looking again at my first book, *Navigating the Collapse of Time.*

## MORE TIPS

When working with vague target information, such as doing distance work for a friend of a friend, ask: "Does the dowsing system know who I am intending to dowse for at this time?"

The original version of the following checklist was given in a two-day workshop. Obviously, we won't be able to go into the same amount of detail and give as many examples here, but you should be able to work with and expand upon all of them. Even doing the first few on a regular basis will have a dramatic positive influence.

After doing the whole list of clearings for yourself, you may want to do just a regular daily clearing, something like this. With left spin, say:

*I ask the dowsing system and my Guides to remove all negative and non-beneficial energies and frequencies from my physical, mental, emotional, and spiritual bodies, transmuting any lower frequencies into pure fifth-dimensional energies of healing, love, and joy.*

Wait for the spin to stop. Then, with a right spin, say:

*I now ask to raise my frequency, protection, and dowsing accuracy levels to 100 percent of their potential for the entire day. Bless me, my family, and my loved ones with divine peace, and allow me the opportunity today to forgive myself and others and to share love.*

## A NOTE ON TIME TRAVEL

With many of the items listed below and in chapter 6, we have found that one of the more effective ways to clear energies, traumatic memories, imprints, emotions, and thought forms is to identify the actual time frame when the event first occurred or was experienced. Although we understand that linear time is an illusion created by the mind and that, in reality all events occur simultaneously in quantum or vertical time, nevertheless the mind believes that these events are time-related, and so we work within that belief. It's as if the mind is given permission to believe its own experience and, in so doing, can identify and isolate the energies and frequencies associated with that memory. Often, you will want to ask about a specific issue:

*Is this a time-related issue? Is it in the highest good to clear this at the point of origin?*

Then you simply dowse the number of digits in the year (which is usually specific enough, although with gestation issues, you will want to identify the week or month) and dowse out the numbers in the year. Validate your findings:

*Did this event first occur for (client) in the year 1833?*

More often than not, you will dowse a year that is clearly beyond the client's current life span. The next question is whether the era is A.D. or B.C.? With your left spin, you then say something like:

*I now ask to go to the year 1833 A.D. and the lifetime that (client) is living then and transmute the emotion at that time that is affecting (him/her) now to 100 percent pure Light, reversing all ill effects in all lifetimes and dimensions, filling all voids with fifth-dimensional Light and love.*

I suggest you quantify the original emotion on a scale of 10 with "10" to represent an intense emotion at the end of a particular incarnation. When you get through a lot of the more recent past-life issues, you may find that you begin dowsing huge numbers, indicating a chance to time travel to lifetimes long, long ago or far, far away before you or the client ever came to the Earth. It is also not unusual when you get to these "advanced" clearings that the number of years you get will be in the future! You are sending a message back to yourself from a future timeline, hoping you make different choices in the "now" so you don't necessarily have to experience what "you" are experiencing in the future timeline determined by your past choices. This is mind-bending stuff!

We like to tell folks in our live classes that that little $15 pendulum is a time machine! Actually, your *mind* is the time machine. And, as time is a product of the mind, it is at your command!

# CHAPTER 4

# The Clearings (adapted from Raymon Grace)

ESTABLISH AN ALPHA STATE. Then ask:

*Can I, may I, should I dowse today for (myself, other person, situation)?*

The first few items are designed to build your confidence. Many new dowsers get discouraged in the early phases because doubt creeps in, or they think they are being too influential in the answers. Put those fears aside, and do the work. You'll do just fine!

## 1. SPIRITUAL PROTECTION LEVEL

Measure the percentage of protection. If it is not 100 percent, ask if there are interfering entities or energies present. If the answer is yes, ask if steps 2 through 9 will clear them. You can also simply right spin your protection up to 100 percent, but this may be temporary, and you should recheck your protection as you go, especially if you start getting inconsistent or contradictory results. Add "without reversal" to your request and avoid the need to repeat it.

Eventually, as you become more awakened and empowered, protection becomes a moot point, as you know the Light you carry automatically transmutes negativity in everything you see, say, and do. But until you reach that point, it's a good thing to check—just don't do it out of fear.

## 2. DOWSING ACCURACY LEVEL

Use a percentage scale for this step. If the accuracy level is less than 100 percent ask if the items to follow will clear up the reasons that your accuracy is low. Spin your accuracy up to 100 percent if necessary, using a right spin.

## 3. OVERALL BODY AND ENERGETIC FREQUENCY

Proceed as described above. If your energy frequency is under 100 percent, the shortcut is simply to right spin your frequency up. The more thorough approach, however, could sound like this:

Is the main factor negatively affecting my frequency physical?

Is it mental?

Is it emotional?

Is it spiritual?

Is it environmental?

Are there more than one category of blockages?

Are there items in the clearings to follow that will address this (these) issue(s)?

The raising of frequencies will speed your spiritual evolution, but may also bring issues to the surface that represent low or incoherent frequencies coming forward to be cleared, much like a metal refining process.. This is sometimes the price you pay for accelerated growth. You may want to ask your Guides and the dowsing system to moderate your frequency increase to a level and rate to which it is easiest for you to adapt.

## 4. LIFE FORCE

This is a little different than frequency and has to do with the strength of your *chi*, or the electrical energy in your field and body. This is a more "earthy" energy. You can break it down into volts, amps, and resistance, if you care to.

Volts are an indication of the strength of your kidney/adrenal complex—the "battery" of your energy field according to Chinese medicine. Amps reflect your brain power—the ability to hold, generate, and create thought and intent. Resistance has to do with the ease of the flow of energies through your body, which can be affected by a large number of factors. Hydration is highly related to life force. Use a percentage scale with an indication of ideal as 10.

## 5. NEGATIVE ENTITIES IN THE ENERGY FIELD

This refers to the presence of disincarnates in your field. Disincarnates are human souls who have left the body, but have not ascended to the higher dimensions. Instead, usually because of their strong mental or emotional attachment to the Earth plane—the three-dimensional world—they become stuck in the dimension that is in the frequency band closest to the third dimension—the lower astral plane, or the fourth dimension.

Entities attach to living humans because they are still playing out some kind of negative drama like grief, revenge, addiction, or sexual deviation. It is when you are in a negative emotional state sympathetic to these "lost souls" that you create an opening for them to hitch-hike on your energy field. These predispositions are sometimes called "attractor fields." Once you pick up this low-frequency energy, you begin to feel or act worse—that is, you can experience an intensification of the attractor-field issue.

Periods of unconsciousness also provide an open door for entity possession. It's not unusual for people who have lost consciousness in a fight, surgery, or accident to go through a personality change after the event. If the personality in these cases goes downhill, suspect an entity possession. Bear in mind that entity possession is more common than not. I'm surprised when someone with whom I'm working for the first time doesn't have at least a few! There are many more disincarnates than human hosts. Think of all the deaths throughout history that were the result of some negative drama—war, poverty, and disease, for example.

Again, we don't want to dwell on or create fear around these entities, as, from a non-dual perspective, they are denied and projected aspects of ourselves—all part of the One, and thus wanting eventually to be healed. You can think of them as disowned and outwardly projected thought forms that we have judged or expressed from a less-than-enlightened state. We send them "out there" in an attempt to distance ourselves from a painful thought or feeling, and eventually they come home to be recognized, forgiven, and healed. They are actually doing you a service in the long run by pulling you into the "deep end" of an area that has perhaps been only a minor issue for you, but one that you will never overcome until you experience it in its extreme polarity. It's like an electrical charge that cannot be discharged until both positive and negative come together and produce a spark of light.

This is consistent with Jung's psychology on the need to face and embrace our shadow selves to become whole. The risk involved in even talking about entities and disincarnates is that the ego will grab hold of the concepts to create fear and victimization, which are never productive or true. That is how you can tell the ego is around—you feel fearful, powerless, and afraid. You can tell Spirit is around when you feel calm, trusting, and happy. There are really only those two choices as to how we experience anything. These entities are attempting to correct a mistaken belief that wholeness can be found in suffering. You can now help them and yourself through your deeper understanding and compassionate will.

With that understanding, the entities often manifest as factors in chronic illness, pain, and depression, and you certainly have the option to release them. Typically, a troubling emotional charge will simply evaporate as you clear these energies. Here's a possible scenario:

Ask if Mary has an issue with negative entities in her field. Answer: yes.

How many? More than 10? Answer: yes.

More than 20? Answer: no.

Using the left-hand scale of ten, ask how many more than 10. Answer: 4.

Ask if Mary has 14 entities in her field. Answer: yes.

At this point, you can ask a lot more questions about the past:

How many years have they been present?

To what degree have they created limitation in her life?

To what degree are they responsible for her depression?

But this is not necessary information. It may be helpful in explaining some events or conditions, but the main point is to clean them up. I can't count the number of pains, headaches, and feelings of the "blues" that magically disappear with this clearing! Even migraines.

Ask if the Spirit Guides will clear the entities. Answer: yes. (I'll address what to do if the answer is no later.) With a left spin, say:

*I ask our Guides to take each one of the entities we have identified by whatever means necessary to the highest, most appropriate dimension for the highest good of all. Please reverse all negative effects, symptoms, or resonant issues they may have had with Mary, and remove from Mary all mental, emotional, physical, or spiritual attractor fields for these and similar entities. Thank you.*

Wait for the spin to stop.

It is not unusual for people to feel a subtle change in their energy as the entities leave. Generally, people report a sense of lightness and relief. The wording does not need to be exact, and you'll likely come up with things to add. As noted, try to avoid getting into a mindless repetition of a stock phrase, but break it up and change the language. It is the clear intent that is paramount.

## 6. NEGATIVE ENTITIES IN THE PHYSICAL BODY

These entities are different from the ones in the energy field in that they can be considered "squatters," while the latter are more like hitch-hikers. As squatters, they usually are more long-term tenants and can be located in a specific place in the body, often a joint. When you send them on, chronic joint pain that may have been around for years can instantly vanish. I have learned that you can combine these entities with the entities in clearing item 5, but it's good to be aware of the distinction. There may be value in going back to the age where the entity was taken on and clear it there. This can erase the memory of life-long suffering—literally rewriting the Book of Life! Ask at what age the entity was first encountered (use your Hand Chart). Then ask if you have permission to time travel there and deal with it then.

## 7. NEGATIVE ENTITIES IN THE HOME OR PROPERTY

This clearing can make a world of difference to the emotional tone of a home. Real estate agents will want to know about this one! You may also want to clear used cars, subway cars, your office, or a school in the same manner. The important thing is to give these beings a destination. "The most appropriate dimension for the highest good of all" works fine as an intent. Ask to reverse all ill effects, release all objects, and return all lost energies to the space. It's one of the rules of the game that, once you identify these energies and their effect on others, they have to obey your command. Gee, that makes us pretty powerful, doesn't it? Remember, *it's all us!*

A related problem can be earthbound spirits on the land. This is often the case where there has been a former burial ground, battlefield, or encampment of Native peoples. Given their affinity for Mother Earth, many of these souls have a hard time leaving the Earth plane when they leave the body. They are often still caught up in the patterns of suffering associated with Earthly existence or are simply reluctant to leave their Mother Earth. Check this if there is a lot of chronic illness, physical or mental, going back for generations with a family or property. The same basic clearing applies. You may need to call on higher authorities than your personal Guides. (See the section below on demonic forces.) You may want to connect with a Guide to whom the Earthbound spirits will listen, like a former chief or a recognized elder. Ask if one is available and willing to work with you in assisting these energies to move on to a "happy hunting ground."

## 8. NEGATIVE ENTITIES AT A DISTANCE

This can include entities operating from another dimension, planet, galaxy, or time frame, or a prior home that still projects an influence. They could be from your childhood, or past/future/parallel lives, in which case determining the year and time traveling is advised. If you don't ask, you won't know. Use the clearing dialogue given above.

## 9. DEMONIC FORCES

The language here is unfortunate, as there is a lot of historical and cultural baggage around the term "demon." The main difference here is that, unlike a disincarnate entity, a demon has never had an Earthly incarnation, and thus is of a purely spiritual nature. Demons are usually associated with the sixth or ninth dimensions, while entities and disincarnates are associated with the fourth. (See *Navigating the Collapse of Time* to further explore this model.)

Demons are among the fallen ones or fallen angels of legend. According to some views of spiritual cosmology, the present universe has been tainted by a rebellious faction that has taken the separated ego experience to its extreme limit. It was inevitable, I suppose, if we go back to the idea that dualistic issues will not be depolarized or transcended until both polarities reach their limit and collapse back into one another—the end of duality, or the end of the knowledge of good and evil. Because of the nature of demons, Spirit Guides will not deal with them.

There is a class of beings, however, who will help clear demons. Raymon Grace refers to them as Spirit Doctors, indicating some kind of specialized credential, I assume. Through dowsing, I have learned that these beings are a group of archangels—powerful beings with whom not many in the universe want to argue! You can be assured that, if you call on the Spirit Doctors, they will know who they are and what you need them to do.

So again, if you get a yes answer to demonic interference or presence, ask if the Spirit Doctors will take care of them. And see what happens. The language can be similar to Clearing 4. You may want to embellish it a bit by doing something like this. With a left spin, say:

*I now ask the Spirit Doctors (after determining their willingness to help) to take and totally bind all demonic forces affecting (person) and render them totally harmless by taking them to the most appropriate dimension for the highest good of all. Help these forces to recognize the spark of Light at the center of their being. Prevent them from wreaking any future havoc on any dimension and clear (person) of all negative affects and attractor fields associated with these beings in all time frames and dimensions. Please fill any voids created with pure life energy of the 5th dimension.*

Wait for the spin to stop.

I did have one case where a demon would not budge. It then occurred to me that this one was ready for the ultimate healing. I asked the Spirit Doctors to take it to the edge of "outer darkness," or the Void. Once there, it was immediately able to snap back to the Light for complete healing. In other words, it had to complete its chosen path, much as we sometimes need to fulfill a vow, contract, or obligation before we can move on.

We must transcend our own tendency to judge these "evil" beings. They are part of the One. After all, "evil" is simply "live" spelled backward! Perhaps they have even chosen a higher path than we assume because of their willingness to endure the suffering implied by their polarized state, so that all can heal eventually.

Now that we've cleared the major spiritual riff-raff, we must acknowledge that there is a whole menagerie of apparent creeps, slime balls, and low-lifers out in the lower astral plane, and some from beyond. Remember, these are just projected thought forms to which we have given life. Not all of these entities are in human form. Sorry for sounding harsh, but that's how they appear and operate until healed through our willingness to offer forgiveness.

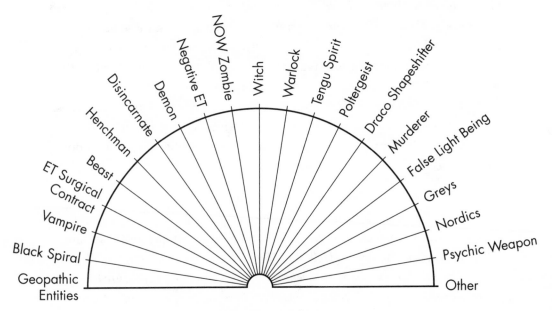

*Chart 4. Spiritual Beings*

Now, for every possible negative thought or emotion, somewhere out in the mind-made universe, that thought form or emotion form has an existence. *All thought produces form on some level.* So again, these beings are just projections of sick minds. As all minds are joined, I am equally responsible for them and in need of healing. That's why any of this has showed up in my experience in the first place. Again, it's not a simple black-and-white picture. The paradox is yes, they do seem to exist "out there"; but "out there" is really all "in here." The Spiritual Beings chart you can use to further identify low energy beings and entities. To use it, ask:

Is there something available here to be cleared for (subject)?

How many entities?

What is the first one?

In order to clear these and similar issues, you are going to have to get the right help. You have Spirit Guides and you know the Spirit Doctors. Chart 5 gives some excellent "helpers" to choose from. For each issue identified in Chart 4, refer to Chart 5 to find which helper will take care of your particular issue. Let's say this indicates Archangel Michael in regard to an energy vampire. With a left spin, ask something like this:

> *I now ask Archangel Michael to take and bind this energy vampire, taking it to the most appropriate dimension for healing, and preventing it from doing any more harm to anyone. Clear (person) of all ill affects of this being in all time frames and dimensions and prevent it from ever returning. Thank You.*

Wait for the spin to stop, while holding your intention.

Remember that it is easy for the ego mind (the analyzer) to buy into these entities as something independently real and therefore something to fear or worship. Neither makes any sense. Always keep in the back of your mind as you work these beings that they are all images representing denied and projected thought forms, all originating from the same One Mind in its dream of separation. Only this (non-dual) perspective can keep you from getting sucked into the beliefs and intents behind these projected thoughts. Remember, with dowsing, we have one foot in the changing illusion we call "reality" and the other firmly rooted in the "real" reality that is the changeless world of Spirit and your True Self.

With that always in mind, here's a sampling of what the items in Chart 4 may indicate. Some of these issues and others are discussed in much more detail further on in this book. These examples are presented simply as a taste of the depth and thoroughness you can achieve once you have charted specific potential problem areas. In each case, we trust the chosen helper to do the work; we simply make the introductions!

## Geopathic Entities

This refers to organized thought forms operating through geopathic stress lines, or ley lines. Send them back (left spin) to their source and reverse all ill effects for all involved.

## Black Spirals

These are energy vortices, either in the land or in a person's energy field, that are "leaking" negative energy into this dimension. Clear (left spin) them back to their source, then bring in (right spin) beneficial positive fifth-dimensional vortices in their place.

## Vampires

Vampires are more likely to be "energy vampires" than the Hollywood type. These may manifest in people who drain your energy and life force, leaving you feeling weak and dazed. Send the source of that energy to the most appropriate dimension, erasing all ill effects for all involved, and ask for the return of all lost energies.

## ET Surgical Contracts

People with ET surgical contracts may find they have "missing-time" episodes and curious scars or marks on their bodies, like those who claim to have been abductees. Ask if this agreement is voluntary or by coercion. Either way, the subject can choose whether or not to continue with the contract. Then dissolve it with a left spin.

## Beasts

Beastly energy is very base and animalistic. This energy may show up in the form of someone controlled by base urges—eating, sex, or power. Send (left spin) the energy behind these behaviors back to its source purified with divine love, and clear all associated thoughts, feelings, and memories from the subject, filling voids with fifth-dimensional light.

## Henchmen

Henchmen are particularly nasty demons. I once knew a lady who completely lost her fascination with horror movies after a simple clearing of these. Ask the Spirit Doctor to clear these, rendering them harmless in all time frames and dimensions.

## Zombies

Zombies are essentially soul-less bodies. They are easy prey for mind control and/or possession.

## NWO Zombies

These entities may be under the control of fear-based groups, and may therefore act erratically and out of character. Do not expect them to have any rational reasons for this behavior. It is best to steer clear of these types. You may want to dowse (right spin) to surround them in white light and render them harmless in all times and dimensions. Left spin out any contracts, vows, or agreements that no longer serve them.

## Psychic Weapons

A physic weapon is usually the etheric trace of a past-life murder weapon—perhaps an etheric bullet, arrow, guillotine, or sword. These can be associated with areas of blocked energy or chronic pain. Consider time travel to reduce the original trauma to zero.

## Negative ETs

Most ETs are friendly, but there are some that are not. Dowse out any vows, agreements, or contracts the subject may have with these, and ask your Guides or the Spirit Doctors to render them harmless. ET types are now understood to be other-dimensional beings, most of whom are benign or friendly. Some may be invasive or working on another's behalf. In all of this, it is paramount not to give in to fear or unwarranted awe. Just think of these beings as no more than mental projections—which is what they are.

## Witches

The witches referred to here are of the negative or "black" type, not the good white witches. So you thought the *Wizard of Oz* was pure fantasy? Black witches are beings that have devoted themselves to the full exploration of a specific aspect of darkness—which, from a non-dual perspective, does not exist. They are thus true believers in their own illusions of power over others. Nevertheless, as all thought produces form on some level, it may be beneficial to ask your Guides or the appropriate helpers to bind their energy and render them harmless, perhaps time traveling to the point of their decision to devote themselves to darkness and undoing that decision and all of its effects. A warlock is a male of the same type. We have found that releasing these energies with the right helpers can relieve depression and obsession with dark or negative energies.

### Tengu Spirits

These spirits are associated with Buddhist practices, and so may have a cultural preference for these practitioners. They are akin to demons, and so require a higher order of assistance to clear such as the Spirit Doctors.

### Poltergeists

Poltergeists can be responsible for things falling or getting lost and re-appearing, and for mischief in general. Interestingly, in psychology, poltergeists have been recognized and associated with a cantankerous teenage girl living on the premises! Send the poltergeist onto the most appropriate dimension for their highest good and clear the home from all negative affects or attractors.

### Draco Shapeshifters

These can be of a positive or negative type. Only 10 percent are of negative persuasion, however. These extra-dimensionals are capable of taking on human or animal form, and are primarily helpful or benign observers.

### Murderers

When murderers show up in a session, they are often associated with past lives. If you are dealing with one in this life, send forgiveness and recall that death is an illusion. Remember as well that we have all likely played both sides of this behavior as victim and perpetrator.

### False Light Beings

This implies that some form of deception is going on. There is something about this person or someone in his or her life that is not as it appears. Create an ethical index or an index for honesty and truthfulness using the Chart of Ten to question someone who seems "too good to be true" (this is one aspect of Chart 4). Many gurus and self-appointed healers may fall into this category, as being a "bearer of light and power" is something the ego loves to take over and use for its own purposes of creating more separation and dependency on the part of the perpetual "seeker."

### Grays and Nordics

These are two of the more commonly experienced ET races active on the Earth plane. There are others—like Pleiadians, Arcturians, and Sirians—who are much more benevolent, but these two seem to be associated more with power and control issues. Dowse out (left spin) any old contracts, vows, or agreements that may be involved. Release these beings to their higher purpose, and send them forward to a time and place (dimension) where they can do no harm.

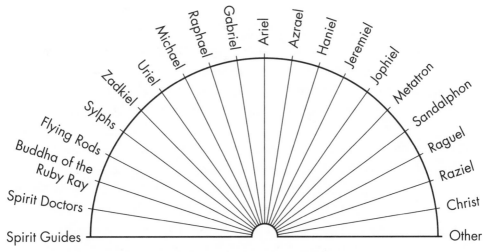

*Chart 5. Who You Gonna Call?*

## Who You Gonna Call?

I don't like to spend too much time on the negative, as the more attention we give it, the stronger it becomes in our awareness. Another one of the rules of the game is that whatever you put your attention on increases. People who are freaked out by entities like the ones above and constantly concerned about protection are doing themselves in. Fear feeds the flames of illusion. So shake off these forces, turn them over to the experts, and get on with filling the world with love, light, and gratitude. These are the vibrations that are destined to depolarize all the negativity in the universe. Use Chart 5 to identify the help you need to clear the negative forces described above.

The best protection is being in joy, which is your natural state and birthright. Darkness is merely the absence of light. It has no power other than the power you give it. Live in the Light, and that is all you need to experience.

## 10. FILLING VOIDS

At this time, ask if you have created any energetic voids. As "nature abhors a vacuum," it is wise to fill any voids intentionally rather than leaving the space open to unknown energies. If the answer is yes, with a right spin, say:

*We ask that all of these clearings remain without reversal. Please fill all voids created by these clearings with fifth-dimensional frequencies of unconditional love, truth, thankfulness, joy, and forgiveness. Seal these clearings for all time and create an impenetrable purple protective field around (client) that will only allow healthy, loving frequencies in and will deflect all negative frequencies back to the universe as love.*

The reason we ask for things to be transmuted into fifth-dimensional energies specifically is that this is the closest frequency range to us in the third dimension that is non-dual. In other words, it is the most accessible realm of perfection to us here in the third dimension, which is obviously dualistic—a world of opposites and the conflicts that opposites imply. Some would say that the Shift of the Ages that is upon us at this time will actually catapult three-dimensional Earth and all who are willing to go into the fifth dimension. So filling voids through dowsing with fifth-dimensional energy is a way of helping prepare for the changes and get a taste of those changes now.

## 11. NEGATIVE ENERGETIC PATTERNS AT BIRTH

We all suffer birth trauma to some degree along with our mothers. Coming back into the third dimension after basking in unconditional love between lives is rather a rude shock—what are we to do with this helpless little body? We experience a lot of pain, noise, and confusion—and possibly regret. "Oh yeah, now I remember. Why the heck did I volunteer for this again?"

If you get a yes in response to this issue, which is very common, ask first for the degree of trauma on a scale of 1 to 10. Ask for the degree of influence of these patterns on the life path, with 10 as extremely bad. Ask the Guides to reverse (left spin) all mental, emotional, spiritual, physical, and cellular memories of birth trauma, transmuting their energies into fifth-dimensional frequencies of joy and love. Ask to reduce the index back to zero.

Optimally, you will want to time travel back to the point of birth and remove the trauma then. I feel this is a much more comprehensive approach. Doing this has the effect of neutralizing all ill effects of birth trauma throughout the entire life path. In quantum time, all events are happening simultaneously, and so are within easy proximity to us in this now. There is something the mind recognizes when we identify the first or original time of a trauma. It's like giving the mind permission to recognize the event for what it is. "Ah, I know what this is about and I remember exactly when it started. OK, let's get to work letting it go!"

## 12. COMPATIBILITY OF SPIRIT GUIDES

This may refer to your compatibility with significant persons, partners, or co-workers. If the answer is yes for this item, it may help explain why certain relationships have hit an impasse—why you always seem to lock horns with certain people and never seem to be able to grow toward a more mature relationship, even when you and they sincerely want to. For instance, ask to what degree (percentage) you and your boss's Spirit Guides are compatible, with 10 as 100 percent. Then ask if your Guides are willing to raise your compatibility. If the answer is yes, with a left spin, say:

*I now ask my Guides to help all Guides involved with (person 1) and (person 2) to release all blockages, resistances, and other issues preventing their 100 percent compatibility, for the highest good of all. Transmute this energy to whatever will support complete harmony and compatibility between these Spirit Guides forever.*

Recheck the question and raise the compatibility level with a right spin if necessary. (It shouldn't be.) You may be surprised how the relationship will shift toward the positive with no other effort on yours or your client's part. Don't forget that you can also do a Spirit Guide upgrade to 100 percent pure Light for all Guides involved as well.

## 13. HEXES, CURSES, SPELLS, BLACK MAGIC, BAD MEDICINE, WITCHCRAFT

These are archaic terms for negative thought forms. Recall that all thought produces form somewhere, somehow, and somewhen. Be sensitive to your subjects and use the modern term if you think they'll be upset or mystified by these concepts. A thought form is simply an energy imprint created by a powerful intent directed with strong emotional energy. These thought forms, especially if shared by many people, take on a pseudo-life of their own and hang out in the lower astral plane, or fourth dimension. They can imprint the DNA of those who are resonant with them. The fourth dimension is the domain of the collective consciousness of mankind. Since the current human mind is split into a dualistic state at this time, it's no surprise that the astral plane is the plane of both angels and demons.

Let's say that, in your lineage, your distant relative accidentally killed your neighbor's cow. The neighbor was understandably upset, and directed to your poor ancestor an emotionally charged thought form like this: "May all your children be cursed with buck teeth from this time forward!" That energy went straight into your ancestor's DNA memory and was passed on to the entire lineage, just as predicted.

Words are powerful forms. Sound is a seventh-dimensional phenomenon. Words are not just inert sounds. They are most powerful when they are coupled with intent and strong emotion. Miguel Ruiz, in *The Four Agreements* (San Rafael, CA., Amber-Allen Publishing, 1997), cautions us not to use our Word against ourselves (his definition of "sin") or our neighbors (his definition of "Black Magic"). Instead, he encourages us to be impeccable with our Word.

If you get yes for an answer when asking if this is an issue, you can certainly ask how many, which type of energy applies to your subject, and even pinpoint the year or years in which the energy was directed. You may choose to release these issues in the generation they first were experienced. Dowse this number of generations back on either the mother's or father's side. I think time traveling to these and other issues feels more complete, because in that way, you can positively affect all beings and relationships involved—past, present, and future.

Remove the issues and their effects with a left spin. Be sure to include the clearing of all time frames and dimensions in your dowsing request. Transmute the energy to fifth-dimensional energies. Check properties and homes for curses as well. Some properties have been the site of previous wars, or may be burial grounds or places of other negative activity. A "curse on the land" was a serious deal in olden times. We moderns need to be reminded of these cultural practices, which we tossed out of our world view in the Age of Materialism (see number 16 below).

## 14. FAMILY CURSES

These are similar to those listed above, but specifically directed to your lineage. Be sure to remove these from ancestors, children, and future generations as well.

## 15. PRE-HISTORIC CURSES

This is a bit more mysterious. My understanding is that this has to do with imprinted negative memories—perhaps imprinted on DNA or even on an elemental level. The DNA in every cell in your body is not just a record of your immediate lineage; it is a record of all life forms on the planet and in the universe. DNA in your entire body is made of elements that existed before life as we know it emerged. The elements in our bodies were literally formed in the explosion of a star that existed before our current Sun was formed. You can take elemental memory right back to the Big Bang.

Our Sun is a second-generation star formed out of the dust of a primal star. The elements in your body carry the energetic signature, or memory, of this creative cataclysm and every other cataclysm that occurred on Earth over the billions of years it took for life to emerge. That is why DNA has been called "the Book of Life" and a "living library." That adds up to a lot of stress and challenges over the eons. Many times in the ancient past, almost all life was wiped out on Earth to be replaced by better-adapted, more complex life forms. Your DNA and cells remember.

If these curses are present, you can dowse them out with a left spin, transmuting their energy into fifth-dimensional energy. Consider time travel to the point of origin. Be prepared to dowse some big numbers!

## 16. CURSES ON HOME OR PROPERTY

These may have been directed toward former occupants, or may represent current issues—like disgruntled neighbors. They may also have deep historical roots—curses on former battlefields, or on sites of massacres or pestilence, or on graves. Ask if there are any Earth-bound spirits involved, and whether your Guides will help them go to a higher dimension. After clearing the curses (left spin), send the spirits onward with a right spin, saying:

*I now ask my Guides and the dowsing system to require all willing Earth-bound spirits in the home and property of _____ to move to the highest dimension appropriate to their soul path and for the highest good of all. I ask that this home and property be cleared of all associated ill effects and blockages, filling any voids with 5D energy.*

## 17. SPIRITS OF VICTIMIZATION

As discussed earlier, thoughts carry vibrations. They can also take on a vibratory life of their own, as it were, and "personify" as specific kinds of spiritual energy. Also, some lower astral thought beings specialize in creating and sustaining specific forms of suffering. A spirit of victimization will try to keep someone feeling powerless, under control, and fearful of making a change for his or her own good. This imprisons the will, and keeps people from realizing their power and potential. Do you detect the fearful ego at work here? Clear and replace it with a spirit of empowerment and responsibility.

## 18. SPIRITS OF CO-DEPENDENCY

I think co-dependency is a somewhat limited psychological concept that gave power to the notion that people can ensnare themselves in unhealthy relationships that are difficult or impossible to escape. This implies helplessness and victimhood. To be interdependent is good, as we are all, on a transpersonal level, the same being trying to wake up to his/her true Self.

A spirit of co-dependency, for our purposes, can be viewed as someone being locked in a mutually limiting, destructive, or enmeshed relationship in which the healthy boundaries of ownership of thoughts and feelings are blurred, allowing for a lot of unconscious "junk" like guilt, anger, and fear to pile up energetically. These relationships have a "heavy" quality to them where true learning has been blocked by a lack of forgiveness. This is a real feast for the ego! Dowsing this spirit out (left spin) can help break the deadlock and enable people to move forward individually. The results of clearing this pattern can go either way as far as the relationship goes, as each person is freed to choose to grow independently, either within or without the relationship.

Another approach to these dead-end relationships in which growth has come to a standstill is to ask the Guides to bring forgiveness and healing to the root of the blockage and cancel all unnecessary contracts, agreements, vows, or karmic issues between them, then to ask to address the Akashic Record of the relationship, bringing it to completion. You may want to have them visualize their personal Library of All Relationships. Use lots of color and sensory input as you describe the scene. Have them enter and ask the Record Keeper permission to complete the relationship, and to recover the "book of the relationship with _____." Have the Record Keeper stamp the last page of the book of the relationship with the word "Completed," then close the book and put it back on the shelf. We can be thankful that we live in a time when we can step out of relationships that are no longer held in love or joy, or that only perpetuate pain.

## 19. SPIRIT OF DEATH

Let's be clear. There is no death! Death is only a transition from one form to another. Freud came up with the concept of the "death instinct"—which he called Thanatos—to explain how some of his patients seemed driven to self-destruction. He may actually have been dealing in some cases with a disincarnate or demon possession. There is a phenomenon, however, in which people reach a certain impasse or plateau with their healing and a part of them does not want to give up the "payoffs" their illness gives them. For some people, being sick gives them the first opportunity to be treated with respect by their loved ones—to feel special or needed. On an unconscious level, this may be very difficult to give up, only to go back to the way it used to be when they were healthy and ignored, taken for granted, or abused.

This is not healthy. We need to heal on all levels—heal from the illness, but also heal the emotions and beliefs that led to the illness.

Another point to consider here is that, contrary to the modern medical model, death is not the enemy. As many ancient cultures recognized, death was a reason to celebrate at the end of a successful life. So, for example, if you dowse for someone who is dealing with a long chronic issue, or perhaps someone who is in a lot of pain and unable to have a reasonable quality of life and the answer is yes to the spirit of death being present, next ask if it is in the highest good of all concerned to remove it. Don't be surprised if the answer is no. If it is, respect the choice the person has made and find other issues to dowse about.

If you determine that the spirit of death is inappropriate at this time and a blockage to healing and learning, ask permission of your Guides, and clear it with a left spin, transmuting its energies into pure life force.

A spirit of death may be appropriate when it represents a conscious choice to graduate from the physical body. What is truly alive can never be destroyed. It is possible to heal mentally, emotionally, and spiritually and still depart the body—like leaving one room and entering another.

A spirit of death is not appropriate when it is coming from unconscious guilt. It is unconscious guilt stemming from the ego that drives us to self-destructive beliefs and behaviors like suicide. Suicide can be quick and dramatic, or slow—as in the case of self-neglect or addictions.

## 20. PSYCHIC CORDS

These are very real etheric lines of energy that connect us—usually with someone with whom we have had a close or intimate relationship in the past. These cords often connect to the lower chakras of the body, and are very likely present in those who have suffered sexual abuse or rape (roughly 30 percent of all females and 20 percent of all males). There is an element of parasitism implied in psychic cords, and we can just as easily be the perpetrators of them as the victims.

Any strong mental/emotional projection sent to or by you can create a psychic cord. Teachers, healers, speakers, and people in the public eye are particularly vulnerable. If you are one of these, check yourself periodically, especially when you feel drained after a session or function. Ever wondered why celebrities are easy prey to addictions? Think of all the emotional energy projected onto them!

First ask if the cords are present. If the answer is yes, you can ask how long they've been there, how many there are, and to what degree (percentage) they are draining the energy of the person.

Left spin to remove all cords and ill effects.

Right spin the healing of the chakra, sending love and forgiveness to the source, or other end of the psychic cord.

Ask for a return through the crown chakra of all energies that were lost to the psychic cord.

A Comprehensive Mini-Course in Spiritual Dowsing

Ask to repair any of the chakras and the energy fields where the cords were attached.

One of my sensitive, psychic friends said that it felt as if vacuum cleaner hoses were being pulled out of his energy field as these cords were being removed. People will generally feel better when they stop losing energy this way. You may need to check this one periodically.

## 21. PERCENTAGE OF ORIGINAL SOUL PRESENT

Your original soul is the portion of total soul energy assigned to your body at "ensoulment" in incarnation. Ensoulment occurs by the third month of gestation. Every Over Soul decides what percent of its total being it will invest in this incarnation. It is my understanding that the average is 15 percent. It is this 15 percent of the total soul being that we call 100 percent of the original soul. Confused? That's okay. No human body could handle the full power of a complete ensoulment. Christ could handle 100 percent for short periods, but kept disappearing when he did! So the average a being can handle seems to be around 15 percent at this time. We will call that portion 100 percent for our dowsing purposes.

It is not unusual to see that less than 100 percent of the original soul is present. This indicates a likely reaction to trauma at some point in time. In many cases, the issue goes back to the original birth trauma. An extreme example of this is found in the case of multiple-personality disorders. People suffering from this disorder usually suffered extreme abuse as children, causing the soul entity simply to leave the scene of a most unpleasant experience. These people enter into a fantasy world (the fourth dimension) where the abuse simply is not happening. Of course, this leaves their bodies essentially unoccupied and available to random tenants and squatters. There are many more disincarnates than there are bodies available! Be glad you have one!

Again, this is the extreme case. It is much more common for a portion of the soul energy to step outside the body in the face of a minor trauma. If this soul displacement becomes permanent, the person may have a sense of reduced vitality and not being "all there." These folks often have diminished enthusiasm in their lives. There is also more likelihood that they will pick up hitch-hikers if there's an empty place for them.

Ask permission to bring 100 percent of the soul back into the body. Better still, go back to the time of displacement, which is often at birth, and correct it then (see the next clearing). With a right spin, bring it all home. You may want to add "not to be displaced by any future trauma or foreign energy" to your intent. Call in 100 percent of the original soul from whatever dimension of time or space it may have fragmented.

A while back, I noticed that, with some folks, I would get a reading of zero percent of the original soul in the body. I was mystified, until I asked: "Is there a soul other than the original soul present in the body?" The answer was yes. I then came across Ruth Montgomery's 1960s work on the phenomenon of Walk-ins called *Strangers Among Us* (Coward, McCann & Geoghan, 1979). Not much has been written about these entities, but the explanation seemed to fit the bill.

According to Ruth, a Walk-in is a higher-level soul that elects to come into a body at a later stage in the human life to accomplish some kind of humanitarian or altruistic goal. Apparently, there are a lot more souls wanting to get here than there are available bodies. Especially now, at this time in history, many advanced souls want to incarnate to assist in the ascension of the planet and humanity to the fifth dimension forseen in the Mayan calendar, the *I Ching*, and many other sources. So the "time sharing" of available bodies seems to be the answer!

A Walk-in transfer is not necessarily dramatic or even noticeable, at least not initially. As with a disincarnate experience, it can occur as the result of a momentary loss of consciousness like a blow to the head or an accident. The difference, of course, is that a disincarnate is not a good thing, and is most likely to feed off some kind of suffering. A Walk-in, on the other hand, is a good thing.

Often after a Walk-in experience, people feel a deep need to change their lives for the better, often embracing a higher goal or purpose. They may lose interest in their former pursuits and circle of friends, and develop a need to learn a new skill or study a new area that ultimately leads to some greater expression of human service. There were some "big years" for Walk-ins: 1972, 1986/7, 1993, and 2003 come to mind. Ask if you are one. I wouldn't be surprised, as not just everyone is magnetically drawn to esoteric subjects like dowsing. If the answer is yes for yourself or for someone else, ask to ascertain the year of transfer. If you are given permission, use the Hand Chart and dowse the digits in the year.

This can be very helpful information for people to know. It can help them accept themselves and the changes they may have gone through. It can also help them commit further to their purpose, now that they know what is behind it.

Being a Walk-in does not erase your history. You still have the same personality, likes, memories, etc. It's just that the quality of Light that shines through these filters has changed. The former soul returns to its Over Soul self and awaits its next incarnation. The former soul is usually a younger soul that needs more experience growing up human, being part of a family, and all the other things that being human entails. Walk-ins are more developed souls with more experience and less need to repeat "grade school." They are here for a higher purpose.

In a few cases, I have come across someone whose original soul had only partially left to make room for a Walk-in. This is a co-habitation scenario. If you encounter this, ask if it in the highest good of all and, if not, invite the original soul to reunite with the Over Soul and allow the Walk-in to incarnate fully.

## 22. PERCENTAGE OF ORIGINAL SOUL AT BIRTH

This question projects the issue above back to the time of birth. Birth trauma often represents the point at which a soul splits—a point that can affect the entire life path. This is another example of when time travel can be effective—giving the ability to shift energies at any point and literally rewrite the personal history and therefore memory.

We generally operate under the stultifying belief that the past is fixed. The only thing that is fixed about the past is our entrenched beliefs about it. Try this idea on for size: The past is not what it used to be!

Understanding quantum time is helpful here. In school, we were taught to think of time as running along a horizontal axis, like some kind of linear, directional process. This created the impression that past events are solid, but somewhere off to the left of us—out of reach and therefore unchangeable. The future, likewise, is somewhere on the right of the line, equally out of reach and unpredictable. And here you are in the present, a measly little point on this infinite line trying to navigate these huge forces of past and future on either side. Have you ever noticed that most of the content of your thought is either reviewing or regretting the past, while worrying and trying to control the future? Your ego is afraid of now, because now is perfect! Right now, you don't even need an ego!

In your mind's eye, take hold of that horizontal timeline and rotate it until it becomes vertical—straight up and down. This view more accurately represents how time works. The past is now above the pivot point of now, and the future is below it. You can best think of this vertical line as a stretched-out point of now in which all events—past, present, and future—are occurring at the same time, which is now! Confused? This may help.

When it was yesterday, what time was it? Now, right? And of course, it's also now now. And when you get to tomorrow, what time will it be? Now again! So the only real time we ever experience is—you got it—now! This idea can help to liberate you entirely from the prison of the past and the fear fortress of the future. I think this is largely what the Shift of the Ages is about.

If you can shift energies in this now—which I am sure you can if you've come this far—what is the difference between this and any other now? There is actually some emerging scientific evidence that this is more than a mind game. The "many universes" theory that emerged from String Theory proposes that, for every potential choice or event in any dimension or time frame, a separate virtual universe exists that supports that event. We choose the universe we wish to experience by the choices we make every moment of every day. So we literally bring universes into being, and can jump from one to the other at the speed of thought. The past or future is not so far away, and we can work with it just as easily as we can work with this now.

If you get an answer of less than 100 percent of the original soul in the body at birth, with a right spin, say:

*I now go back to the time of birth for _____ and recover 100 percent of the soul back into the body for as long as is necessary or beneficial, for the highest good of all.*

You can use time travel to seek out the root of current mental, emotional, physical, or spiritual issues. This ties into the issue of past lives as well. There is something about doing this that gives the conscious mind an anchor, as it were, to accept the need for or possibility of change. After all, we made time up to begin with and, on some level, you know this!

For *any* issue, you may be guided to ask whether the issue has a root in another time frame. Is it rooted in the past? In the future? Is it necessary or helpful to identify the year? Then ask if it is possible to go backward/forward to that time and remove, scramble, and deactivate the cause of this current issue.

## 23. IMPLANTS

Implants are either physical objects or etheric (immaterial) patterns inserted into the body or energy field for specific purposes. I know this sounds vague, but nobody really has the final word on implants. If you get an answer of yes when you ask about their presence, you can ask if they are beneficial and if it would be beneficial to have them removed. You can also ask if they are physical or not, how many there are, and when they were implanted. While this background information may be very interesting, it is not necessary for their removal.

Some people feel that implants are "tracking devices" for observing and perhaps even controlling or limiting us—working in much the same way as the tags we put on cattle. They may be placed there by Earthly or ET beings. If you get an answer of yes to this situation, I think you'll want them out of there!

You may need to apply to special helpers for their removal—helpers like the Spirit Doctors. Be sure to release all associated blockages, contracts, or agreements and fill any voids with fifth-dimensional loving energy.

## 24. FEELING WANTED AT BIRTH

This is a very formative factor in our emotional lives. Even while in the womb (you may want to check for prenatal emotional influences as well), we experience all our mother's emotions, whether directed toward us or not, as if they are our own. We also directly experience hormonal shifts, allergies, toxins, and other stress factors.

If the percentage of feeling wanted at birth is less than 100 percent, first remove the negative beliefs and emotions from the entire life-path (left spin), then raise the feeling to 100 percent joy. You can also check energy levels and the "love index" of the parents, doctors and nurses and birth location on a scale of 1 to 10 and adjust accordingly.

## 25. COMPATIBILITY WITH BIRTH LOCATION

If the compatibility of the subject and their birth time and location is less than ideal, raise the energy level to 100 percent compatibility. Check physical, mental, emotional and spiritual compatibilities.

Here's a novel approach. If the compatibility with the birth location or time on your percentage chart is dismal, and you or your subject would really like to change the entire experience, you can! Choose a location in which you would like to have been born—maybe a paradise like Hawaii, or a power place like the Andes or the Pyramids at Giza—and ask your Guides for the compatibility with the new location and if you can change the energy of your birth location to match the energy of your chosen location at 100 percent compatibility. See what difference this makes in your current energetic state. Since the past is not fixed, you can always make another choice. You'll still have to use the former birth location on your passport, however!

## 26. NEGATIVE BELIEFS, THOUGHTS, OR MEMORIES

These can be inherited, learned by association, or self-imposed, and they represent much of the mental and emotional baggage we all pick up as a result of living here in the third dimension. True learning—that is, Self-knowledge—has been described as more of an unlearning process—ridding ourselves of the weight of the remnants of unawakened human collective consciousness.

Psychologists say that 99 percent of the thousands of thoughts we have each day are the same ones we have every day—that is, they are entirely conditioned. Westerners have a particularly hard time with this, as we are all very cerebral at the expense of the more nonverbal types of intelligence of which we are capable. In addition, the ego has convinced us that our thoughts are uniquely our own and entirely private. Not so! We are all joined on the level of the One Mind in the fourth dimension. The trouble is that the One Mind is having a bad dream called "separation." Awakening from the dream is our homecoming. Remove these beliefs and transfer the emotional energy attached to them to positive energy.

Ask your Guides to help you become more conscious of your everyday stream of thoughts, or inner dialogue. Part of you can actually separate from the "thinking" process and observe it from an inwardly detached perspective. The value of regular meditation is in cultivating this inner healthy detachment as a habit. Remember, it can take twenty-one days of practice before a new habit becomes spontaneous. Once you have established the perspective of the neutral observer of thought, you are more likely to think *consciously,* rather than just from the collective conditioned mind. It is like waking up in a dream. Most dreams seem real while you're in them, and you feel you have no control over events. But sometimes, you wake up in the dream and realize: "Hey, I'm dreaming!" You can then start directing the dream the way you want it to go.

You can dowse this issue by asking to what percentage you are awake in your dream-world or illusion of separation. If less than 100 percent, ask if there are blockages that can be dowsed out. If the answer is yes, with a left spin, say:

*I now ask that these blockages to my complete awakening within my mental/emotional dream world be removed and transmuted to pure awareness from this time forward, and that this awakening occur at a safe natural pace, allowing me to assimilate it fully with grace and ease.*

## 27. NEGATIVE ARCHETYPES

These are persistent personality patterns, often with a past-life association. Caroline Myss has written extensively on this subject, identifying over 300 possible patterns. This may be more than is practical or needed. Unlike disincarnates, these patterns are typically aspects of your own past-life "story line."

Personality archetypes may create behavioral patterns or shortcomings that interfere with your ability to work, have positive relationships, and just get along with other people. For example, people with a King or Blueblood archetype may have a hard time working for anyone else, as they carry the unconscious memory of being everybody else's boss. I specify negative archetypes here, because some archetypes may be serving you well, and you can certainly investigate and raise the influence of these if you want to. A short list of common, potentially limiting archetypes follows. You will find more extensive charts for both beneficial and non-beneficial archetypes in chapter 6. Use your number scale to determine how many apply to you, and to identify specific ones. Left spin to remove all cellular memory of these archetypes in all time frames and dimensions.

| | |
|---|---|
| King | Slave |
| Queen | Simpleton |
| Blueblood | Outcast |
| Master | Criminal |

| Priest | False Healer |
|---|---|
| Priestess | Charlatan |
| Gambler | Victim |
| Militant | Seducer |
| False God/Goddess | Miser |
| Psychic Manipulator | Cheat |
| Martyr | Drug Addict |

## 28. OLD ISSUES

Unresolved mental/emotional attachments to prior dramas can create significant drag on your happiness. We all have a story that becomes embellished with time and often reinforces some of the negative archetypes we were just discussing. Ask first if old issues are holding you back, then ask to what degree you or your subject are willing to let go of attachment to the drama. One of our typical unconscious fears is that, if we give up our dramas, which we feel are part of our identity, we won't know who we are. You can dowse up the willingness and motivation to let go of the drama, then dowse out and transmute its energy to fifth-dimensional pure Light.

## 29. VOWS, CONTRACTS, AND AGREEMENTS

These may be from either past or present lives. Along the same themes as above, these issues involve heartfelt commitments that we made at a time when we felt they were necessary, not realizing that, in another life, they could become blockages. These are often vows made within a religious context, or from a place of servitude. A vow of poverty may be contributing to an inability to hold a job or manage money. A vow of obedience may be keeping you from taking initiative or complete responsibility with your life. A vow of chastity may be involved with sexual fears, frigidity, or impotence. A vow of vengeance can be part of a problem with anger or aggressiveness. After removing the vows with a left spin and releasing all relationships from their ill effects, transmute their energy into positive emotional energy in the present with a right spin.

## 30. POLLUTED THOUGHT PATTERNS

These can be the result of education, media influence, and negative human or non-human associations. Scramble, deactivate, and adjust their frequency to pure thought forms. Time travel to their source in time and do the work there. Remove their impact on the future.

## 31. LACK OF DESIRE FOR IMPROVEMENT

Positive change requires at least some degree of motivation, or will. If the desire for improvement is low, remove inner resistances and raise it to 100 percent.

You can likely see, at this point, how many of these issues and clearings become self-reinforcing. You may find that you are approaching one or a few core issues, but from a variety of perspectives. This is good positive reinforcement, and the more angles from which you approach an issue, the less likelihood there will be of reverting to former patterns.

## 32. SELF-DESTRUCTION, SELF-JUDGMENT, SELF-PUNISHMENT, SELF-HATE, SELF-SABOTAGE

This is getting very specific with self-destructive programming. These kinds of subconscious programs can drag down your immunity, contribute to depression, and even lead to disease and suicidal thoughts. They do not have to be conscious impulses to be active. Usually, they aren't conscious at all. Be sure to transmute their energy to positive, loving energies as you clear them. Also clear all negative effects of these patterns on your subject, and on their loved ones and families.

## 33. BRAINWASHING AND MEDIA PROGRAMMING

It doesn't take a genius to realize that the majority of media and entertainment (read: entrainment) is aimed at the lowest common denominator of human consciousness and is, at least on the surface, motivated by market concerns focused on lower egoic drives, fears, and instincts. I have also read very well-documented evidence that the 50- to 60-hertz AC field in everyone's home disrupts the biological energy field, and that cell towers, which are ubiquitous, operate in a frequency band that is ideal for mind control. What do you expect from a world mirroring an insane wish to be separate?

Young minds are particularly vulnerable. Read *The Plug-In Drug* by Marie Wynn (New York, Penguin, 2002) for an exposé on the effects of television on young brains. I have found that, often, a specific media experience at a young age can imprint a deep fear or phobia. Go to the age of exposure and work there.

Dowse for the degree of influence from these sources. Reduce the desire for media, which can be a form of addiction. I have actually found violent and disturbing visual media to be a potentially deep traumatic trigger in children younger than seven—one that can affect intellectual development and emotional security. Raise the desire for truth and the ability to discern truth from lies.

## 34. CELLULAR MEMORY PATTERNS

This refers to what science now recognizes about DNA. Len Horowitz's latest book, *DNA: Pirates of the Sacred Spiral*, documents that DNA is an ideal medium for the storage and transfer of information. It does this via laser emissions (bio-photons) and by utilizing the extra-cellular matrix of water and specific proteins in the body capable of information transfer on a quantum level.

The DNA "Book of Life" carries a record of all life on Earth going back to creation. Specific traumas are stored as memories in the DNA, and can predispose us to re-experiencing similar experiences by resonant attraction. In homeopathy, these memories are called "miasms" and can contribute to the probability of developing certain physical ailments or weaknesses. Ask for their removal in all time frames and dimensions, and ask to reverse all negative effects of these patterns for all time. Invite higher Light to come in and repair the DNA disordered by these patterns. You may want to dowse in the frequency 528, an ancient musical or *Solfeggio* frequency known to have positive effects in restoring DNA. Dowse it in at the most beneficial frequencies and potencies for the client's highest good.

## 35. UNWORTHINESS, FEAR, DOUBT, SHAME, AND GUILT

These patterns are particularly important to remove, as they are the five top emotional immune depressors. You may want to get time-specific for the deepest clearing. I like to dowse for which pattern in particular needs clearing, and sometimes will inquire as to the time frame of first exposure. Check and reduce their effects on immunity. Raise immunity and self-love to 100 percent.

## 36. HERITAGE, CULTURE, AND RELIGION

The vast majority of our ancestors lived in a much smaller world. The parameters that worked for other generations thus may no longer work in the era of globalization and emerging higher consciousness. It is good to acknowledge and honor traditions. Try to see the root of traditions as respect for life, family, and nature. These are the beneficial effects of heritage, culture, and religion. When, however, these serve to divide rather than join, to criticize rather than accept, and to fear rather than love, they do not work for us, but against us all. They become part of the separatist agenda of the ego.

The notion that spiritual knowledge can be passed on by traditional or religious affiliation from one generation to the next is simply unqualified wishful thinking. These practices have more to do with the passing on of wealth or dynasties historically than they ever did with spirituality. True spirituality, which is everyone's birthright, is only experienced on a deep, subjective, and personal level. No creed, doctrine, or set of beliefs will ever substitute for the real thing—direct contact! You don't want to step in the dogma!

If you find these patterns present, ask for their degree of influence. Ask that they be cleared for past and future lineages as well. Replace them with frequencies of love, tolerance, and acceptance.

## 37. REPRESSED POSITIVE EMOTIONS

These can be the result of childhood conditioning, cultural or religious influence, or self-defeating thoughts and emotions. They are evident if you find yourself often avoiding fun, laughter, and the enjoyment of life's natural pleasures, or if you feel guilty for enjoying them. They can be tied into past vows. Dowse to remove the repression, and to liberate positive emotions.

## 38. NEGATIVE MENTAL, EMOTIONAL, AND PHYSICAL HABITS

Habits are ingrained behavior patterns that often go unnoticed—at least by us. "It's just the way I am!" Habits are entrenched thought forms that have a frequency, and so can be removed by dowsing. Remove their triggers and the thoughts and feelings that may accompany them, transmuting their energies into self-love. Ask to substitute negative habits with positive, life-affirming habits. It takes twenty-one days of conscious effort to establish new habits.

## 39. FEAR OF SUCCESS

It doesn't seem as if success would be something anyone would fear. We all aspire to succeed at something. This is a basic cultural value and human need. To some, however, the memory of success may not be so positive. Some may unconsciously feel that success would threaten their current self-image, which would then need reinventing. We may unconsciously fear others' rejection as we begin to outshine them with our achievements. I think it's the fear of the "little gap of unknowing"—perhaps suspecting that we are "nobody" and destined to fail—that keeps some locked in their current limited self-image. This is classic ego operation. The ego would much rather keep you "in your place" than face the possibility that you will no longer need it at all, once you discover who you really are—that is, limitless Spirit!

Success may also threaten your closest relationships, which are often based on a compromised image you have created and projected. Once this has been minimized or removed by dowsing, dowse in confidence and a desire to succeed for the highest good of all. Success in life need threaten no one. To quote Golas' *Lazy Man's Guide to Enlightenment* (Gibbs Smith, 1995): "We are all equal beings, and the Universe is our relationships with each other."

## 40. BALANCE POINT FOR NEUROTRANSMITTERS AND NUTRIENTS

Use the Balance Chart to determine the over- or under-supply of crucial neurotransmitters and nutrients like serotonin, noradrenaline, melatonin, lithium, electrolytes, and dopamine. This is obviously a short list. You can do a complete nutritional assessment if you desire by using a good resource book on the subject. I knew of a naturopath whose entire practice was based on dowsing nutrients. As far as remediation goes, dowsing may represent the future of nutrition. Let me explain.

The principles of nutrition, although outside mainstream medicine, are still largely based on materialist assumptions. The common perception is that every nutrient you need must somehow enter your body from outside. This belief has spawned an incredibly lucrative supplement industry. Back in the 1960s, a pioneering French scientist named Louis Kervan (*Biological Transmutations*) observed chickens in the South Pacific producing robust eggs each day with zero calcium in their diets. His work revealed that the chickens were making calcium out of silica, which was abundant in the local sand. Now, chemically, this is impossible, but the chickens didn't know that. What they were doing falls under the rubric of "transmutation of elements"—an idea previously called "alchemy" that was tossed in the historical dustbin by much wiser modern scientists years ago.

It stands to reason that, if chickens can do it, so can we. And that we can assist the process with intent and dowsing. Ask to what percentage your transmutation potential is active. Ask if there are blockages that can be removed. You can dowse the intent into your water so that it will support you with all your nutritional needs. What is food, when you think about it, but reconstituted sunlight? So dowse that your body will be able to receive its needs directly from the source! Think of the savings! Of course, you may want to eat as well, as we all seem to enjoy it. But is eating solid food just an old habit? It may be our spiritual destiny to live eventually on Light alone!

## 41. CETYL MERISTOLATE

Raising this biological substance to optimal levels may be helpful in relieving aches and pains in joints. The production of this natural lubricant seems to decline with age. Raise it to 100 percent, and raise your body's ability to continue to produce optimal levels. Many folks can feel the improvement in their joints right away. This is a good one for skeptics!

## 42. LYMPH

Measure the degree of overall function on a scale of 1 to 10. Left spin out any toxins or blockages. Raise the functional vitality of the lymph system to 100 percent. Encourage daily exercise. Even a twenty-minute vigorous walk can help dramatically. Rebounding is great!

## 43. CHAKRAS

The chakras are energy vortices that unite our multi-dimensional bodies with our physical bodies. Although there are hundreds of minor chakras, we are concerned here primarily with the seven major chakras and a few that extend below our feet and above our heads. You can use Table 1 and Chart 13 to discover more possible issues with individual chakras.

Chakras can be either too open or too constricted. They also can be subject to psychic cords, which we discussed earlier. Chakras also hold memories of past and future lives and need to be in harmony with each other.

For general dowsing, ask to bring all chakras into ideal spin, alignment, and functioning, removing any blockages, emotions, or memories that need to be released.

## 44. MERIDIANS

These are light-transmission channels throughout the body that provide the means, along with the extra-cellular matrix, for inter-cellular communication and overall body harmonizing. Light equals information. You may dowse the entire meridian system or specific meridians with the Balance Chart looking for yin or yang imbalances

Think of the meridians as the body's "fiber-optic" network. Dowse to balance excess (yang) with deficient (yin) meridians, and to bring individual points into resonance with their ideal values, removing any energetic, emotional, or spiritual blockages in the system and transmuting them to pure Light energy. You may want to chart individual meridians and points for yourself, or use a good reference book if this interests you.

## 45. ENERGETIC IMBALANCE WITH EARTH FREQUENCIES

Imbalances in this area are widespread and often overlooked. Some scientists are admitting to a puzzling reduction in the Earth's magnetic field and a corresponding frequency rise, especially in the last 500 years. They say that this could be a precursor to a "flip" in the direction or location of the North and South Poles. There is evidence that this has occurred many times in the past based on the magnetic signatures left in core samples from the Earth going back eons. There is further correlation with these events and major epochs of time recognized by the Mayan and Hindu calendars.

As the Earth's magnetic field weakens, which is being driven by similar changes in the Sun having to do with its periodic alignment with the Galactic Center, our energy fields and physical bodies are being stressed to the limit. There is some evidence, or conjecture at least, that dramatic changes in the DNA of species that led to "leaps" in evolution in the past have been driven by dramatic changes in the nature of cosmic radiation, especially in the gamma-ray range. What we are experiencing may be the beginning of a natural event—potentially both disruptive and creative—that happens regularly in cosmological time.

You can measure current levels of adaptation on a scale of 1 to10, with 10 as 100 percent or ideal, Adjust these to 100 percent, and extend that adjustment into the future by stipulating the correction be irreversible. By most accounts, the current round of changes culminate at a time coincident with the arrival of a Golden Age of enlightenment to replace the previous age of control, exploitation, and ego dominance. Do the same for adapting to changes in the Sun and in galactic energies.

Remove all ill effects from the movement of Earth, the solar system, and the Milky Way through space.

## 46. ELECTROMAGNETIC FIELDS

We are talking here about artificial EMFs (electromagnetic fields) and microwave radiation. This is a challenge with which our ancestors did not have to deal. It is best to neutralize your living space as much as possible. See *www .stetzerelectric.com* for inexpensive technology to create an EMF-free haven in your home.

Dowse for the degree of EMF stress on your body, then in your home or workplace. Remove the effects and raise your resistance to these energies. Also raise to the maximum your body's ability to recover from EMF stress. Do not knowingly expose yourself to these fields, especially where you sleep. Electric blankets, heating pads, and clock radios are highly toxic and can literarily "scramble" your energy field, inhibiting healing and regeneration. The pancreas is especially vulnerable to these fields. Sixty-cycle EMFs can cause and/or exacerbate diabetes. You can dowse the degree of stress from EMFs on the pancreas, and dowse out their negative effects. Do this for anyone with a blood-sugar disorder, and have them remove themselves from all unnecessary and "hidden" EMF exposure.

## 47. GEOPATHIC STRESS

This refers to natural lines of energy that run along the planetary surface and underground that are caused by water running underground, by magnetic fault lines, or by underground mineral concentrations. In some cases, these lines become unhealthy, especially in cities where they can be negatively energized by EMFs and microwave technology. In Germany, geo-stress is a recognized cause of disease, and the building authorities there can tell you where to build on your property based on a geopathic stress analysis.

Traditional dowsers can help locate where these lines may enter your home or property and, by placing copper brackets (like huge staples) in the ground, divert them. Likewise, a coat hanger bent into the shape of an omega (like an open O with feet) will divert these lines back in the direction of their source when placed in the path of the lines.

You can use traditional "L rods" made out of coat hangers or your own pendulum to assess you own home. First, use your pendulum to determine if this is a problem. Ask how many lines there are and what their strength is on a scale of 1 to 10, with 10 being lethal. Ask if they are playing a role in any health or behavioral problems in the home. Hold the rods, out in front of you so they swing loosely in your hands and point them out in front. Ask to be shown where the stress lines are by their swinging apart or together as you walk the perimeter of your property. Then ask for the direction of the energy in the line to be shown by the rods swinging together one way or the other. Some lines will be entering the home; some will be leaving. You really only need to deal with those that are entering.

There have been associations made between geopathic stress and crib death (SIDS), as well as learning and behavioral problems in children, migraines, bedwetting, and other sleep disturbances. Even cancer and other degenerative diseases have been associated with geopathic stress, which has been documented by German health practitioners. Practically any dis-ease can be partly or entirely due to geo-stress factors. Use either of the above methods, or simply ask your Guides and or the elementals to divert these lines back into the second dimension within the Earth and to place a protective field around your home to prevent their recurrence. With children especially, consider moving the bed as well. Cats will be drawn to spots that are negative for humans; dogs will be drawn to spots that are positive. Geopathic dowsing is an extensive field, and might be considered a sub-discipline within dowsing. See Chart 28 for other possible issues.

## 48. ASTROLOGICAL ALIGNMENTS

This is similar to assessing and adjusting birth location, only, in this case, you are assessing unfavorable or unnecessary astrological alignments and neutralizing non-beneficial astrological aspects or challenges that are no longer serving you or the highest good.

## 49. CELL COMPATIBILITY WITH SIGNIFICANT OTHERS

This is a very important thing to check, particularly when there is the presence of *any kind of auto-immune disease.* This incompatibility relates to a disharmony of vibration on a cell-frequency level that is misinterpreted by one of the individual's bodies as an attack on the system, triggering an immune response. Often the "other" to whom we are reacting is someone to whom we have been physically close over time—a parent, a pet, or a partner. This is a purely energetic incompatibility and has no bearing on mental, emotional, or spiritual compatibility.

After asking if this is an issue, ask to what degree it is contributing to ill health or auto-immune imbalance. Left spin to dowse out the negative effects of the incompatibility, and right spin to raise and correct the vibrational disharmony, including past, present, and future time frames.

## 50. ATTRACTOR FIELDS

This is a general issue that applies to practically any of the prior clearings. I have lately been adding it to whatever I am asking to be cleared. An attractor field is whatever is in you that drew to you the particular experience or energy you want to remove. This again refers to the principle that all you ever experience is yourself, that the world "out there" only exists as a reflection of the world "in here," and that, if you do not carry a particular attractor field, you will never experience the issue associated with it. Not everyone you work with is ready for this concept—yet. It implies total responsibility, which is a prerequisite for total freedom. If you get yes in response to this issue, narrow the cause down to a physical, mental, emotional, or psychic (multi-dimensional) attractor, asking if it is time-related. Clean with a left spin at the time of first encounter.

## 51. DOWSING FOR SPECIFIC CONDITIONS

In this modern era of society's upside-down version of freedom, you must be very careful not to claim to heal, cure, or prevent disease. This is the sacred domain of the medical profession and purveyors of iatrogenic disease, which is death by medicine. (See the article by that name at *www.nexusmagazine* *.com*.) Even if you do this clearing for yourself, be mindful of with whom you share your experiences. These corporate clods actually believe they own you! With the dialogue below, substitute your favorite symptomatic definition or condition. Please, do not make any claims in this area. Keep the dialogue to yourself. And while you are at it, you may want to spin out the belief in the diagnoses—70 percent of which are wrong, according to the AMA's own admission.

With a left spin, say:

*Banish the spirit of _____. Scramble the frequency of its reproductive intelligence and programming. Deactivate any emotional blockages, causal memory, or mental precursors to it.*

*Remove from the DNA/RNA any damaged or inherited factors contributing to this condition.*

*Neutralize the factor that turned off any _____-limiting gene. Clear the brain and all cell memory of all programs, thoughts, beliefs, and memories associated with the condition.*

With a right spin, say:

> *Restore immune awareness of _____ to 100 percent. Raise the probability of healing on all levels—mental, emotional, physical, and spiritual—to 100 percent. Bring in the appropriate Guides, angels, Ascended Masters, and other helpers to assist in complete healing. Heal the mind of its belief in _____. Heal the mind of its belief in separation from the Creator. Allow the mind to accept complete healing now.*

## 52. ALLERGIES

With a left spin, go back to the womb and adjust the DNA before birth not to express the target allergies. All true allergies can be traced back to a "stuck" emotion. Time travel is best here. Neutralize the energy and emotion causing the allergy and the ill effects of the allergen on the body. Neutralize any contributing past-life trauma. This can be a main cause of many serious allergies.

Many apparent food allergies involve a sensitivity induced by enzyme exhaustion from the overuse of certain foods or a pancreatic weakness. As such, they are more accurately called intolerances. Check the percentage of enzyme availability to digest this allergen completely in the body.

For example, you can ask to be shown the percentage of available enzymes to digest wheat completely, and/or the percentage to which the pancreas is able to produce sufficient enzymes to digest wheat completely.

I have found that, in many cases, the pancreatic insufficiency, which can also contribute to chronic acidosis due to bicarbonate of soda under-secretion, is due to the holding on of an old memory or emotion around the "loss of sweetness" in life—an old broken heart, for example. Check for this and time travel to the event and unwind and raise the energy to the fifth dimension there.

Chronic enzyme deficiencies are very common, especially as we age. It is one thing we all can supplement to our benefit by eating more raw, enzyme-rich foods and limiting cooked "dead" foods.

## 53. BALANCE OF HEART AND MIND

This is necessary for ascension, as we must bring our mental intelligence into harmony with our heart intelligence. You can use percentage to determine to what degree the heart and mind are harmonized, or use the Balance Chart to determine what is out of balance. Many of us are challenged with too much mind and not enough heart—especially males, as this is how we are encultured. Have the client visualize a golden cord connecting the two areas as you dowse for optimal results. Ask that the improved connection remain as the new default ratio. An ideal ratio would be 90 percent heart intelligence and 10 percent brain intelligence—a brain ruled by the heart, in other words.

## 54. SURFACE TENSION OF ALL BODY WATER

The degree of surface tension, or electrical charge, on water molecules determines their "wetness"—i.e., their ability to bind easily with toxins for their removal and with nutrients for their delivery to the cells. Surface tension impacts the pH of the water with high surface tension associated with acidic states. Adjusting the units, called "dynes," down to the ideal has tremendous health benefits. Check the charts in chapter 6 on this very fundamental physical correction.

Measure current dynes first either on a Balance Chart or on a Scale of 10, with '0' representing the optimal minimal dynes. Then left spin and adjust downward. Next, imprint each molecule of water in the body (right spin) to remember and transmit this ideal dyne to every future molecule of water with which it comes in contact.

In chapter 6, you will find a variety of dowsing charts that will greatly expand the scope of our work together. Remember to use them first on yourself. Sooner or later, you may have a chance to offer the willing an opportunity to experience the power of intention and the healing of the mind through spiritual dowsing.

# CHAPTER 5

# Specialty Dowsing

"ASCENSION" IS A TERM APPLIED to the notion that we can elevate ourselves to a point where we break through to a higher dimensional aspect of our selves. The timeline of the Mayan calendar, for instance, centers on the possibility of this phenomenon for planet Earth. Individually, ascension involves raising our frequencies regularly, and avoiding everything that drains or lowers them. It also means not empowering anything negative with our fear or undue attention, only giving attention to what brings us joy and harmony.

There is some indication that ascension will involve the Earth herself rising to a higher fifth-dimensional expression, leaving some people behind on a three-dimensional material planet to continue on in duality as their free-will choice. There is no judgment implied here—some souls are ready to graduate, some are not—yet. Ultimately, we all do.

You can dowse to find out if a person is destined for fifth-dimensional Earth at the time of the Shift. Be sensitive with whom and how you share this information. Some higher beings will actually elect to continue on in the third dimension out of love and a desire to help those humans who remain there. No matter what your choice, everyone can benefit from experiencing their highest potential—and eventually, we all ascend!

Dowse the following affirmations into all levels of your Being:

I am always at the right place at the right time

My body, mind, and spirit adapt effortlessly to all past, present, and future Earth, cosmic, multi-dimensional, and energetic changes.

Then determine the current percentage of adaptability to present and future Earth changes by asking the following:

Are there blockages to (my, subject's) 100 percent adaptability to Earth changes?

Are these physical?

To what degree are physical blockages contributing to my total blockages?

Do the same for mental, emotional, and spiritual blockages. For the different aspects, ask if their energies can be dowsed out. With a left spin, ask for their removal and transmutation into fifth-dimensional energies. Then ask what is the percentage of your connection with the Christ Consciousness Grid—the fifth-dimensional golden healing grid that is in place now on the planet. Raise it if it is under 100 percent.

Commit to the practice of gratitude, for even the smallest of things. Gratitude conditions the mind to expect the best. You will experience the world you want! Consult *Navigating the Collapse of Time* for more practical ideas to support you and your loved ones through this time of transition.

## HARMONIC (RADIONIC) RATES

Harmonic, or radionic, rates are number values that carry inherent healing energies. They were originally determined by early radionics researchers like Abrams, Drown, and Copen. These and other researchers used their own biological energy fields to connect at a distance with a client via a "witness"—or sample of the person's energy signature. This witness could be a drop of blood, a lock of hair, or even a picture. They used electronic boxes powered by a quartz crystal wrapped in a "mobius coil" and with multiple knobs, each of which measured a specific range of subtle electrical resistance, to come up with a group of numbers that represented the energetic electrical resistance pattern of a specific symptom or disease.

It turned out that many of these rates had universal benefit and, even without the boxes, an experienced dowser can, by focused intent, determine and send harmonic rates at a distance with healing benefit. Just how this works cannot be understood with Newtonian principles or linear logic. It can be approached, however, with an understanding of quantum physics. David Wilcock has documented much of the alternative research that was largely ignored or suppressed in the last century by mainstream interests in his recent book, *The Source Field Investigations*. Essentially, we all see what we want to see. If you have a vested interest in the status quo, you will see the right evidence to support that view. The paradox or joke here is that, even in denial, we are proving the observer effect.

Just as in homeopathy, there is a point at which physical and even quantum explanations do not fully address what is going on here. We have to admit that, when things work that are beyond our ability to describe, there's a chance we don't know how things really work at all. As described in Barbara Hand Clow's nine-dimensional model and in my own book, numbers are sixth-dimensional. This is the dimension of the basic geometric and numerical templates of creation expressing through the lower and physical dimensions. As such, groups of numbers, especially if dowsed for a specific purpose, carry their own subtle energetic signature. This signature can be carried on a non-local quantum level by thought focused with intention to affect any disharmonious energy pattern in any place or time in the universal quantum soup. Mathematics is the "language of creation," in this sense.

For a free list of radionic rates, see *www.sulisinstruments.com*. Personally, I prefer to dowse rates with my Chart of Ten for a more up to date and pertinent rate for the unique individual I am working with. I consider these rates to be the perfect fallback choice for stubborn issues or when you just don't have time to go into details. First, they are powerful and beneficial; second, I have never been told no when asking my Guides if there is a rate for a particular person around a particular issue.

Here is an example of how we can come up with a rate on the spot. Let's say a youngster has a tummy ache. You can:

Ask if there is a rate that will help remove the tummy ache. Answer: yes.

Ask how many digits are in the rate. Answer: 3.

Dowse out the first number. Answer: 4.

Dowse out the second number. Answer: 2.

Dowse out the third number. Answer: 9.

Confirm the number by asking if the most beneficial rate to remove the cause of this tummy ache is 429. Answer: yes.

Administer with a right spin as indicated below.

Rates can be associated with specific dimensions or realms of influence. I have found lately that ninth-dimensional rates are usually three digits, while fifth-dimensional rates are typically four digits. The energies on Earth are accelerating so quickly now that shorter rates seem to be able to accomplish "more with less," especially compared to many of the very long rates from decades ago. This is another good reason to dowse for rates rather than looking them up.

In order to send a rate, first ask if it is appropriate. You can measure the degree of benefit if you wish. Although you can dowse the rate directly to a person's energy field, you can also have the client hold a bottle of water and send the rate into the water at the same time to make a nice energetic back-up formula.

Once you have identified the rate, with a right spin, say:

*I now broadcast the rate 429 to (name) at the most appropriate potency or potencies and intensity. I ask that this rate continue to resonate in (his or her) energy field and continue its benefits for as long as necessary or beneficial.*

Wait for the spin to stop. You may want to ask if there is a personal rate that will help you through the ascension process.

Rates can also be written out and pasted to water bottles, as with the work demonstrated by Emoto. Perhaps it is the high water content of our bodies and water's ability to be programmed by the mind that explains some of the direct physical benefits of dowsing.

## BASELINES FROM BIRTH

Baselines are the potentials with which you came into this life. You could say that this is the hand you are dealt at birth. Your baseline also often reflects where you left off in a previous incarnation relative to specific issues or challenges. A low baseline can set limits on your ability to heal and grow beyond these limits. They may represent long-standing lessons that you are working out over numerous lifetimes. Being the captain of your destiny means that, once you identify these areas of limitation, you have every right to change your mind about them.

Suspect a less than ideal baseline in areas of stubborn resistance or with issues that present as general themes over the life path. If you suspect this is an issue in, for instance, the area of finances, just measure your baseline at birth for financial prosperity on a scale of 1 to 10, with 10 being ideal. If the answer is less than 10, go ahead with the following guidelines in mind. With a left spin, say:

*I now remove the emotions, beliefs, thoughts, and memories of my ancestors to the dawn of time that limit my _____ baseline.*

With a right spin, say:

*I now transform these energies to the most appropriate energies to raise this baseline at birth permanently and in all time frames and dimensions to 100 percent.*

Here is a by-no-means definitive list of possible baselines to consider. Any area that is showing up as a theme in your life can be checked. Check each item listed and see if it applies—yes or no? Then measure the baseline on a scale of 1 to 10 at the point of birth.

| | |
|---|---|
| Taking responsibility | Ego |
| Independence | Detachment |
| Self-regulation | Non-judgment |
| Trust in physical safety | Sense of equality |
| Business integrity | Commitment to purpose |
| Guilt-free success | Devotion to truth |
| Humility | Mental clarity |
| Honesty | Emotional balance |
| Self-forgiveness | Spiritual evolution |

## ENERGIZING WATER

Water is particularly programmable. As noted, this may explain many of the physical benefits of dowsing, as our bodies are mostly water. The water molecule is a unique liquid crystal that has all of the energetic and informational properties of a solid crystal, but in a liquid state. It is sensitive to subtle energies, like those produced by a thought carried by strong feeling or intent. The technique below can be applied to bottled water or bodies of still or moving water like lakes, wells, and springs. You can "taste test" between each phase. The differences in taste can be quite obvious—another one for the skeptics!

**Step 1:** Just notice the taste of the water; don't label your experience. Left spin out all toxins and toxic information. Clear the memory of the water in all time frames and dimensions. Clear the spirit of greed (water was never meant to be sold!). Lower the surface tension to the lowest level for optimal chemical bonding for both nutritional delivery and detoxification. Check to see if the water is 100 percent neutralized before going on.

**Step 2:** What differences do you notice? Have clear intent and focus all your mental and emotional energy on the water. Raise (right spin) the frequency of the water to the optimal frequency for the healing of all illnesses, imbalances, and deficiencies. Invite back in the spirit of the water. Spin in the intent and ability to detoxify continuously all mental, emotional, physical, and spiritual toxins. Program the water to communicate instantly all of these benefits to every subsequent molecule it comes in contact with from this time forward. Once the spin stops, check to see if the charging is complete and optimal. Even one drop of this "mother tincture" will now have amazing effects on any body of water into which it is introduced. Take it to a community pool and see for yourself!

**Step 3:** Can you tell the difference?

## CLEARING SPACE AND LAND

Working with homes and properties can lend tremendous support to the folks living there. Obvious issues include geopathic stress and electromagnetic interference. Some homes with an unpleasant feel may carry the energy of past tenants, drug use, or strong negative emotions. What some call "ghosts" may actually be etheric shells—non-living imprints that are stuck between dimensions. Ask if they are ready to be united with their souls. Move them out to the most appropriate dimension for their highest good.

Suspect geopathic entities when any persistent geopathic stress patterns keep returning after clearing. These are beings that attach themselves to geopathic stress lines; they can literally "follow" you as you, for example, move your bed. There may be a negative elemental being tracking someone through the geopathic stress lines. Send the elemental back to the second dimension to be purified.

Most space-and-land clearing involves releasing the memory of trauma or conflict from matter in the area—specifically, formerly "live" matter like wood, rubber, or fabric in which intact DNA can still act as a subtle energy capacitor. There may also be toxic issues in the environment to consider. Once cleared, ask your Guides to place a fifth-dimensional energy cell in the geographic center of the space (home or property) to absorb negative frequencies and energies on an ongoing basis, purifying them into fifth-dimensional healing energies. See Chart 28 for more on this topic.

# CHAPTER 6

# The Charts

AS OUTLINED BRIEFLY IN THE PREVIOUS CHAPTER, a quick and easy way to get helpful information from your superconscious mind is through the use of dowsing charts. About three fourths of us are visual learners, so using visual charts is easier for many people than navigating text or auditory learning modalities alone. Charts are hands-on tools that can be made quickly and easily to measure and affect practically any issue imaginable.

How do the charts work? Let us review for a moment some of the dynamics of dowsing by reinforcing its core concepts. With dowsing, we experience an interface between the physical and non-physical dimensions. This occurs in part because of certain physical structures in the body that respond to subtle, or non-physical, forms of energy. The most obvious of these structures is the autonomic nervous system, or ANS, which responds to subtle waves of unconscious thought and memory.

The ANS is designed to operate automatically to regulate body functions like breathing, heart rate, and countless physical processes so you don't have to consciously think of them. The ANS also responds automatically to what it perceives as a threat—the so-called fight-or-flight response. We share this kind of survival reflex with all living things, down to the smallest microbe. It is part of what is also called "electrophysiological reactivity"—the ability of life forms to react instantaneously in order to adjust to changes in their environment.

When you make a conscious decision to act on the physical world, you make a choice and your body acts on your command. These kinds of actions involve the conscious mind sending information through the central nervous system (CNS) to the larger motor muscles in the body. You do this when, for example you type on a keyboard, or pick up a glass of water. However, the ANS is wired into the superconscious mind, which operates beneath conscious awareness, but actually makes up 90 percent of our brain capacity— compared to the 10 percent of capacity used by the conscious mind. Given this proportion, into which aspect of intelligence would you put more confidence to give you more complete information on a situation? And why do we rely so heavily on such a small part of our brains?

When you put a question to your superconscious mind, it responds through the ANS and the smaller, or micro, muscles of your body—in the same way that it would respond to a life stressor through the fight-or-flight response. This is especially true if you have consciously programmed your mind and nervous system to respond with a pre-determined signal, as we did when we programmed for yes and no responses earlier. The difference with dowsing is that you are consciously tapping into this deeper intelligence, rather than just relying on it as a kind of fire alarm.

What, then, is the superconscious mind? A traditional materialist scientist would say it is the product of millions of years of physical evolution. Somehow, we evolved a biological computer we call the brain. Of course, this computer, though amazing, is pretty much limited to perceiving sensory data, and is thus chained to the physical world. Thus the empiricist's oath: "Anything measurable is real; anything not measurable is imagination."

Quantum physicists offer a different view, pointing out that we now can demonstrate that the brain supports quantum functions as well as physical ones. As such, the brain is not limited to operating within the sensory world, but is involved in non-local reality and can affect matter and energy through the power of attention and intention. The term "non-local" implies not being limited by linear time or space. We find that the brain is a vehicle for the Mind, which can exist without a brain! By capital "M" Mind, I refer to the collective mind, rather than the limited local sense of the personal mind. This expanded mind is what Zen Buddhists call "Big Mind." It is a non-local field of awareness not limited by the body, time, or space. Big Mind literally fills the universe.

Quantum physicists, although recognizing the unity of all things in the form of what they call "entanglement," have not quite yet made the leap of acknowledging a primal cause and the causal directionality of these processes. Many researchers have observed the strong correlations between quantum functions and traditional views of metaphysics and spirituality, while many still hold on to the wish (read: fantasy) that we, as distinct biological forms, are still somehow the foundational cause of the Mind. In other words, "we made ourselves." This fanciful wish represents one of the final defensive bastions of the ego as a set of conditioned beliefs built on the false foundation of separation and individuation, and the fears this imaginary condition fosters.

The experiencer of non-dual reality, or Oneness, has "stepped out of the mirror" enough to appreciate the possibility that a pre-existing intelligence, preceding the material universe and thus the brain, is the causal root of even Mind itself. This implies a divine "Thinker," or Creator. Dare we say God? Interestingly, some physicists now agree that the universe is best understood as an idea existing in a Mind with a will to create.

If this is true, then all seemingly separate aspects of the universe are unified in this prime intelligence. As an expression of this intelligence, your superconscious mind is holographically wired into, not only all possible knowledge, but also the appreciation of your true Self as One with that intelligence. Ponder this, and you may even glimpse the magnitude of who you truly are.

Again, to what aspect of your self would you prefer to refer for accurate and helpful information? The choice is limited to two; the time-bound conditioned and fearful (although logical in its own terms) ego, or your superconscious mind, which retains the memory of and potential for communication with All That Is.

Think of the charts given below as roadmaps to expanded possibilities. Do not be limited to their use, but use them to help clear out the debris of old memories, traumas, or toxins that only obscure your experience of your divine Self.

## MIND-SET FOR USING THE CHARTS

The skills you have developed in the foregoing chapters will play a major role in the constructive use of the following charts. If you are not sure what these are or are not fully confident in your use of them, please review the earlier chapters on basic skills like yes and no answers, reading the Chart of Ten and the Balance Chart, and left and right spinning. These charts can also be used as an extension of or in addition to the clearings you learned in chapter 4. Be sure to be coming from a clear place when approaching the charts—assured of your protection, accuracy, and optimal frequency, and of course, working from an alpha brain-wave state.

A Comprehensive Mini-Course in Spiritual Dowsing

Dowsing works best when it is used for healing or a return to wholeness, as this is the common solution to all perceived problems. All of the charts involve holding the pendulum over the fulcrum or center point, asking the appropriate question, and allowing your superconscious mind to direct the movement toward the answer. There are explanations with suggested questions and approaches for shifting energies with each of the charts. Trust your intuition and Guides to help you. We have been amazed at the results we have gotten with the use of these charts.

The charts included here represent the accumulation of dowsable issues that have come to us over the years. Some of them evolved out of workshops, or were modified from others' work. Whenever I read about or heard of a new set of variables or a new way of seeing something, it would occur to me: "Hey, this could be dowsed." The result was often a new chart. I highly recommend that you do the same. Use these charts for as long as they are helpful, but consider adding to these with your own personal set as well, based on your own learning and what is revealed to you. Nobody has the patent on the right way to dowse! We have provided a set of blank charts at the end of the book that you may duplicate for your own non-commercial use.

Most of the charts will provide information that will lead to the opportunity either to remove or improve something. I again refer you to earlier chapters on techniques for the removal and enhancement, or bringing in, of energies. This form of dowsing, which we like to call active dowsing, goes above and beyond just getting information (passive dowsing). I thank Master Dowser Raymon Grace who introduced me (David) to this way of working. I also want to thank our friend and colleague Montgomery Young, who generously provided his skill and time to help put these charts together from my rough sketches. I also acknowledge the work of all the clients and teachers I have met along the way. Every client has taught me something new. Thank You!

And finally, a word on the value of non-attachment to outcomes. As with any healing art, the practice of dowsing can be offered in the service of Spirit for true healing or can be taken up by the ego for its own purposes—to keep up the illusion of separation and "specialness." There is a tendency, especially as the first results from dowsing begin to manifest, for the ego to jump in and make you feel somehow "special" or particularly powerful. Actually, any feeling or idea that makes you feel better or worse than anyone is coming from the ego. One of my favorite maxims is: "We are all equal beings, and the Universe is our relationships with each other" (from Thaddeus Golas, *The Lazy Man's Guide to Enlightenment*, Layton, UT: Gibbs Smith Publisher, 1995).

Give the power of your superconscious mind back to its source, and leave the results up to Spirit (God, or the Divine, or whatever word or symbol works for you). We are all operating within the One Mind of the Divine. Our wholeness and healing are already accomplished on the level of spirit. It is only on the level of form—the body, time, space, and the world—that it is possible to suffer or that change or correction are needed. All we as healers can ever do is to shorten the time it takes to awaken to our true Selves. Eventually, we all awaken. There are no losers in this game.

So there is nothing, really, to be accomplished here, other than realizing that who we really are is not "here" at all! We are One with the One. So please don't take what you think of as your self or the issues you appear to be addressing too seriously. And let's help each along the way as best we can by sharing whatever we do from this place of inner peace, confidence, and knowing. It is said that, with the movement from the Age of Pisces into the Age of Aquarius, we are moving from the age of belief to the age of knowing. May your dowsing be a help to you on your path toward knowing who you really are! And you are amazing beyond words!

Here are a few suggestions on how best to use the charts:

1. Open each chart and ask if it is an appropriate chart to use for the person or situation at hand. Wait for a yes or no response.

2. Ask how many of these charts may be helpful for the person or situation under review. Go down the list of charts and wait for a yes response, or use your hand chart to dowse out how many charts in the list apply. Dowse the number of digits in the answer to this question, then ask for the number of the first chart, the second chart, etc.

3. After a number of clearings, don't forget to fill any voids with fifth-dimensional energy.

4. As you work with a few charts, you may want use your percentage chart to ask how complete the session is. I have found that, with first-timers, there may be a limit to how much can be cleared in any given session. I respect the limit the client's superconscious mind tells me. They can always come back later and go deeper.

# GENERAL GUIDANCE

Use the General Guidance chart to get a general idea of the direction in which to proceed. You may want to skip this step if you already have an idea of what to do or address. With this chart, you are actually asking at what level the mind of the client is ready or able to accept healing.

## Physical Issues

These can represent entrenched emotional energy or spiritual factors. But if the mind is fearful of approaching things on this level, you may need to start on the physical level. In addition, it is very difficult for the mind to settle and go deeper if a physical issue is demanding attention.

Measure pain, circulation, and inflammation on a scale of 1 to 10. You can left spin out pain and inflammation, then right spin increased circulation and oxygen to a certain area. You can also dowse in (right spin) energy fields of natural remedies. In the case of a headache, you may try dowsing in (right spin) the energy of Willow Bark, a natural form of aspirin, or cayenne to improve circulation. Harmonic rates can work very well for physical issues. Caution: Do not in any way make claims to be "healing" anything, unless you are a licensed physician or other practitioner. You are simply adjusting the energy associated with these physical concerns.

## Mental Issues

These may be entrenched ideas accepted by the mind that now operate automatically, below conscious awareness—like "default" programs. These thoughts were often first entertained in moments of stress or at a young, impressionable age. They can come from well-meaning authority figures, the media, friends, or just about anywhere.

"Groupthink" is a term used to describe how groups take on a shared identity through their mutual acceptance of certain beliefs or ideas. This can be dangerous, as people often suspend their good sense in exchange for allegiance to the group in order to be accepted and feel part of something bigger than their current limited self-concept allows. We suggest that you time travel to the point of origin of the thought for the individual and clear it there while reversing all ill effects in all times and dimensions.

Ask if the thought first occurred in this life.

Ask at what age it occurred and how many digits in the age.

Ask if it became active in a past or future life.

Dowse the digits of the year and clear it there, thus relieving all life-paths of the limiting effects of that thought.

## Emotional Issues

When emotional issues are indicated, the chart is asking you to explore the emotional roots of an issue with a dialogue similar to the one above. We have found that emotions that have been with the client for life—that is, since birth—were, in many cases, associated with a trauma in a previous lifetime, usually from the end of that life. Ask if this is the case and time travel there by dowsing the year of the trauma. Clear it there "for all lifetimes and dimensions."

## Spiritual Issues

When this comes up, my next question is usually to ask which dimension is implied. Usually, spiritual factors resonate with the fourth, sixth, or ninth dimensions, as these are dualistic dimensions where both positive and negative aspects manifest. The remaining non-dual dimensions typically do not present problems per se. Recall from the first chapter the non-dual perspective on these spiritual issues. Although we describe them as if they were separate beings, they are only mental projections that have been denied and are "coming home" to be healed. There is nothing in all of creation to fear.

## Environmental Issues

These typically refer to the physical environment, but you may want to ask if they refer to the mental, emotional, or spiritual environment of the client. Ask to clear (left spin) all negative effects of the environmental stressor and transmute the stress factor to positive energy.

## Social Issues

These are issues in relationships, especially with groups like families, co-workers, townspeople, or organizations. Relationships offer us the greatest opportunity to grow spiritually through true forgiveness. Raise the probability (right spin) that the client will see the "forgiveness opportunity" with the group and take responsible action to correct his or her own judgments and perceptions of others. Check the identified group's overall integrity, honesty, and love index on a scale of 1 to 10. It may be that the client needs to reconsider his or her allegiance to the group.

## Radionic Rates

Dowsing this indicates the benefit of a special "number" to assist the client. Any topic or issue under the Sun can be addressed with a rate. As numbers, these rates represent sixth-dimensional energetic templates that are implied in the esoteric sciences of numerology and sacred geometry. First ask how many digits there are in the rate, then dowse to identify them one at a time. Once you have the rate, deliver it with a right spin, saying:

*I now send the rate of (rate) to (client) at the most beneficial potencies and strengths, and ask that the rate and all of its benefits continue to resonate with (client) until no longer necessary or beneficial (optional) to address the issue of_____.*

The last phrase is optional. Have clients write the rate down in pencil and carry it with them. They can "charge" their water with it by placing a glass on the paper, or by using the paper to label a bottle.

## Deservingness

This issue is measured on a scale of 1 to 10. It can give a quick idea of how much someone may be blocking his or her own healing with thoughts of unconscious guilt or undeservingness. This condition, common to students of Earth School, can mask as humility as the ego attempts to keep us small and powerless, crediting our low opinion of ourselves over the Creator's opinion, which is that you are divine, perfect, invulnerable, and innocent. Until you discover deeper areas to clear, if the measurement is less than 10, simply right spin to increase it for now. You may find a time-related factor to clear.

## Love Index

Check this for a person, as well as for his or her home or work place. Raise this to 100 percent "without reversal" for best results. I can't think of any space or condition that would not benefit from raising the love index. Here's an experiment: The next instance you hear of any form or level of suffering, check into the love index, raise it, and see how *you* feel. Quantum healing on the level of the mind is *always* a shared experience, as we truly are One Mind and One Self. Love is the principle of inclusion, negating separation on all levels.

## Open to Insight

This is another index measured on a scale of 1 to 10. If the measurement is less than 10, you can raise it to 10 (right spin) or, better still, left spin out the resistance to insight. You can not add anything to a full cup. The mind that thinks it "knows" is not open to the light of new information or inspiration. It actually dwells in the false and shaky confidence of the ego, and thus can quickly become defensive, even attacking anyone who challenges the unstable sense of self.

Check your client's attachment to thoughts and beliefs using the appropriate index and reduce (left spin) it to the most tolerable minimum for now.

## Other Modalities

Dowsing is not for everyone. Well, yes it is, but not everyone is ready to accept it! If you get an indication of other modalities, look at what other tools you may have at your disposal, or pass the client on to someone else. True professionals know the limits of their practice. Be humble enough to know that you don't know what's best for every person in every situation.

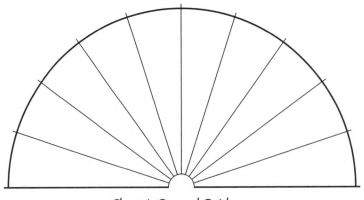

*Chart 6. General Guidance*

A Comprehensive Mini-Course in Spiritual Dowsing

# IDENTITY FOCUS

This chart has to do with what the superconscious mind knows about the client's identity—or those areas with which the client is currently ready to accept consciously. Bear in mind that, aside from divine love or Universal Consciousness, none of these identities are essentially "real." They are more like "stations" or concepts in our awareness where we may be lingering. We can get stuck in the station, especially if there is an ego payoff attached to that identity. Figuring this out can motivate you to hop back on the train of awakening!

## Soul Imprisonment

This implies that something causing spiritual limitation is likely going on in another dimension or time frame. The soul is eternal, but we can fall asleep to our identity as soul or spirit, and thus be imprisoned by our own beliefs. You may need to release some old contracts, vows, or karmic issues, or remove interfering spirits or ETs.

## Fear

Fear is the antithesis of love, and is at the root of all illusions. Transmute fear (left spin) into love at the point of origin in time, if given permission. Fear is not so much a thing or condition as it is simply the absence of love or truth, just as darkness is only the absence of light. As real love is without opposite, being non-dual, love's "opposite" is clearly an illusion. There is nothing real to fear.

## The Pain Body

This concept is explained elegantly by Eckhart Tolle as a parasitic emotional memory field that creates suffering to feed its addiction. A good definition of the ego! Dowse down its influence and life force to zero. Release all mental and emotional attachment to the need to feed it at all.

## Mind, Body, and Emotional Identification

This indicates a general over-identification with the ego, or false self. This observation is without judgment; it is just the condition of humanity in the dream of separation. As these facets are always in flux, identifying with them leaves us feeling basically insecure and cut off from goodness or the Divine.

And, of course, this is exactly the ego's purpose. Reduce these factors after measuring them on a scale of 1 to 10.

## Spirit Identification

Even spirit identification can be out of balance—as in when you fail to integrate all the dimensions or get ungrounded. When you over-spiritualize everything, this is another ego ploy to create an identity around being more "spiritual" than others. Use the Balance Chart to determine under- or over-identification with these items.

## Planetary, Galactic, and Universal Awareness

This has to do with stages in the expansion of your true Self-identity. This is being facilitated by the activation of the corresponding new chakras described below. When clients receive these responses, it likely means that they are ready to become aware of and accept this expanded sense of themselves. Raise the conscious awareness of the item that comes up, and suggest that they begin to visualize and activate the corresponding chakra. Have them visualize themselves actually "as big as" these realms, perhaps embracing the planet or standing in the center of the galaxy or universe. Since these domains are all projections of the mind anyway. As the mind moves toward accepting its true magnitude, we can "play along" and reduce the fear of the conscious mind as we expand into our universal mind—our One Self.

## Spirit Awareness

Spirit awareness, of course, transcends the limits of normal awareness and goes into the formless nature of pure Being. This is a very abstract concept that defies further description, although it can be "felt" and discerned nonverbally. Spirit Awareness only emerges out of mental silence as it lies beyond concepts. Measure on a scale of 1 to 10, with 10 as completion or Unity Consciousness. After spinning it up to 10 and/or dowsing out all resistance to further growth, suggest a regular practice that cultivates mental silence. There is no substitute for this kind of discipline as long as we are here in Earth School.

## The Divine Messenger

This refers to the active aspect of the Divine, even within the dream of time and space. In *A Course in Miracles*, this is called the Holy Spirit, a term that may have limiting religious overtones for some. Receiving this information means that you may actually be receiving divine messages, without knowing to whom or what to attribute them. The Holy Spirit often "speaks" in dreams, through inspiring literature, music, or art, or through more direct inspirations or revelations. The messages often come through everyday relationships and encounters, which we may easily miss if we are not asking to receive inspiration in the first place. Raise (right spin) the client's awareness of these messages, and clear (left spin) any resistances to receiving what Spirit has to offer.

## Divine Love

This implies a more direct and personal "heart connection" with Source. Receiving this may indicate the need just to "be" with the Divine and open to a greater loving relationship—a relationship that is patiently waiting for each and every one of us until we decide we want it above all else.

As the extra chakras come on line as a natural part of the evolution of the fifth-dimensional Light Body, we expand by stages from awareness of our connection to Mother Earth (Earth chakra below the feet) to our solar, galactic, and ultimately our universal chakra above the head. This is how we come to realize that all within our awareness is *us*, that we *are* One with the Source of the universe. We are moving now as a species toward a twelve-chakra system.

## Avatars

An avatar is one who has mastered existence in the multi-dimensional universe of form, yet, like an Ascended Master, has volunteered to "walk among the sleeping" to help in the Great Awakening. For clarity's sake, an Ascended Master is a self-realized fifth-dimensional being, while an avatar is fully tenth-dimensional in its scope of experience and knowing.

## Planetary Ascension Team

This term describes those volunteers who are here to raise the frequency and thus the awareness of the planet and of humanity through their presence and their actions, often as healers, artists, or educators. Some are first-timers on the planet or in human incarnation, and so may feel somewhat detached or naïve when it comes to understanding human affairs. They may even feel a sense of not belonging here until they become aware of their higher purpose.

Dowse the percentage of awareness of these identity foci and simply raise or lower it, depending on the nature of the issue, to optimal. For instance, if emotional identification comes up, the Balance Chart shows this as under-identification (left of center). This person may be in emotional denial and not fully experiencing the richness of his or her emotions. With a right spin, say:

*I now raise the awareness of (client's) emotional life to optimal balance, enabling them to experience and learn from all emotions without fear.*

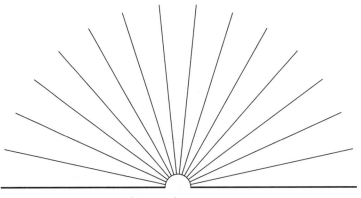

Chart 7. Identity Focus

## EXPANDED IDENTITY

We are all multi-dimensional beings. We are all also One with the Divine. Within that Oneness, we are having multiple experiences simultaneously due to our mutual choice to experience separation. Knowing these other hidden identities can help us better understand and accept parts of ourselves. As we gather in these parts of ourselves, we grow in our spiritual identity, with the ultimate goal of Self-realization. From the space of Oneness, you are all beings in all times and spaces. There is only One of us here! Until we get to that realization, we expand into our true identity in increments that the mind can accept. Until we do so, we can expect to feel occasionally that we don't belong or are somehow incomplete. Frankly, we don't, in fact, belong here in a dream-world of illusion and separation. So if this is you, you're right!

A Comprehensive Mini-Course in Spiritual Dowsing

Yet self-acceptance of these levels of being can be part of our total healing and return to wholeness. And it leads to other acceptance as well. It's also fun to know ourselves on other levels. Just don't let the ego suck you into thinking you are special; everyone is, and no one is! We are all equal beings, aspects of the One, having a human experience.

## Human Humans

A Human Human is one whose primary focus has always been evolving on the Earth. These people will be very close to Nature, and do not feel the need to venture into esoteric worlds. Many native and aboriginal people may qualify here. They can easily become Earthbound spirits when they die because they are happy just to be here with Mother Earth. Human Humans will not be happy to live in noisy, modern cities. They will feel much more at home in Nature.

## Fairies

A fairy is someone closely aligned with the elemental kingdom, or the second dimension. People with fairy connections are often inspiring to be around; they carry a lot of Light in the form of good humor and sociability. They can also be very energetically sensitive and will need to avoid abrasive energies like violence, conflict, and the media along with other toxic energies in the world in order to stay balanced. We need folks like that to keep us light—and to keep us from taking ourselves too seriously!

## Galactic Federation

A person from the Galactic Federation is tied into the council of beings overseeing the planetary ascension process on Earth. As such, they can hold a sense of the bigger picture, a feeling of confidence in the plan, and perhaps a sense of participating in something big. It helps us to put our problems in perspective when we can see the big picture. These folks will be drawn to information on prophecies about the planetary ascension. Most of their galactic work at this time is done in the dream state.

The different star systems (Pleiades, Arcturus, Orion, Sirius) and the Andromeda galaxy are simply locations where we have, or are having, another experience—part of our total education in this quadrant. You may feel a connection to some of these societies, and there are good books channeled from beings from these places. This is not so unusual when you consider that most of your ancestors came from elsewhere on the globe. Just expand the notion that we are all immigrants from somewhere out a little bit. We will be learning an expanded picture of human history as we begin to discover artifacts on Mars, for example, that resemble Earthly structures. Barbara Marciniak's *Bringers of the Dawn* (Santa Fe, NM: Bear and Co., 1992) is a good book to start with, especially for information about Pleiadians. *Songs of the Arcturians* (Hillsborough, OR: Beyond Words Publishing, 1996) is another.

## Ascended Masters

Ascended Masters are fifth-dimensional beings who are here by choice to help the planet and humanity. They don't need to be here like the rest of us to learn lessons; they learned them already, but they love you enough to come back and help. They carry a very strong unconditional love vibration, having transcended dualistic love, or "love-fear." Ascended Masters are associated with Venus, a planet that, although it is uninhabitable by third-dimension standards, is apparently home to an ascended fifth-dimensional culture, as Tesla once affirmed. There's a lot of good information coming through now and many materials on the lives of the Masters. This is the "big show" they've been waiting for!

## Incarnate Angels

Incarnate angels are humans operating from the upper fourth dimension with a strong connection to the fifth dimension. They live from the heart. They are often very sensitive to things like cruelty and violence, and do not tolerate this kind of energy very well—in fact, it makes them sick. They are prone to showing up at the right place and the right time to do the right thing—to give a hand or encouragement, or even a healing touch or prayer. Keep your eyes open for them. They will shine through the eyes of that loving person—old, middle-aged, or very young—and leave you feeling as if, well, as if you've been touched by an angel! Incarnate angels bring hope to a despairing world and light to what darkness claims as its own.

## Elementals

Elementals often have a pixie or gnome-like appearance, and an affinity for Nature. They may have an impish personality and love to play tricks. As they are aligned with Nature and the second dimension, they have a hard time in cities. Once they have been identified, they can consciously decide to align more with Nature, and feel more at home here.

## Walk-Ins

Walk-ins represent the positive side of entity possession. Knowing you are a Walk-in can be helpful in explaining life events, especially if you dowse the year of "transition." This was usually a time of significant change in life direction, usually toward a more altruistic service-oriented life. Walk-ins are typically more mature souls with a higher purpose in service to mankind. Others may not appreciate the change. Walk-ins therefore can easily feel rejected or misunderstood by those who still see the old persona only. Once Walk-ins realize who they are, it becomes much easier to move on and forgive those who don't yet understand. (See Ruth Montgomery's *Strangers Among Us*.)

## Wizards

A wizard is someone who is likely playing that role in a parallel life. Wizards will be drawn to magical possibilities—perhaps healing arts like energy work or homeopathy. One goal of a wizard is to master the transmutation of elements or the limits of form. Thus they are often able to turn lead into gold—that is, they may have amazing healing skills, or invent or use new healing modalities like crystals, sacred geometry, and other ancient arts. A wizard will look at a problem or situation and just know that "It doesn't have to be this way!" They are playful optimists, and know that anything is possible.

## Star Beings

Star beings have directly incarnated here from a stellar home. There is a belief that all humans are evolving toward this status on our way home, and that our Sun itself is a being of high magnitude. Consider how the ancients worshipped the Sun, and how sunlight is the source and sustenance of all physical life on the planet. A star being is here to contribute a particular quality of Light to the planet and is part the greater Planetary Ascension Team.

## Buddhas

Buddhas are part of a venerated lineage of awakened beings. As the Buddha energy came to Earth 500 years before Christ, we can say that the awakened state that Buddha represents is a prerequisite condition to accepting unconditional love. After all, when we awaken, we must awaken *to* something. Someone with Buddha energy in their profile will flourish in an atmosphere or practice of silent devotion and the cultivation of compassion.

## Final Incarnation

This is a reason for celebration. It means that a soul has neared the end of its third-dimension life lessons. Many here at this time have waited until now for their final incarnation, as they want to graduate along with the Earth and all three-dimensional life forms during the Shift of the Ages that we are in. If you are one, however, be on the lookout for your final forgiveness lesson—a crowning achievement in forgiveness drawn from the deepest recesses of your being. It's okay, however. Since this is your final incarnation, you will most likely pass the test with flying colors!

## Ascending with Gaia

This implies that you will be among those who move into the fifth dimension with the Earth in your current physical form. This means that your physical form will be going through some fundamental redesigning, which can be weird temporarily. Research Light Body activation for more insight. Support your body with light, rest, water, and patience! Trust that you will be guided to be at the right place at the right time!

## ET Visitors

An ET visitor is either a shape-shifter disguised as a human or someone who has direct ET parentage—a hybrid. Ninety percent of ET visitors and observers are of the Light. Negative ETs can easily be identified by their motivations and actions. Although they may be "light on the outside," they are here with ulterior motives. Dowse with which variety you may be dealing. Celebrate the ET presence on Earth, as they are here to celebrate with us our Galactic Initiation.

## Remaining on 3D Earth

This implies the choice on some level not to "ride" the ascension to a fifth-dimensional expression. It means that, you are choosing to remain in the third dimension out of love. This does not carry with it any form or level of judgment. One dimension is not better than another. The different dimensions just represent different kinds of experience.

If a soul chooses to remain in the third dimension with the Earth, or to incarnate onto another third-dimension planet, it is because it knows what kinds of experiences it needs on its sojourn home to Oneness. It may be that these are simply "young souls" going through the same curriculum as all of us! Although a future third-dimensional Earth may be dealing with some of the same challenges we see today on Earth, it may be that, with a diminished population, there will be less pollution, more available resources, and a new perspective on how to draw upon the lessons of history. Some may be transporting to another third-dimensional world. Eventually, we all make it home. Our paths may vary, but our destination is the same.

## Cosmic Beings

This is a general term for a universal explorer that lies outside the scope of the other definitions here. Dowse for more information based on the questions you can imagine. These beings may be vessels for a unique form of energy that we need in order to become whole as one united Being.

## Eighth-Dimensional Beings

These beings come from highly developed non-material civilizations located much closer to the Galactic Center than Earth. As this is the dimension of the Mind of God, these are pretty highly developed beings who are here as ascension helpers. They hold the frequency of Divine Will for all of us, which is love.

## Ninth-Dimensional Time Lords

These are part of the executive planning committee for our experience of time. Ninth-dimensional beings will likely be here to help usher in the next time wave and help us adjust to the next cosmic plan, which promises to be a Golden Age of unlimited potential.

## Incarnated Fourth-Dimensional Beings

These may be angelic, or may simply manifest as beings with many lifetimes of rich experience and knowledge from many incarnations. The spirits of great artists, healers, and scientists are all willing and available at this time to lend their talents and gifts in fulfilling love's purpose on Earth. They are here to share their specific gifts and guidance.

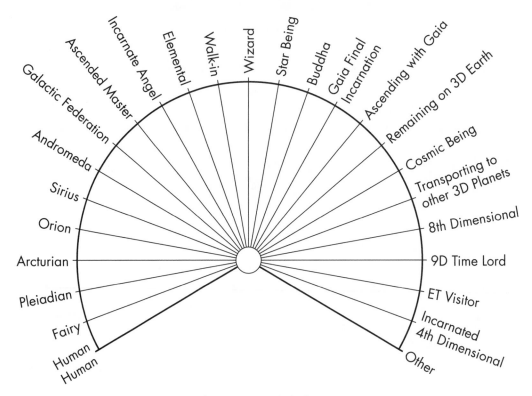

*Chart 8. Expanded Identities*

## LIFE ARENAS

This chart can be used to focus on general areas for deeper investigation. Ask how many apply.

### Forgiveness

This invites clients to look at areas where they may be holding a grievance, or a relationship or situation where the thought of it brings a loss of peace. Consider introducing them to the simple *Ho'oponopono* forgiveness method. Without necessarily feeling it, just have them bring the person or situation to mind, and tell that person: "I love you. I am sorry. Please forgive me. Thank you" until the feeling becomes lighter. This technique works to shift relationships permanently, even if the receiving person is unaware it is being used or is deceased.

There are two kinds of forgiveness. Only one works. The old style looks at the fault, thus making it real, and then tries to forgive. This keeps the "fault" alive under a sense of moral superiority. True forgiveness sees no fault at all, only the radiance of the divine Creator behind the face of the "criminal" calling to be recognized and loved. True forgiveness eventually leads to the realization there is nothing to forgive. When we get there, we realize that we too are forgiven on this level.

## Creative Expression

If this comes up, there is either too much or too little creativity in a person's life. In most cases, it is probably too little. Ask to see if there is a primary blockage in this area, in what domain this blockage resides (mental, physical, emotional, spiritual), and whether the factor is time-related. See what other kinds of questions come to mind and trust your intuitive sense and Guides.

## Chakras

If chakras are indicated, ask if this is a general issue, or if there is a more specific chart that needs to be checked. It may be that they are all under- or over-activated.

## Past and Future Lives

This refers to parallel lifetimes being lived by the Over Soul in different experiential versions of now. Ultimately, as there is only One of us here dreaming of separation, we are living *all* possible lives in all time frames and dimensions at once! Although this idea is mind-boggling (the mind needs a good boggling now and then!), it is in line with the non-dual metaphysics of thought systems like *A Course in Miracles*, which states that, as separation is an impossibility—only a crazy mad idea—the universe of separate time and space never occurred in reality, only in a state of sleep or hallucination. We are, in fact, "safe at home while dreaming of exile."

However, as we are here untangling the web of our belief in guilt, pain, and suffering, there are certain timelines or life experiences that are more pertinent to our individual pathways home. Often, these parallel life issues represent patterns of belief or behavior that we are working on multiple levels simultaneously. Thus, the issue can seem to have a continuity that may appear to set these lives apart as somehow "special." This is only true as far as the opportunity they may present for us to understand and forgive the issues, completely negate them for ourselves and everybody, and move on back to Oneness and full God Realization.

Check to see which domain needs to be looked at, and make further enquiries as you are guided. Dowse the year implied by the issue, checking to see if the era is A.D. or B.C. and go there with your intention to remove or improve what comes up in your investigation.

## Life Purpose

These issues may or may not have to do with clients' jobs or physical situations. Ask. The answer may indicate the reason or purpose behind what they are doing in life. Ask, for example, if their current motive for living is for survival or growth. If survival, ask to go back to the original thought/fear/belief that set that pathway, and clear it. Raise (right spin) the awareness and motivation to discover their true life's purpose. Hint: It often has to do with other people. You can never discover your own life's purpose yourself. That is always a joint venture!

Ultimately, the highest purpose one can aspire to on Earth is forgiveness. This practice is the fast track to awakening and graduation. In this sense, it matters much less what we do than the reason or purpose we give to what we do.

## Lineage DNA

This has to do with a memory caught in the DNA—typically behind a repeated pattern or predisposition in the lineage. It may be physical, as in the risk of certain illnesses, or mental or emotional, as in the case of certain family traits that we take for granted, but that can be changed. Time travel back through the lineage to the source of the thought/feeling/belief behind the pattern and clear it there for all past and future members of your lineage. Quantify the number of generations back on the mother's or father's side, go there, and clear the issue at its root.

## Cell Memory

This is a similar issue, but may involve more than just your lineage. Or it may simply be something in your individual experience. What is important to understand is that these things are held there and revealed now for a reason—because you can change them! Mind is the cause of matter. Change your mind, and matter will follow. You do not have to accept anything less than your perfection, which is each and everyone's birthright.

## Energy Work

This points to the benefits of seeking out healing energy work. For many who already work with energy, this will only validate or reinforce its benefits for them. For the uninitiated, this may show up as an invitation to begin to explore something out of the box, which can be an important step in spiritual growth. You may know of certain modalities you can test on a scale of 1 to 10 to indicate the degree of benefit. Working with energetic healing techniques or tools can be a great introduction to spiritual awakening. We first awaken from the material realm to the energetic; then we move beyond energy, which is really only expanded matter, to the further realms of Spirit.

## Primary Relationship

When this shows up, it should by no means be taken as an excuse to dump the other person in the relationship or make radical changes. Rather, it is an invitation to see the relationship and person differently—through the eyes of Spirit rather than ego. In Spirit's view, relationships offer us the greatest opportunities for growth through forgiveness. When relationships are healed by these means, they transcend the ego's limited view (as another excuse to suffer) and help us begin to see the divine purpose in the relationship.

## Spiritual Identity

If you dowse spiritual identity, it may bring up the question: Is this person aware of their spiritual identity? Perhaps this person is in denial of his or her spiritual identify, or has mis-identified him- or herself. Ask. Dowse out all mental and emotional resistance to their spiritual awakening.

## Highest Purpose

This chart refers to the spiritual purpose one has given to their lives. We serve either fear and the ego, or Spirit, which is Love. The timing of this awakening is pre-set, and inevitable. Check levels of self awareness and willingness to awaken, and adjust in order to "save time and reduce suffering."

## General Relationships

This response implies the same issues as with primary relationships, just applying to other areas of life like family, work, or organizational relationships. Usually, people know which relationships are offering the top forgiveness opportunities at the time. Dowse out the blockages to forgiveness (left spin), which can involve past-life issues, and raise the motivation to forgive (right spin). We actually don't forgive others as much as we forgive our own perceptions and judgments of others. Lack of only hurts you. Ask Spirit to raise your awareness of your forgiveness opportunities. They show up whenever your inner peace is disturbed, even slightly.

## Health

In this case, health implies physical issues. Although we accept that physical issues are always the tip of a greater iceberg and not a cause in and of themselves, nevertheless, it is often necessary to reduce the pain and worry around physical issues before the mind can settle down and focus on deeper issues. Harmonic (radionic) rates can be very helpful here—i.e., to reduce pain, increase circulation, speed healing, reduce fear, etc. Some of the clearings in chapter 4 can help as well. Be careful not to make any claims regarding diagnosis or curing. This is the sacred domain of the priests of reductionist medicine, at least at the time of this writing.

## Occupation

When this comes up, you may want to use the Balance Chart to see the overall effect of clients' current occupation on their minds, their bodies, or their spirits. Do they have any unfulfilled vows or agreements keeping them in an unpleasant situation that can be cleared? Is this a self-identity issue? Use the Chart of Ten to determine the probability that they could find an occupation more in line with their highest purpose—in a week, in a month, in two months, etc. You may want to dowse in a team of helpers like angels or Masters to lead a client to the perfect occupation. Think of these helpers as the "job committee," and ask which one will work on specific aspects of the career change. This idea of helper committees can be applied to any project.

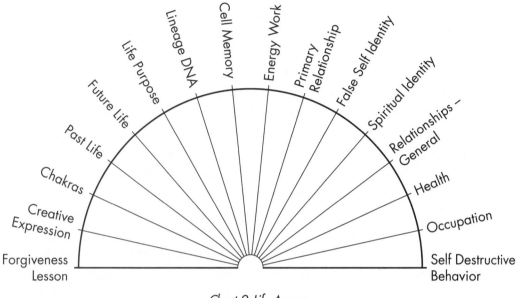

*Chart 9. Life Arenas*

## MEGA-HERTZ SCALE

This chart captures the average range of the vibrational speed of the human energy field in mega hertz, which are reflective of a variety issues both physical and non-physical. One mega hertz (MHz) is equal to a million hertz, or cycles per second. This very high-frequency range implies the non-physical or multi-dimensional aspects of the energy body, or aura.

This chart provides a panorama, if you will, of many of the possible states within the illusion of separation, form, and time. These can be viewed as experiential "stations" along the pathway to the recovery of our memory of Oneness with Source. As such, there is no hierarchy implied here, just perhaps opportunities to appreciate where you are on this universal journey, and the opportunity to accelerate the process through recognition and a choice to "fast-forward" the movie we call life. Simply ask where you or your client are on this scale today. The answer can provide a thread of questions around these issues. For a quick fix, simply raise (right spin) the value to optimal.

Happiness lies at 70 MHz, which is also the chart's 3D Limit. The implication here is that, in order to be happy, we must transcend limited material consciousness. We must be able to see beyond the narrow range of our senses, and know beyond the cognitive prison of judgment and perception. Spinning up the frequency can hasten the shift to expanded awareness.

This kind of knowing is more feeling-based than information-based. The beginning of the inner shift is the awakening to the will—the desire to see things differently. If there were any value in suffering, this would be it—that is, to get to the point of throwing up your hands, giving up on your own strength, and looking to a higher power to carry you through. Something wonderful happens when you get to this place. Your emptiness makes room for the Divine, who says: "Now you're getting it! Let's do this life together from here on!"

Prosperity consciousness has nothing to do with material gain, by the way. We make a grave error when we limit ourselves this way. Prosperity is a state of mind in which you begin to intuit your limitless value in the eyes of the Creator, and begin to see this abundance reflected in your perceptions. To love and be loved is true prosperity, which does not depend on any outward cause.

Note that, below 68 MHz, it will be difficult to maintain any consistent degree of happiness or experience prosperity of any kind. If you dowse your client's frequency at 70 MHz, right spin and say:

*I now ask to raise (client's) frequency to the maximum optimal level for their highest good at this time, and that this new frequency become their new baseline frequency from which there is no reversal.*

Raising someone's frequency on a regular basis covers a multitude of issues and yields maximum benefits from minimum effort. Why not do it daily until it "sticks"? Then recheck the frequency.

## Soul Reabsorption

This refers to a last-ditch effort to salvage the soul substance of a being that is totally committed to its own destruction. The soul can be salvaged from a dead-end situation and start over on the evolutionary journey. As nothing real can be threatened, according to *A Course in Miracles*, we can never truly destroy life. There will always be a chance to start over. Just as in every moment we can release ourselves from time and choose peace, so there is no condemnation in the Divine's creation. If you get this reading for living (embodied) people, simply release them to their higher selves and the decision they have made to start fresh. You may raise (right spin) the probability that they will awaken through the next timeline they choose to experience.

## Physical Death

Death, like everything else, has a frequency. In truth, there is no final death except for the body. Use discretion, obviously, if you receive this for a living person, and ask your Guides if you have permission to spin him or her upward and out of this frequency. We cannot judge another's decision to leave the body, so you may get a response of no when you ask if this can be adjusted. You may need only to release the fears around the issue of death, and welcome (right spin) the frequency of peace into their lives at this time.

## Cancer, Candida, and Flu

These terms are not to be construed as diagnostic. They only show the frequency that would be supportive or reflective of these states. Raising or neutralizing these frequencies may be indicated, as may further investigation of levels of cause (mental, emotional, spiritual, environmental).

## Normal and 3D Limit

Notice that the indication of "normal" lies below the 3D Limit, showing that, at the time of this writing at least, the majority of the population is vibrating well within the limits of the third dimension—or, more accurately, are asleep. As we start to enliven the mind, we can begin to vibrate up into the gifted and genius range, which is everyone's potential. I expect this level will continue to rise as humanity embraces Unity Consciousness, the great promise of the New Age.

## DNA Indicators

Notice that DNA indicators range from three- to twelve-strand, with twelve showing a passage beyond the fourth dimension. As the 12-strand DNA begins to manifest (a natural part of the evolution of the fifth-dimensional Light Body), the frequency rises. Scientists agree that most of human DNA is dormant, or operating in an "off" position. This implies that we, as a species, are at a very early stage in our evolution. The energies the solar system is moving into at this time hold the potential to "vibrate awake" this latent DNA. The cosmic alarm clock is going off. Why not assist in the process, by accelerating your evolution and consciously intending and spinning up your frequency?

## Multi-Dimensional Portal

This reading indicates a path whereby you will be able to transcend time and space consciously, and move about the universe at will. Others have achieved this. Why not you? Ask if this portal is already open to them, to what percent they have stepped into this potential, and if there are any blocks to clear in this area.

## Ascension

This refers to the transition from carbon-based physicality focused in the third dimension to a silica-based, or crystalline, physiology, often referred to as the Light Body. When you achieve this, you enter a fifth-dimensional experience. This describes the achievement of the Ascended Masters who, through personal devotion to truth and the undoing of illusion, paved the way for all of us to do the same. The time has come when conditions can support large numbers of people in this transition. Imagine, a whole planet of Ascended Masters!

## The White Brotherhood

The White Brotherhood is a council of Ascended Masters playing a major role in the planetary ascension. As the color white includes all colors of the visible spectrum, the implication here is of a group of beings who recognize and exemplify all as a unified Being, the One Mind or Created One. Receiving this item may indicate a need to connect through prayer or meditation or, to open to downloads of information from a higher plane.

## Divine Human or the One

By the time you dowse someone as a Divine Human or the One, you are seeing someone who, on a light-energy vibrational level at least, is holding the energy to move fully and consciously back to the original state of Oneness with Source. The fact that the individual may still be in a body does not negate this. It simply shows that he or she has chosen to appear as limited and physical while the rest of us "catch up."

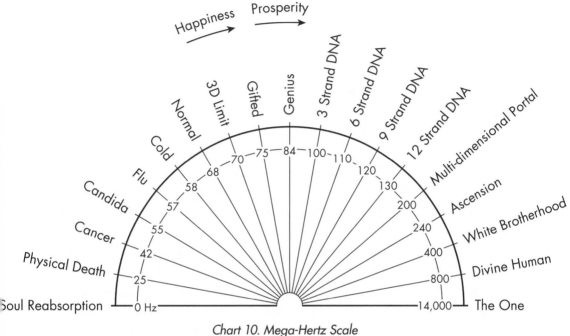

*Chart 10. Mega-Hertz Scale*

## BRAIN-WAVE FREQUENCY

This chart measures the electrical activity of the brain, which can also be read with standard biofeedback equipment. Using this chart, you can reset and establish an optimal default or dominant brain-wave pattern. We operate in all brain wave frequencies, but often gravitate to a specific range as a conditioned default pattern. Start by asking what is the subject's current predominant brain-wave pattern or frequency. This measurement reflects the quality of consciousness moving through the brain. Contrary to the materialist scientific view, the brain does not cause the mind; rather awareness or consciousness causes the brain and body, and uses the brain as a medium of communication.

Generally, the lower the brain waves, the more efficiently your brain is functioning as a unit and the deeper your connection to All That Is. The higher the brain waves, the more focused, and thus limited, your awareness. Kind of puts the brain in context, doesn't it? Despite its elegant physiology, the more your brain is out of the way, the further you can expand your awareness!

With this chart, you will find it beneficial in most cases to lower (left spin) the brain waves to facilitate higher states of awareness. However, if you will be writing an exam in the future, or doing something that requires a lot of clear, focused attention, you can dowse an ideal beta frequency of 13 Hz into that future time period. Notice that we have noted Annunaki Access in the range between 14 and 20 Hz. This refers to the male-polarized state that these beings represent in the ancient records of Sumeria. It is an energy tradition-ally associated with empire-building and conquest, and the mind-set inherent in this orientation to the world. We find that the ego is hell-bent, literally, on keeping us immersed in unsolvable problems—always looking to the future, but never quite getting there. This is consistent with a dominance of beta brain waves and an obsession with problems.

Notice also the role of TV and the media in keeping us out of the more expansive lower frequencies. You can cultivate alpha states by imagining tracing a large horizontal figure eight over your eyes. This connects the hemispheres of your brain so they are operating in a balanced fashion. Notice how this calms you down and puts you in a relaxed, pre-meditative state. Even better, elevate your field of vision about 20 degrees upward. If you close your eyes and imagine a full-sensory experience, you will also drop into an alpha state.

Check first to see what the dominant or default brain-wave pattern is for your subjects at present. Then ask what their ideal default brain-wave fre-quency is. Dowse the brain waves down (left spin) or dowse in the specific frequency (right spin). Consider this chart for group work as well. Perhaps teachers can help students perform better, or perhaps we can improve the harmony and creativity of our homes, work places, and political servants!

## Alpha, Theta, and Delta States

Delta waves on the left of the chart are associated with deep sleep, near-death experiences, astral travel, and lucid dreaming. Although these experiences seem unreal upon awakening, if you consider that the waking state is simply another level of dreaming, these are no less real than any other. In a delta state, the conscious mind is out of the way, so you are free to break the rules of physicality.

## Ideal States

If you look at the brain-wave frequency associated with gratitude, you can see a pathway, as we lower our brain waves from here, taking us through the states of meditation, on to channeling, and to mental silence, which is the goal of meditation. Etheric vision implies a state like dreaming, but with more of a feeling of direct contact with higher realms or beings.

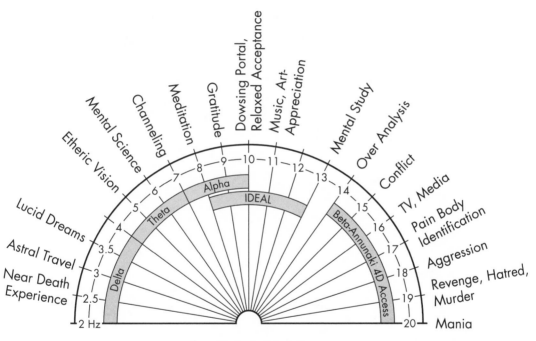

*Chart 11. Brain-Wave Frequency*

Note also that, especially if you are an aspiring dowser, you must be operating at or below the brain waves associated with the dowsing portal at 10 Hz. My dowsing mentor, Raymon Grace, was at one time a top trainer for the Silva Mind Control method, a system that teaches techniques to get into an alpha state and work from there. It is in alpha that we tap into our own whole-brain usage, and also into the field of collective consciousness. We are thus much more able to affect other minds positively, and, being in a relaxed accepting state, are much more likely to intuit what is best for another person without trying to fix or solve temporary problems. When we are in "fixing" mode, we are operating in beta, and we tend to make the problem more real and solid, just as when you "fix" a chemical compound. Would you rather be fixed or healed—that is, made whole?

When we bring the right hemisphere of the brain "online" through activities like music and art appreciation and meditation, the efficiency of the brain goes up, even as the overall frequency goes down.

## Beta States

As you can see, as the brain waves get more active, we move more into the potential for conflict, even to the point of extreme negative behaviors. When awareness is polarized toward the left hemisphere (analytical "male" brain), we drop down to a busier, but much less efficient, brain state.

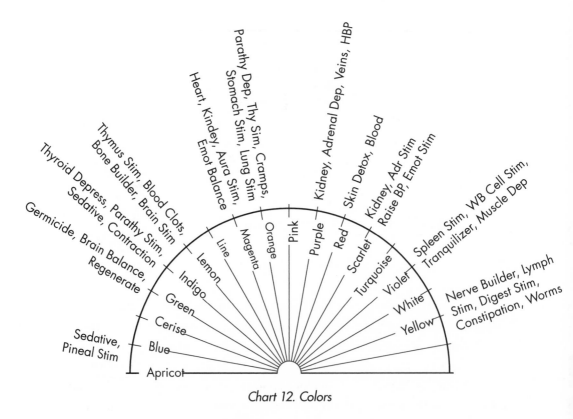

Chart 12. Colors

A Comprehensive Mini-Course in Spiritual Dowsing

## COLORS

Color therapy has a long history. Ask how many and which colors are out of balance for your subject. Assess colors with the Balance Chart, increasing deficiencies or decreasing excess accordingly (deficiencies are more typical). Ask to make the adjustment irreversible. Suggest that clients follow up by wearing garments, eating foods, or exposing themselves somehow to their deficient colors.

Note that many of the colors have physical correlations. You may decide to dowse for how many hours a day and for how many days they need to be exposed to the color to completely balance out these issues. Color therapists use colored lights or gels directly on the body. The medicine of the future will use these harmless, non-invasive therapies once we understand their value and get over our dependence on harmful and expensive drugs.

## CHAKRAS AND TONES

The chakras are subtle energetic vortices centered over the endocrine glands. They extend in front of and out from behind the body. They connect us as "vortex portals" to all dimensions of existence, and can hold or give access to stored memories from other time frames and existences. They can also be entry points for energetic connections to others, either beneficial or non-beneficial, as noted earlier.

We call these "psychic cords." They can be the means whereby others can access and drain our energy at a distance—especially those with whom we may have had a prior intimate relationship. Ask if this chart is an issue. It very often is, especially for healers, teachers, or others in the public view. People who "want what you have" may unconsciously send out a psychic cord. Ask how many chakras have "leaks." You can also ask what percentage of the chakra energy is being drained, if there is a cord involved, or if the draining involves past or future lives or a relationship from this life. After removing the cord (left spin), transmuting it to pure Light, and bringing forgiveness into the relationship, ask to recover (right spin) all lost energies and restore the chakra to full function.

When measuring the overall functionality of a chakra at, say, 70 percent, ask what percentage is being lost to the past (this is often where the missing 30 percent is hanging out) or to the future of course. Psychologically, when a chakra is leaking into the past, it may accompany emotions of regret, guilt, or other past-oriented feelings. Likewise, a chakra leaking into the future may involve fears, apprehensions, and insecurities. Use the Balance Chart here, with the left side indicating past reference, and the right side indicating future reference. The balance point represents "all present and accounted for." My experience has been that traveling to the points in time and clearing the emotions there will automatically bring the chakra back to full, present-time functioning.

The different chakras also have their correct direction of spin. As there are different schools of thought here and different spins for the front and back chakras at different times, simply ask for each chakra, or generally, whether the chakra is spinning correctly. You can then ask to be shown the correct direction of spin for that chakra *at this time*, as the optimal direction can change depending on what the superconscious mind is up to!

## Extra Chakras

The planetary, galactic, and universal chakras refer to energy centers formed over the head at one, three, and six feet above the body, on average. The Earth chakra is situated three feet below the feet. Some theorize that these "extra" chakras are coming on line as part of the shift in planetary and human consciousness at this time, and reflect a general expansion of our awareness beyond the constraints of the physical body. You can meditate on these centers and see if you notice a greater sense of connectedness with these realms.

There is a musical note or tone associated with each chakra as well. Ask if it is deficient or over-energized (Balance Chart). Dowse it in or out as needed. If you have access to a musical keyboard, you can also play the note or major chord of that key as sound therapy.

Chakra 5, the thymus, has also been called the energetic or new heart chakra. It is a presently developing chakra, reflecting the evolutionary changes humanity is experiencing at this time, as are the four extra chakras connecting us with the earth, the planetary grids, the galaxy and the universe. We are evolving a twelve-chakra system, consistent with the evolving twelve strands of DNA. There are actually many secondary and micro-chakras in the body—for instance, in the palms of the hands and the soles of the feet, behind the knees, and at the back of the head. Every cell has a chakra by virtue of the electrical spin of the RNA/DNA. You may want to inquire into these extra and cellular chakras as well.

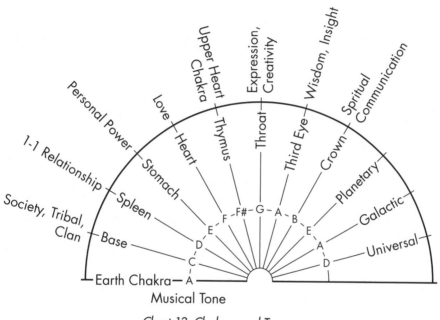

Chart 13. Chakras and Tones

## WATER SURFACE TENSION

We move now from the esoteric to a few more physically based issues. This particular issue has many implications for your physical well-being and optimal health—all part of being a healthy and "whole" person.

The surface tension of water molecules is relative to the amount of electrical charge held by the molecule. The stronger the charge, the less "bondable" the molecule. It's as if it's so bound up in itself that it can't easily bond with other molecules.

Our work, thus, is typically to reduce the water surface tension to the optimal minimal charge, measured in this case in "dynes." You can do this for individuals, for any body of water, or for bottled water—either locally or at a distance. There's something about the water molecule that makes it an ideal "sub-space antenna." The perfected, or "clustered," water molecule forms a crystalline lattice that is sensitive to overt and subtle energies of light, sound, temperature, pressure, and even thought (scalar energy). Water is the universal solvent and is necessary for the completion of the trillions of biochemical events that occur in your body every second. It is critical to nutrient transport and toxin release. You can survive forty days without food, but only three without water.

Surface tension is directly related to pH, which is directly related to oxygenation. By extension, surface tension is highly related to oxygenation as well. High surface tension equates to an acidic pH; low surface tension equates to greater oxygen transport potential. The two strongest predictors of cancerous cellular changes are acidic pH and low oxygen. Are you getting the picture? Therefore, of all the physical things you can dowse for, this one seems to produce some of the most tangible results. People literally feel a rush of oxygen to the brain, creating calm and mental clarity. This is because the brain uses up 80 percent of all available oxygen in the bloodstream.

Do a pre-test measurement on the scale. Left spin the surface tension of the water in the body to the optimal minimum level. Dowse in the memory (right spin) of this ideal level to be remembered and instantly communicated to every water molecule introduced into the body from this time forward. Re-test to see the results, then ask your client: "How do you feel?"

Radionic Homeopathics were added to this chart just to give you an idea of how bondable, and thus absorbable, these remedies are. This may help explain their efficacy and how they are easily communicated to every cell in the body when ingested. You may want to experiment with some water by dowsing the surface tension down to this level and then mentally imprinting (as you right spin) your intention (or a rate) into the water. This can be done at a distance, by the way, with the subject on the phone in front of a glass of water. Make sure you get the person to taste the water before and after; practically everyone notices a difference! These remedies can also be made on a device like the Sulis Remedy Maker from the UK.

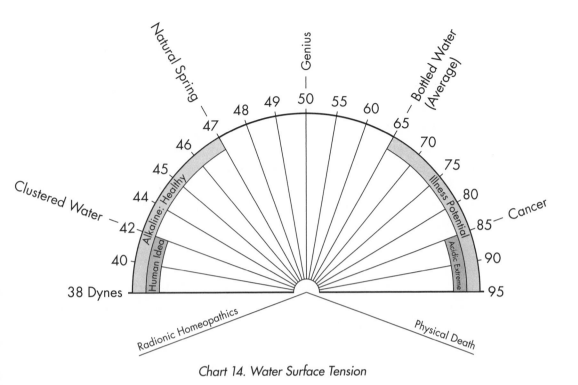

*Chart 14. Water Surface Tension*

# HYDRATION FACTORS

Ample hydration is such a fundamental factor, for physical as well as energetic health, that we will look at the many factors that can go into assuring that we are adequately hydrated.

When you are born, your hydration level is at 100 percent, or ideal. In addition, the water in your new body is in its purest state, with 100 percent of bodily water in a "clustered," or ideal, molecular state. Very quickly, with external and internal toxins becoming part of your existence, these values begin to diminish and, with aging, simply get worse over time for most people. Depending on your sense of thirst alone to tell you of your hydration needs is an unfortunate mistake, as a strong sense of thirst usually means that you have begun to dehydrate on a cellular level, and that your body is in panic mode.

## Good Source

Dowsing "good source" indicates that your current water supply is not optimal, thus the need for a good source of healthy water. City water is often adulterated with chlorine, which may be beneficial as a disinfectant, but wreaks havoc on the body, especially the thyroid. Fluoride was used by the Nazis in concentration camps, added to the drinking water in order to dull the brains of the inmates and make them more compliant. Its use as a dental preventative and water additive is unwarranted and is not backed by solid research. The solution?

Good filtration is one option. Leaving drinking water out overnight to let the chlorine evaporate is another. Moving to an area with clean water may be the best. You can dowse out pollutants from your drinking water and dowse rates that will counteract toxic chemicals. You will actually taste the difference when you do this.

## Misidentification of Hunger

This means you are eating when your body is really asking for water. Dowse up (right spin) the ability to recognize thirst. A common dieting technique is to drink water when hungry, then wait twenty minutes before eating. You may still want to eat, but your appetite will be satisfied more easily. Drink only up to 4 oz. of liquids with meals, however, as more will dilute your stomach acids. Misidentification of pain can be similar to this.

## Cell Wall Permeability

This can be affected by a diet low in essential fatty acids, which give cell membranes their elasticity. Cell membranes are made of two layers of fat molecules separated by water, creating an electrical flow potential like a tiny battery. Cellular dehydration shuts down the electrical functioning of the cell, including nutrient delivery and detoxification, and is implicated in toxic cell conditions that can contribute to cancerous damage to the DNA. Measure the permeability on a scale of 1 to 10, as well as fatty acid intake and metabolism and cellular hydration (see also Chart 26).

## $H_2O$ Metabolism

This refers to the body's ability to absorb and utilize water. There may be a deficiency of the associated water-digesting enzymes known as hydrolases. Check the levels on a scale of 1 to 10. It also may be a membrane issue, or surface tension and pH-related issue. Exposing your water to a negative-north magnetic field can help to make it more bio-available. You can place a magnet on an intake pipe or near your drinking-water container. Check the magnet with a compass. Negative north, which is biologically healthy, will attract the south point of the compass.

## Surface Tension and pH factors

These have their own charts (Charts 14 and 17), which you should investigate if these come up in a session.

## Emotional Aversion

Emotional aversion may have to do with childhood issues of being forced to drink water, or perhaps past-life trauma. There are people who just do not like water, which seems so unnatural, given water's essential role in all life forms. Time travel to the point of original aversion and clear there.

## Replace Substitutes

This identifies the need to stop addressing thirst and hydration with substances that cannot do the job—and very often negatively affect health, especially over time. This includes coffee (which dehydrates), sodas (which are a double whammy of refined sugar and carbon dioxide—both very acidic), juices (which can be high in sugar), and alcohol (another dehydrator). Diuretic medications, although helpful in the short term, can also lead to dehydration if water is not being steadily supplied. Often, these lifestyle habits are simply due to a lack of awareness. Digestive concerns and constipation, depression, back pain, and headaches can miraculously disappear as you increase your water intake.

## Inadequate Intake

This indicates the need to increase water intake. Many experts agree that the optimal number of fluid ounces of water we should consume each day is determined by the body weight divided in half. It is more valuable to sip frequently than gulp it all down at once.

Water, as noted, is the most highly programmable substance in your body—and perhaps on the planet. You can dowse your body's water by right spinning and saying:

*I request that my body's water be 100 percent bio-available, achieve its ideal frequency, become free of all toxic memory, and spontaneously recover its ideal clustered molecular state, communicating this ideal state to every subsequent water molecule entering the body from this time forward.*

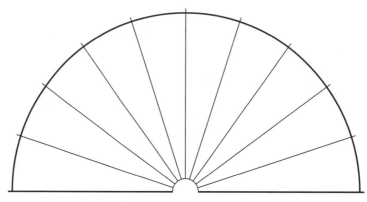

*Chart 15. Hydration Factors*

## ORGAN OF PRIMARY CONCERN

This chart is fairly self-explanatory. Once you have identified a primary concern, ask about "co-organs" that may be involved or affected. Measure the stressed organ on the Balance Chart for yin/yang status. A yang state implies that a current stressor is producing some kind of reaction, like an injury, allergy, toxin, or infection. A yin state typically implies a more chronic stress condition—perhaps one to which the body has adapted, no longer reacting to it in the form of a symptom. A yin issue may take longer to address and for recovery, and may require nutritional or homeopathic support. Check the organ's frequency level, life force, and functional status (using a percent chart). Because organs, like cells, can be considered beings in and of themselves, treat an unbalanced organ like a client. Ask about emotional trauma, toxicity, mental stress, circulation, and oxygenation. Some organs still retain the memory of childhood diseases, vaccinations, surgery and injuries, or drug use.

I have found the correlation between specific organs and emotions used in Chinese medicine to be very true. Here's a basic list:

Kidneys—fear

Lungs—grief

Stomach and digestion—lack of acceptance ("I can't stomach that!")

Heart—sadness

Spleen and immune system—worry

Skeletal system—support (emotional, financial)

Knees (reflect kidneys)—fear of moving forward

Colon—"mother" issues,

Senses—what it is that you refuse to see, hear, or feel

Pancreas—loss of "sweetness" in life

Check also for miasms or etheric weapons and entities.

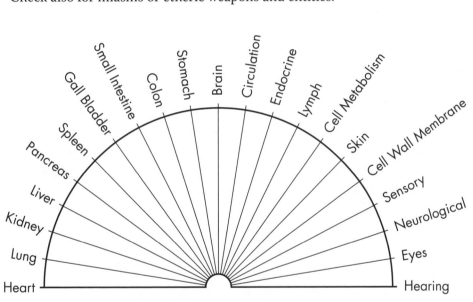

Chart 16. Organ of Primary Concern

Check to see if the imbalance you measure is at root physical, mental, emotional, psychic, or environmental. Time travel to the point in time of the original trauma can often be beneficial. When you use this line of enquiry, each answer will guide you naturally to the next question. For example, if you find that the root issue for the organ imbalance is physical, ask if you are dealing with an injury, toxicity, developmental issue, nutritional deficiency, etc. If it is mental or emotional, very often these are memories stored in the organ. In this case, ask if the emotion (or mental pattern) is from *this* life. Is it time related? Do you have permission to time travel to the original trauma and clear it there? You can then dowse the number of the year, or the age if you prefer. Go there with a left spin and do the removal, remembering to fill voids with fifth-dimensional energy. I generally also request that the organ now recover "according to its ideal template." With this method, we are truly undoing time; time is not what it used to be! Consider making your own chart for anatomical areas not represented here.

## PH AND ACIDITY/ALKALINITY

As noted, pH (acid/alkaline balance) is closely related to water surface tension and oxygenation. Most typical is overall hyperacidity. Aside from a sugar/grain/meat-based diet, the top causes of acidosis are dysfunctional shallow breathing (a stress response that can become habitual) and suppression of the pancreatic secretion of bicarbonate of soda. Shallow breathing is a fight-or-flight response to stress that occurs when we try to avoid threats by attempting to become "invisible" to a potential threat. Think of the prey holding its breath as the predator walks by. In modern life, this response automatically occurs just as often with mental and emotional threats as it does with physical threats or stress. As carbon dioxide is acidic and heavier than air, it tends to settle in the bottom of the lungs and recycle through the body when we are not breathing fully.

Bicarbonate of soda, a natural alkalizer, is normally secreted by a healthy pancreas to neutralize digestive HCl; but an exhausted pancreas can't keep up, so we pass our own digestive acid into the bloodstream and body. The pancreas can be exhausted either from over-stimulation of insulin and enzymes from a sugary grain-based, cooked-food (read: typical) diet, and/or from holding on to emotions of loss. Time travel to the source of this emotion and clear it there (left spin).

Another factor affecting the pancreas can be a virus transmitted in dairy products. This virus apparently survives standard pasteurization. This may explain some cases of Type 1 diabetes, which behave more like a contagious disease, appearing in families, often in children, with sudden onset. If you get a yes to this possibility (you are only asking for the presence of the energy signature of this virus, not diagnosing its physical presence), appeal to the deva or consciousness of this virus and respectfully send it home to the second dimension where it belongs. Reverse all ill effects in all time frames and dimensions with a left spin. Right spin to bring the pancreas back to optimal health and functioning.

A final factor to consider with pancreatic weakness or blood-sugar imbalances is the effect of 60-cycle EMFs on the pancreas. Although overlooked by mainstream science, researchers who operate outside the box of pharmaceutical control have validated this effect, and one in particular (*www.stetzerelectric.com*) has come up with simple, effective, and inexpensive devices to neutralize this effect. These are use in some hospitals. Stetzer even produced a scientific paper validating what he calls Type 3 diabetes, which is caused by EMFs.

If a client measures below 6.6, or overall ideal, determine what percentage of the imbalance is due to either the first or second factor. Teach the client deep, abdominal breathing while you spin out (left spin) the memories of stress or trauma that started the unhealthy breathing pattern. You may want to pinpoint the time of the habit formation and spin it out there. Check the pancreas against Chart 16 and the discussion above.

Once these issues are covered, go back and recheck the overall pH level. Right spin it toward alkaline if need be. You may also want to spin in a memory program for the ideal pH into the body's cells, organs, and water content.

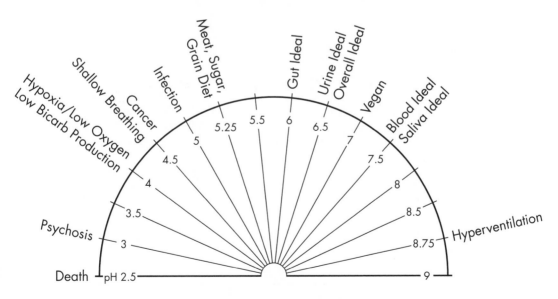

*Chart 17. pH and Acidity/Alkalinity Scale*

With a specific issue in mind, ask what the ideal pH value is to help correct or balance this condition. Simply dowse it in (right spin) "without reversal until the desired balancing is accomplished, or until no longer beneficial."

## CORE FEAR STATES 1 AND 2

These issues often have to do with past-life memories, DNA memories of when we were in non-human form, or even back to the level of elemental memory. Going to the point of origin to clear is advised. Remove (left spin) the DNA, cellular, mental, emotional, muscle, tissue, and organ memories associated with each fear. Clear all relationships in all time frames and dimensions of all associated factors. Fill voids with fifth-dimensional divine Light and love.

Here, soul imprisonment refers to a state in which you felt spiritually or psychically disempowered. This is more of an illusory belief state than an actual condition, as your understanding of the soul is that it is forever free and dwells safely in the eternal Mind of God.

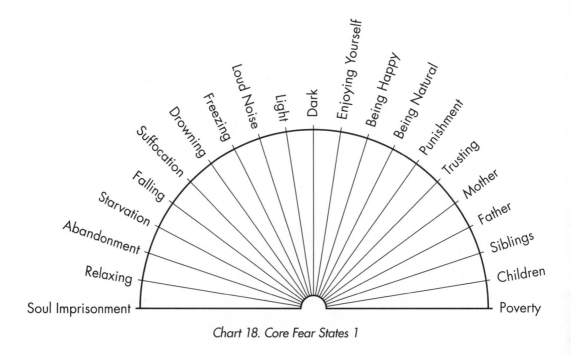

*Chart 18. Core Fear States 1*

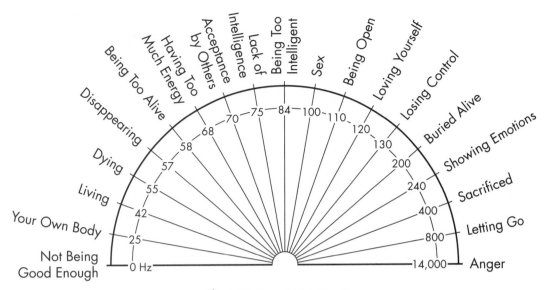

Chart 19. Core Fear States 2

Consider the rest of these items, which are all fairly self-explanatory, as "triggers" for more deeply held memories or associations. Don't necessarily expect them to make sense to the verbal or logical mind, although they can and sometimes do. These are unconscious fear patterns, perhaps held for lifetimes, and thus may simply be overlooked by the conscious mind. Nevertheless, their energy is a constant drag on your energy, and they will act as attractors for similar kinds of life experiences until you recognize and acknowledge the pattern, then choose to let it go consciously and willingly.

## MENTAL, PHYSICAL, AND SPIRITUAL EXTRAS

Each of these issues will imply its own set of further questions. By getting specific measurable data on any item, you can get a before-and-after reading by rechecking after doing a removal or correction.

### Metals

The presence of metals may lead you to ask which ones are present in the body. Top suspects are lead, mercury, cadmium, aluminum, and nickel.

Each of these substances, although toxic in the body, is harmless in its home dimension—the second dimension in the body of Earth. They each have a governing consciousness, or organizing principle if you will, that we can call an elemental. So, contrary to the typical attitude toward Nature, we respect all Nature, but reserve the right to put limits on parts of it that are not being helpful or supporting life.

Have the client place both feet on the floor. With a left spin, address the elemental:

> *Gather yourself up and leave the body now, returning home to the second dimension where you belong. I reverse all toxic effects in the body, and retain only enough of the substance to maintain perfect order and balance in the body.*

You may only need one molecule of an element, but it still plays a pivotal part in your overall biochemical make-up. You may also use a radionic rate to reverse a toxic substance in the body.

## Herbicides, Pesticides, and Vaccines

These can be approached in a similar way. You may want to check, on a scale of 1 to 10, the overall efficacy of the natural detox pathways, which include the liver, bowels, and sweat glands, and the kidney/urinary and lymphatic systems. Natural approaches to diet, improved hydration, and toxin-chelating substances like diatomaceous earth, clays, chlorella, cilantro, and zeolite may all apply. Dowse to see which ones would be beneficial at 10, and dowse for daily dosage and duration.

## Blood Flow to the Brain and Heart Circulation

These are measured in percentage and may require a schedule of regular left-spin dowsings to "stick." Ask if the blockage is physical or emotional, or both. Blood vessels constrict when we are stressed. Physical blockages may require medical referral, but can be helped along with natural arterial clearing formulas like Strauss Heart Drops. (Note: the FDA requires that these natural formulas be used for "experimental purposes only." It's okay to experiment and take your chances with Nature, but you need a prescription to take a drug that just may have death as a side effect!)

## EFT

This implies the benefit of learning the Emotional Freedom Technique. This simple and effective method of clearing old emotions is outlined at *www .mercola.com* and *www.emofree.com*. Anyone can learn this technique, even children. It is based on the idea that old emotions and thoughts can be lodged in the acupuncture meridian system, and only need our willingness and a little physical nudge (tapping) to release. This technique is highly recommended as a drug-free alternative to mainstream therapies.

## Processed Foods, GMOs, and Sugar

These are easily overlooked areas that can have deadly effects over time. Educate clients as to their effects, then left spin them out as you would metals and other toxins. Left spin out the desire for these so-called "foods" and their effects on the metabolism, brain, and nervous system particularly.

## Heart/Brain Balance

This is another issue that some say needs to be addressed in order to ascend. Use the Balance Chart to check and correct, with the left side representing heart intelligence (yin) and the right side representing brain intelligence (yang). Spin either up or down to bring in the balance point, which represents 100 percent harmony.

## Mass Consciousness

The effect of mass consciousness implies the effects of what Deepak Chopra called the "hypnosis of social conditioning." This shows a need to break away from beliefs that we inherit from friends, family, tradition, education, religion, or media and to begin thinking for ourselves. Left spin to remove all the ill effects of negative mass consciousness and reduce the desire or appeal it may hold. Right spin in the resolve and ability to discern the thoughts, feelings, and beliefs that come from mass consciousness, and to counter these with love, truth, and forgiveness.

## Programmed Death

This has to do with our entrenched belief about what will happen "when our time is up." This may have to do with family patterns. Surrender the belief (left spin) and give your time to the Divine! You may also want to reprogram any limiting cell memories based on life expectancies of generations before. Currently, human cells are programmed by Nature to live to 120 years (the Hayflick limit). In the new energies, this may all be changing. Check to see what your "real" potential life span is, and dowse out the old programming.

## The Love Index

The love index of the home, office, or institution can be measured on a scale of 1 to 10. Raise it to 10 if it is below that. This is, of course, a temporary band-aid approach until you discover and clear the issues behind a low index. In a pinch, however, it can help. And with repeated application, it just may hold. You dispel darkness by turning on the light!

## Self-Acceptance and Self-Forgiveness

These are two sides of the same coin of Self-love. Measure it on a scale of 1 to 10. Left spin all blockages and resistances to 100 percent. Right spin in the recognition of all opportunities to express these to yourself and others.

## Elemental Transmutation

This is a latent ability in humans to transmute elements within their bodies into nutrients, and thus, ultimately, receive all of their nutritional needs from the air or sunlight, as do "breatharians" and "sungazers." In ancient times, this was called alchemy. With 10 as optimal, measure your regular progress daily or weekly on the scale. You may also want to dowse to optimize the related enzymes, called *transmutase isomers*. An adjunct here would be to dowse your water to meet all of your nutritional needs. See Louis Kervan's *Biological Transmutation* for scientific backing for this concept. Experiment if this interests you, or if you just want to cut back your grocery bill!

## Dark-Side Influences

These items identify areas where we are being negatively affected through secondary means. These imply attachment issues, especially if you note an emotional charge around any one of these areas. Ask to release the negative thought form, beliefs, or entity working through these means. Investigating your feelings around these areas may help you see how you have become inad-vertently "attached." If you find yourself thinking that you could *never* give up your beliefs, treasured possessions, friends, etc., this may be a clue that these are the things that are helping to keep you in an energetic trap.

On the other hand, there are belief systems that involve cursing objects, for whatever reason. This sounds like egoic power-tripping to me. If you get one of these, consider checking chapter 4 for the appropriate clearings.

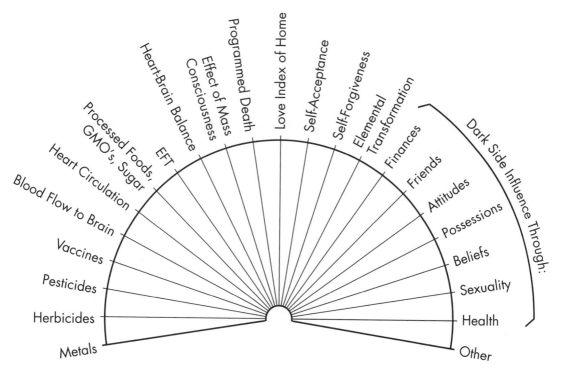

Chart 20. Mental, Physical, and Spiritual Extras

## HOMEOPATHIC POTENCIES

This chart is one of my personal favorites, as it can cover a wide range of issues at once. You don't even have to know what the issues are for it to work. If you only have time for one chart in a session, consider this one.

With dowsing, anything under the Sun can be broadcast or sent at a distance as a remedy to a known target. Let's say your husband or wife calls you and says that he or she has just been stung by a wasp. Ask the dowsing system for permission to send a homeopathic remedy. Use the chart to determine the best potency. The principle here is that "like treats like." A homeopathic dose of wasp venom at the right potency can reverse the symptoms caused by the same venom! Once you identify the potency, with a right spin, say:

*I now send the frequency and energy signature of the specific wasp venom that caused the sting to (name) at a potency of __. I request that the remedy will continue to resonate in (the person's) field until the symptoms subside, and is no longer necessary or beneficial.*

This is an example of "non-local virtual nosode homeopathy" in action. "Sarcodal homeopathy" supports the tissue, once the nosodal homeopathy has done the clearing. After clearing the nosode—which can also be a bacteria, virus, fungus, or other infectious agent—you can measure the potency and send a sarcodal remedy for the skin, organ, or muscle affected. This can also help with allergies and toxins.

You can send an inverted pattern of a toxin, allergen, or addictive substance in the same manner. For example:

*I now send (right spin) the inverted form of refined sugar at __ potency for my sugar-addicted grandson, Billy.*

The potencies listed are the most commonly used ones and have fixed values up to "50 m" that require that you dowse a specific potency value for "cm" and higher. The potencies on the left are used mainly for physical issues. As you go to the right, you are addressing higher vibrational aspects.

Ask how many potencies are required for the situation. You may need to schedule different potencies in succession, in which case you can dowse out the number of days between. For example, you may send an X potency for a tummy ache on day 1, but on day 3 send an M potency for the emotion behind the issue.

A more universal approach to this chart is to use it as a Master Reversal chart. Ask to send back to the person *all* of the unresolved issues, trauma memories, and incoherent energy patterns held in the person's energy field potentized to the appropriate dowsed potency. This is like asking all of the past stressors to stand up and be cleared at once! You may want to specify all of the physical, mental, emotional, or psychic stressors as separate categories at their potency to ensure a more thorough or gentle approach. We use a specified (dowsed) potency because sending the wrong potency can be either ineffectual (too low) , or harmful (too high). A potency that is too high can cause a worsening of symptoms, an effect known as "proving" the homeopathic.

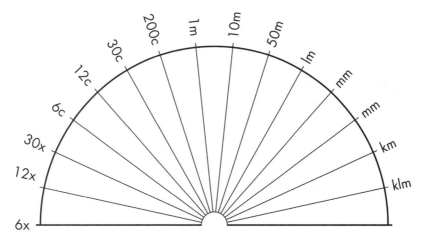

*Chart 21. Homeopathic Potencies*

## WEIGHT CONTROL

There are multiple factors that can go into a weight issue—which may be either too much or not enough body weight. Ask how many issues on this chart apply to your subject. Ask to be shown the issues in order of priority. Then ask which of these need to be dowsed for daily, weekly, or monthly periods, and how many days, weeks, or months for each.

I suggest writing up a plan and teaching your clients how to dowse these things for themselves, as well as how to make the lifestyle changes implied. You may also dowse in (right spin) the memory of the ideal levels into the cellular and tissue memories for as long as they are beneficial to support ongoing results. Check the following issues using the Balance Chart, with the right side indicating stress, over-energized, or excess levels, and the left indicating weakness, chronic stress, or deficiency.

### The Glands

The pituitary gland, among numerous other things, stimulates the thyroid gland. Low thyroid is fairly common. Because it regulates body temperature and the rate at which the body burns nutrients, a low-functioning thyroid can contribute to weight gain as well as sluggish digestion and elimination, not to mention mood swings. Measure the vitality and functional efficacy of the thyroid on a scale of 1 to 10. The thyroid requires adequate iodine and selenium. Check to see if the root cause of the thyroid imbalance is physical, mental, emotional, spiritual, or environmental. Emotionally, a low thyroid often reflects buried emotions like "I give, and give, and give . . . but when is it *my* turn?"

Stressed adrenal glands are another reason for a low-functioning thyroid, as the thyroid tries to compensate for low hormone production by the adrenals. Stressed adrenals also put out too much cortisone, with abdominal weight gain as a primary symptom. Use the Balance Chart to measure and bring cortisone levels back to normal. The two biggest dietary stressors on the adrenals are sugar and caffeine.

The hypothalamus is another master regulator that is tied into both the pituitary and pineal glands.

## Starvation Fears

These may stem from early upbringing or from past-life memories. Identify the time frame of the acceptance of the belief and go there to remove it. Family patterns and conditioning can be handled in the same way. An example may be guilt-laden programming to "finish everything on your plate—what about those starving people in China!" Another common pattern is gobbling your food when there are too many mouths to feed and not enough food, as in large families or institutional life.

On another note, genuine starvation can be the result of malnutrition or the malabsorption of nutrients. Modern industrialized foods are depleted of many important trace minerals. Suggesting a good green-foods product and a liquid colloidal mineral supplement or natural sea salt can compensate for a typical modern diet. Check for the integrity and vitality of the small intestine. Fungus (fed by a sugary, grain-based diet), parasites, over-the-counter pain medications, and gluten can seriously damage this organ, leading to "leaky gut" syndrome. Check the levels for this on a scale of 1 to 10, with 0 as ideal and 10 as lethal. For a reading of 10, check for celiac disease or extreme gluten damage and intolerance.

Left spin out all stressors affecting the small intestine, along with all associated symptoms and effects. Right spin in the ability of the small intestine to recognize and conform to its ideal within the energetic template of the body. You may need to dowse this for a number of days, along with dowsing in the motivation to make basic lifestyle and dietary changes.

A sedentary lifestyle seriously limits proper digestion and elimination. Encourage at least a vigorous daily walk. Rebounding is fun and convenient if you can't get outdoors. Suggest a return to more water-based foods (fruits, veggies), a reduction in dense animal proteins (meat, cheese), and a bread-free diet. Grains are simply not suited for the human digestive system. They are relatively new foods for our hunter-gatherer bodies to process well. The exceptions are sprouted grain products or gluten-free grains. Constipation must be addressed for proper digestion and detoxification. Encourage self-education or refer clients to a good nutritional consultant.

## The Obesity Virus

The obesity virus (adenovirus-36) implies contagion. Check other family members if this comes up. Neutralize viruses and pathogens (left spin) by saying:

*I send the life force and collective consciousness of the (virus, bacteria, fungus, worm) back to the most appropriate dimension. Scramble and deactivate its reproductive intelligence, and reverse all ill effects of the pathogen.*

## MSG

Monosodium glutamate has been called the "nicotine of the food supply." Unfortunately, it can now legally be labeled as a "natural flavor." This is rampant in many foods. Look for junk-food addictions, and send an inverted virtual homeopathic remedy (see Chart 21). Stay away from all fast foods. Watch the videos *Super Size Me* and *Food, Inc.*

## Glycogen

Glycogen is the hormone secreted when we eat proteins. It causes a release of glucose from fat cells. It has the reverse action of insulin, which triggers storage of excess sugars as fat. "Low-fat" foods that are high in sugars and refined grains (which turn to sugar upon chewing) are the biggest scam of the food industry. Dietary fat actually reduces body fat eventually, as it is a very concentrated and satisfying food that reduces the low-blood-sugar states that cause sugar cravings. Here we have another example of upside-down thinking in the world. Dowse glycogen up to optimal levels and efficacy. Dowse the insulin response down to optimal levels, and reverse the many symptoms and ill effects of excess insulin on the body.

## Sugar Addiction and Fungus

These issues usually go hand-in-hand, as fungus, especially candida, stimulates the brain to crave sugar, which in turn feeds the fungus (and cancer). You'll also find an acidic pH here, as fungi love an acidic body and hate oxygen. Fungus is actually just doing its job as a recycler of dead bodies. Best to send it a message: "I'm not ready to check out yet!"

Consider inverting the energy signature of sugar into a homeopathic solution, or dowsing a rate that will facilitate aversion to refined sugar in all its forms.

## Emotions of Holding On

These have been associated with weight gain. Unrecognized emotional pain may create a pattern of self-defense with a need to insulate the self from the world and turn to food to comfort an inner sense of lack. If this shows up, go to the time of the emotional trauma or decision, and reverse it there. Left spin the emotions around the beliefs, memories, impressions, and false decisions made at that time. Restore (right spin) self-love and forgiveness, and ask for the healing of all relationships implied by this event.

## Food Addiction (Oral Stage)

This refers to unfulfilled oral satisfaction in infancy. Being put on formula too soon or not bonding with your mother by being able to suckle naturally, or simply failing to bond emotionally with your mother in infancy at all, may set up a pattern of unsatisfied gratification needs, leading to compulsive eating or smoking later in life.

## Water Awareness and Motivation Index

According to Batmanghelidj, the author of *Your Body's Many Cries for Water* (Vienna, VA. Global Health Solutions, 1992), what we label "hunger" is, in many cases, thirst. Increasing (right spin) your water awareness and motivation index can help remind you of this basic misinterpreted impulse.

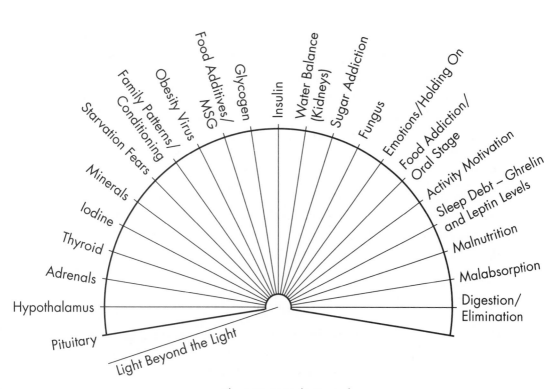

*Chart 22. Weight Control*

Batmanghelidj goes on to say that any pain is a cry for water and that a glass of water will satisfy hunger in most cases. Not enough can be said for reducing stress generally, and finding the riches of our inner resources or divine Self. Weight gain implies taking more energy in than we need because, on some level, we feel inadequate within.

One definition of an addiction is that you can't get enough of what you don't really want. What we really want is to feel full at all times—full of love, joy, and self-respect—with a positive outlook on tomorrow. Without these things, we can't help but look for satisfaction "out there" in the things, objects, people, and food around us. Understanding this can be a first step in learning to self-nurture in other ways.

Fall in love with your self—not in a selfish egoic manner, but by giving yourself what you need to be truly happy. Take time to go within—take a vacation, learn meditation or yoga, or find some kind of creative outlet that can be the beginning of new self-respect. How can you love others if you don't start loving yourself by ensuring that you meet your needs? Live life from the inside out, and you may find that your outside needs —including food—will demand less of your attention. The *Light Beyond the Light* is an energetic exercise that involves forming a triangle with your thumbs and forefingers and laying it over a chakra while you stand in the sunlight and get nourished with solar light. It works! Simply stand and say: " I call in the Light beyond the light to fulfill all of my needs." Continue until you feel a sense of fullness.

## Sleep Debt

Sleep debt is the accumulated effect of sleep deprivation. It increases levels of the appetite-stimulating hormone ghrelin and reduces the satiety (I've had enough!) hormone leptin. Check both of these on the Balance Chart and adjust accordingly.

## PARIETAL-LOBE ACTIVITY/SEPARATION

Before the age of two, we do not have a clear sense of separation between ourselves and our primary caretakers or our environment. Around age two, the parietal lobes of the brain, situated along the side of the head behind the ears, kick in and begin the natural trend toward individuation—the beginning of a sense of a "separate me."

Neuroscientists call this part of the brain the orientation association area (OAA). Hence, we learn to say "no" and "mine" and enter the "terrible twos." Hopefully, we learn to temper that period, and gain some basic cooperative skills. The trouble is that the temporal lobes continue to affect us in the same way throughout life, contributing to an ongoing sense of alienation and a separate self into adulthood. Meanwhile, Western cultural values exemplify the value of the rugged individual ("I've gotta be meee . . . "), while, at the same time, many suffer from the resulting existential angst in the form of depression, suicide, and psychosomatic diseases. You could say that all our suffering stems from our sense of separation—from each other and from our divine Source. Why should this be? Because separation is neither true nor real.

Anthropologists point out that a natural transitional point of maturation occurs in individuals in primitive cultures at around, if not before, the age of eighteen. This time is often marked by some kind of ritual welcoming of the person into a new phase of maturity, which usually involves absorption into some kind of collective identity—hunter, craftsman, medicine man, warrior, etc. Thus the drive to individuate is subsumed into an identity that now serves the greater good (tribe, culture). In Western society, we do see weak versions of this ritual (family gatherings, campus fraternity rites, induction into service clubs or the military), but by and large, we grow up without the benefit of being able to shed the separate self in a clear, transformative ritual setting. Adjusting this imbalance through dowsing can be a critical factor in reducing suffering and hastening your awakening to your true Self, which is our shared collective identity as One.

## State of Permanent Oneness

You can see that, before birth, we dwell in a state of permanent Oneness. This is descriptive of the reprieve we enjoy between lives as we take a breather before the next incarnation. This state is forgotten when we pass into the third dimension through physical birth. We are still close to this state in infancy, but, by age two, we fall under the spell of separation as true believers. The more we invest in and subscribe to the state of illusory separation, the more we incline toward war and insanity, which are synonymous.

## Dissolving Sense of Separation

It is possible, through devotion to mental silence and meditation, to lose your sense of separation. As you do this, you move consistently away from complication and over-dependence on left-brain logic and problem obsession, toward a simpler appreciation of reality and the experience of inner peace. "Except you be as a little child . . . ," as the Master said.

Measure your client on the chart. In most cases, there will be a benefit to reducing (left spin) the over-activity of the OAA. To balance the situation, consider the role of the left frontal lobe and its potential for saturation with the neurotransmitter dopamine in facilitating states of union or Oneness. In many, this is under-activated. Use a scale of 1 to 10 for the left frontal lobe and for dopamine saturation, with 10 as optimal and 0 as dormant.

For instance, if your client measures 75, left spin and say:

*I now ask to reduce the over-activity of the parietal lobes in maintaining a sense of separation for (client) to the optimal minimal levels for (his/her) highest good.*

Then right spin and say:

*I now raise the functional level of the left frontal lobe and levels of dopamine to optimal to maximally support (client's) enlightenment process and stabilize these new optimal levels as a new baseline without reversal.*

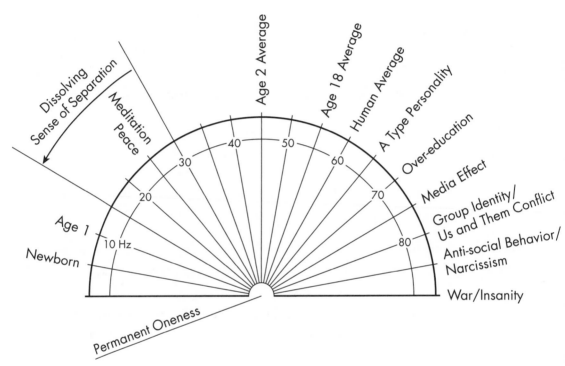

*Chart 23. Parietal Lobe Activity/Separation*

## SOLFEGGIO AND HEALING FREQUENCIES

The Solfeggio frequencies are derived from the musical tones of antiquity that we no longer hear in modern music. Len Horowitz (*Emerging Viruses: AIDS and Ebola: Nature, Accident or Intentional?*. Tetrahedron Press. 1996) points out that these same frequencies have appeared lately in numerological studies of ancient sacred texts. It turns out that these frequencies, when applied to the body as electrical frequencies at biological levels or simply heard as sound, are effective at neutralizing man-made pathogens. These are normal bacterial and viral forms that have been altered deliberately in human laboratories for the express purpose of biological warfare. Yes, I know this may be hard to believe, but this is the documented source of commonly known health issues like Lyme disease and AIDS. Dr. Horowitz has the evidence! (See his *Emerging Viruses.*)

The frequency 528 is apparently used in standard DNA research, as it has been seen to "reset" the DNA back to its ideal template. Unexplained syndromes and symptoms may have a basis in bio-warfare microbes. We have all been exposed to the mad creations of the military-industrial-congressional complex that Eisenhower tried to warn us of as he left office. I suspect that chronic fatigue syndrome and fibromyalgia are simply default diagnosis for sets of symptoms associated with these dark forces. Thankfully, the global agenda of control and domination by these factions is grinding to a halt, making room for a much more egalitarian planetary society. We do not want to empower the "dark forces" with too much attention. Rather, we can choose to see them as misguided brethren, who, at heart, want the same things as the rest of us. They are just operating under some erroneous assumptions—that we are separate egos living in a world of lack, for example.

Included in this chart are some other more esoteric frequencies. Ask if any of these frequencies will benefit your client, then identify them. Ideally, you want to use these with a frequency generator like the GB 4000 available from *www.quantumbalancing.com.* However, you can still dowse them in (right spin) by saying:

*Allow all the benefits of the frequency of \_\_\_ at the most appropriate potencies and strengths to continue to resonate until no longer needed or beneficial.*

## The Great Pyramid and the King's Chamber

This frequency is significant if we consider the possibility that this chamber, which sits in the exact center of the Great Pyramid at Giza (*pyra-mid* means "fire in the middle"), has been viewed as a multi-dimensional transformation portal connecting those who lie in the granite-and-crystalline sarcophagus with the energy of the star Sirius, whose light penetrates into the chamber via a perfectly aligned tube or extended window. This very well may have been an ancient stargate. When Napoleon spent a night in the King's Chamber, he appeared shaken in the morning and never spoke to anyone about his experience there.

## The Christ Consciousness Grid

This is an energy matrix in the form of a dodecahedron of golden light around the planet, consistent with Edgar Cayce's prediction in the 1930s that a "new energy" would come to the planet that would represent the "next major phase in human development." The term "Christ" does not here refer to the historical figure who embodied this frequency 2000 years ago and whose identity was absorbed into and usurped by the dualistic state religion of the time. Rather, it refers to the unconditional divine Light and love that Jesus introduced into the collective mind at that time. His promised "return" indicated a time of opportunity in which each and every one of us will have access to this redeeming energy as a common, unifying experience. Reduce (left spin) any resistance to and raise (right spin) the degree of connection to this grid on all levels.

## The New Schumann Wave

The Schumann wave effect is based on conjecture that the heartbeat of the Earth produced by the resonance between the body of the planet and the upper atmosphere is reflective of, or in concert with, the range of brain-wave frequencies in the individual and collective brain. As the previous established limit of the wave of approximately 7.6 Hz corresponds to daydreaming—an apt analogy for the human condition under the spell of separation—the suspected next step in an organic process of wave acceleration would be 13 Hz, based on the natural harmonics of the Fibonacci Scale, which is consistent with the waking state. Whether true or not, this provides a tantalizing analogy for the awakening of human consciousness as a whole as the awakened Global Brain. The wave itself is not considered static at 7.6 Hz—in fact, various atmospheric and magnetic conditions can create a wide fluctuation from this base rate. Given the electromagnetic implications of the galactic alignment and other changing cosmic conditions, the means for this shift becomes more imaginable. Do I hear an alarm clock?

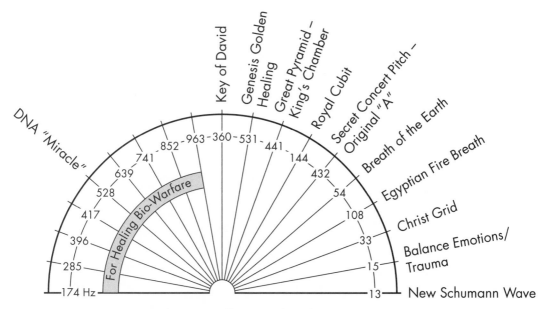

Chart 24. Solfeggio and Healing Frequencies

## MIASMS

Miasms are energetically inherited patterns of pre-disposition to disease identified by Hahnemann, the father of homeopathy, almost 300 years ago. He observed that when people survive a disease, it leaves an energetic imprint in the cells (DNA) of future generations that may predict a greater probability or predisposition to that disease or an associated biological weakness. According to Hans Selye, who looked at the effects of stress on biology, miasms are more likely to manifest when we are in a state of exhaustion or depletion from too many accumulated life stressors, leading to a weakening of immunity and regenerative potential. In other words, a miasm is not necessarily predictive. It is more of a potential.

For example, a miasm for tetanus (or lockjaw) can be part of a profile for TMJ (temporal mandibular joint) disorder. A miasm for cholera may predict a tendency toward bowel weakness, etc. Think of miasms as rocks in a farmer's field. As long as they are underground—no problem! But you never know when one will pop up as seasons change, and then it needs to be dealt with, or it could ruin your tractor!

Dowse out the miasm (left spin) on a cellular memory level, and ask that it also be cleared at the point of origin and at all points in the lineage—past, present, and future. Replace the miasm (right spin) with the energy and memory of perfect vibrant health for all affected. You may want to identify the year of the establishment of the miasm in your lineage and go there to clear it at that time.

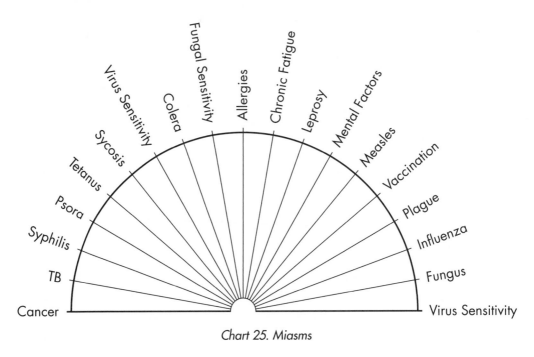

Chart 25. Miasms

## CELLULAR TRANS-MEMBRANE POTENTIAL

According to Bruce Lipton's recent work, *The Biology of Belief* (Hay House, 2008), the cell nucleus is no longer considered the brain of the cell. Rather, all of the internal cellular processes and exchanges within the body are mediated by the cell-wall membrane. This structure requires adequate fatty acids and water in the diet. The electrical charge on the cell membrane is reflective of its overall functional state and vitality. Fresh and raw foods, as well as exposure to sunlight, provide an abundant supply of healthy, free, negatively charged electrons to the body that normally supply adequate electrical "food" to the cells. In the short term, small doses of bicarbonate of soda can do the same.

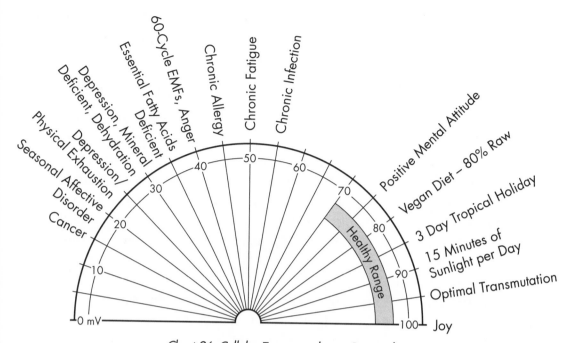

Chart 26. Cellular Trans-membrane Potential

The normal electrical voltage in the body is a function of the kidney/adrenal complex. In Chinese medicine, these are considered the "batteries" of the body. Check on their status on a scale of 1 to 10, or using the Balance Chart. Do a separate reading for both left and right kidneys and adrenals, as one may be functioning quite differently than the other. Find out if what is stressing them is physical, mental, emotional, spiritual, or environmental. Again, you can treat an organ as if it were a being—because it is!

## The Healthy Range

Obviously, you want everyone to be in the healthy range. Another emergency electrical first-aid tip is to hold one terminal of a 9-volt battery with a finger on your left hand, and tap the other terminal with your right. This sends an electrical "transfusion" into your body that can temporarily "top up" your biological battery. A minimum of fifteen minutes a day of direct sunlight with no UV-protective sunglasses will provide you with an optimal daily dose of free electrons as well.

You can see how many states and conditions are correlated with low electrical flow across the cell membranes. Note that the optimal transmutation potential is associated with optimal sunlight exposure. This again describes the inherent ability of living organisms to manufacture the nutrients they need from what is available around them—even in the form of air and sunlight.

## FIVE ELEMENTS/MERIDIANS

Chinese medicine has a 6000-year history of research, documentation, and success. Do you think they are on to something? Compared to Western drugs and surgical medicine with perhaps 300 years of history, I'm inclined to say yes.

You need to study basic Chinese medicine to appreciate the value of dowsing these issues. However, there is some balancing you can do with the help of your Guides, good intentions, and the dowsing system. First, with the elements in mind, ask if there are any de-compensating elements. If the answer is yes, identify and measure them on the Balance Chart. Simply raise or lower the element accordingly.

Do the same with the meridians. Ask to be shown any imbalanced meridian, check it on the Balance Chart (left/yin; right/yang), and correct accordingly. You may want to ask if there is any emotional information that needs to be released from the meridian, as repressed emotions can clog the meridians

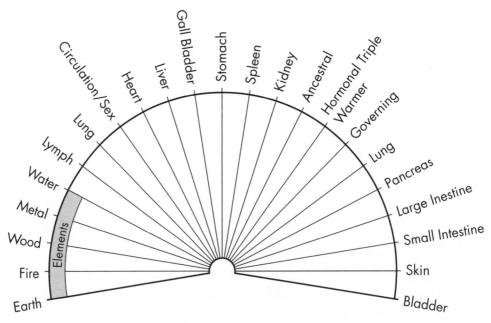

*Chart 27. Five Elements/Meridians*

*A Comprehensive Mini-Course in Spiritual Dowsing*

or specific points. Ask if time travel is appropriate. We have seen chronic physical issues disappear using this method.

Tip: A laser pointer, available at most office-supply stores, can charge the meridians at the terminal points in the corner of each fingernail. Running the laser over the finger tips along the bottom line of the nails can give you an energetic boost and charge up the meridians. It is advisable to confirm with dowsing that this is beneficial, as a yang meridian may go into stress with extra energy running through it. Don't overdo it, and avoid ever exposing your eyes directly to laser light.

## EARTH ENERGIES AND GEOPATHIC FACTORS

These factors are often unseen and thus easily overlooked. Geopathic stress may be involved in as many as half of all diseases and medical conditions. Suspect this possibility and check this chart when there is any kind of chronic health issue, especially when the issue is associated with moving to a specific location, or is multi-generational and involves the same home and property, or is endemic to a specific area.

Geopathic stress is a recognized disease-causing factor in many European countries. It is rooted in the idea that Mother Earth is a living entity and has streams of energy flowing throughout her body much as we do. Consider that the Earth involves complex networks of minerals, metals, and water, often flowing in specific pathways and intersecting with each other. Consider also that the moving molten core of the Earth is responsible for generating the electromagnetic field of the planet. It is thus a source of tremendous energy, constantly charging all of these "hidden" systems, many of which are electrically conductive. Here on the surface, we live in la-la land, believing that out of sight is out of mind.

These influences can be strongest in places where we spend a lot of time—in bed, at the office, or on the living room couch. One way to find out if geopathic stress is an issue for you is simply to move the offending bed, office chair, or favorite easy chair and see what happens. Cats are natural geopathic stress detectors, as they seem to be drawn to and like places that may be unhealthy for humans. Dogs, on the other hand, are attracted to places that are energetically good for humans. So take my advice, boys. It's much better to be in the doghouse than the cathouse! If you want more on this fascinating subject, there are many good books, mainly out of Europe. You may also want to check out the local chapter of the American Society of Dowsers (*www.dowsers.org*), as this is the home of many skilled and experienced dowsers in this more traditional application.

With any of these issues, ask your Chart of Ten the overall effect of the item on your physical, mental, and emotional health—on your sleep patterns, digestion, or other areas of consistent concern. You may be surprised. As these are all Earth-related issues, appealing to the elementals in their healing or undoing is recommended. And be sure to consult your Spirit Guides. Consider also the plant and animal spirits that are in your environment.

Quantum physics has given us a means to reconsider the ancient belief in pantheism or animism—the belief that everything is alive and has a spirit or life force. This belief was tossed out in the Age of Reason as science attempted to release itself from the stranglehold of religion. The more you call on these energies, the more you will begin to discern their effects and presence. We will all be getting a big opportunity to reconnect with the forces and forms of nature once the military-industrial complex goes out of business due to the current extreme electromagnetic effects on the communications and electronics systems involved. Do you get a picture of Mother Earth shaking off the old nets and snares of misguided humanity?

Other approaches may involve asking the elementals to redirect (left spin) any lines or energy patterns back to their source and render them harmless. Or you can ask that the frequency of the item or issue be shifted (right spin) to one that is beneficial for life. Always ask to reverse (left spin) the ill effects on the home, property, and individuals involved. Ask as well to clear any attractor fields involved—the mental or emotional factors of the occupants that are acting as a resonating antennae for some of these energies. There may also be objects or structures that need to removed or dismantled.

Consider as well the potential of negative elementals or other negative spiritual entities being involved. Remember that Jesus was reported to go underground and work with the souls trapped there during the three days before His resurrection. Be open; listen to your inner Guidance. And try new things all the time. This is an endless learning curve!

## The Hartmann and Curry Lines

These lines are named after the medical doctors who first identified them many years ago. They run in latitudinal and longitudinal patterns over the entire planet, like the grid map you see on a typical globe. Their intersection can create a point of energy that is stressful to human life, with the Hartmann lines associated with cancers. If your home or property tests positive for either of these lines, consider the following approach.

1. Walk outside and dowse the outer perimeter of the home or property to determine if there are non-beneficial geopathic energy lines present. Traditional dowsers use L rods for this purpose, but a normal pendulum will work as well. Start with the pendulum in a neutral position or negative movement and ask for a yes response when you cross a non-beneficial energy line.

2. When you detect such a line, ask if it is going into the home, or coming out of it.

3. Mark the spot.

4. Continue around the entire perimeter of the building or property.

5. Get some 18- to 22-inch lengths of copper wire; multi-strand electrical wire is fine. It can be either insulated or uninsulated, but it needs to be bendable and to hold its shape.

6. Make some giant staples with ends of 3 to 4 inches each.

7. Drive or plant the staple in the ground at the point where you want to intercept the line and perpendicular to it.

Do this for every entry and exit point you have identified.

This will re-direct the energy back into the Earth and keep your home clear. You may need to re-check the place in a few weeks or months, as sometimes the lines can drift, especially if you are in a seismically active area—near a volcano or in a place prone to earthquakes. Areas of underground water movement like lake or sea shores are suspect, especially if they are in mountainous areas where water runs downhill regularly. Clay beds around river deltas can also accumulate negative energies.

## Grave-Linked Spirit Lines

These indicate some kind of energetic connection to a gravesite or site involving Earth-bound spirits, like the site of a massacre or battle. Ask your Guides to trace the line to its start and clear the energies at the source as you would for entities at a distance. Consider that there are no coincidences, and that you may be being called or gifted with an opportunity to release beings in other dimensions from suffering. Always give thanks when the clearing is complete.

## Toxic Bed Springs

These occur when the metals of springs get magnetized through repeated movement over time. This is more common with actual spiral springs, although flat metal springs can also be a problem. Metal spirals are ideal antennae for picking up and amplifying energies and signals indiscriminately. You may be able to "de-gauss" them with the appropriate equipment, but I suggest that, if there are other geopathic or chronic health issues, you consider switching to a non-metallic sleeping system. A quick scan over the bed with a simple compass will show you if you have a "hot spot" on the mattress. The needle will spin crazily over a charged spring. Placing a powerful negative-north magnet over the spring for a day will help to discharge it.

## Positive and Negative Ionic Fields

A positive ionic field produces unhealthy charges that can contribute to many chronic imbalances. The language can be confusing, but a negative ionic field is actually healthy. An example of this is the nice feeling you get at the seashore or near a waterfall, which both release cascades of negative ions into the air. If a positive field shows up, see if you can discover its source. Ask how close the source is and if your Guides can go there and negate or reverse the pattern. Or perhaps the energy can be diverted from your home and grounded back into the Earth.

## Hydro Lines and High-Tension Power Lines

These lines are a documented source of cancer-causing (immune-suppressing) frequencies. They have been particularly implicated in blood cancers and leukemia. The research is there, although suppressed. Suggestion: Find another place to live. There can also be problems with electrical leakage through the ground from a power source to a conductive building, body of water, or simply mineralized soil. This is a huge, but largely unrecognized, problem with the world's aging electrical grids. Dowse to ground and divert any such leakages vertically into the Earth.

## Deadly Orgone

This was Wilhelm Reich's term for "*chi* gone bad." Deadly orgone can make you ill. It can be produced around devices of high electrical output like transformers, cell phone towers, and microwave devices. Microwave ovens are banned in Japan and Russia. Why not here? They are just the right size, however, for footstools, and can stimulate some helpful conversation in that harmless role! Factoid: Microwave ovens were invented by the Nazis. Need I say more?

## Cell Phone Towers

A major source of deadly orgone is cell phone towers. If you live near one, you need to do everyone a favor and learn about simple orgonite tools to protect life from these invasive energies. Google "orgone clearing" or "tower busters" and educate yourself.

On one level, these towers are literally intended to create a frequency fence in an attempt to keep us from ascending at the pivotal time. Don't worry. It's not working. But in the meantime, we can do our part! See *www .littlemountainsmudge.com* for more information.

## HAARP

The HAARP project is located in Alaska and elsewhere. This experimental array of powerful transmitters can literally tear holes in the ionosphere and can bounce psycho-active data off the upper atmosphere, literally affecting the mental state of targeted populations. If this shows up in a profile, consider raising the client's frequency beyond the range of HAARP, and dowse a radionic rate for protection from it. Suggest placing an orgonite grid around the home and property by placing orgonite in every corner of the location.

## Apex Grid Points

An apex grid point is a focal point of a larger energetic planetary grid, of which there are many. Check the Balance Chart to determine its effects as positive or negative. In and of itself, this may just indicate an energy concentration. If negative, ask the elementals to relocate it to somewhere that is harmless to all.

## The Gravitational Grid

Gravity is considered an aspect of the first dimension and is pivotal in keeping all the dimensions aligned. Thus, gravity plays a part in the stabilization of third-dimensional Earth's dualistic nature. As such, it may also be part of what is inhibiting ascension, or the rise to fifth-dimensional experience. Think of the implications of "psychological gravity" as both a stabilizing and potentially limiting factor. Ask your Guides if this is manifesting at a specific point and can be shifted if need be to another location, or if you may simply need to move away from or avoid this limiting factor. Some informed sources claim that UFOs utilize gravity grids in navigating their craft around the planet. As the term "grid" implies, any point on the grid may tap into the grid's total power or provide an entry or exit point for energy around the planet—or beyond.

## The Electromagnetic Grid

This grid may be viewed as the Earth's nervous system. As such, it can be under- or over-activated, and may need some stress reduction of its own. Use the Balance Chart to determine its influence. Ask the two-dimensional elementals to help direct or tone down this energy if you find it too high or stimulating. Recently, and for many centuries, there has been a steady drop in both the solar and planetary electromagnetic grids. This may be a precursor to a literal pole shift, and at the least may be allowing for a general rise in the frequency of other grids and systems as part of a natural evolution. Use your skills of discernment and determine the best action to take, if any.

## The Light Grid

This grid, on the other hand, is associated with the planetary Light Body, or merkaba, and is part and parcel of the shift to fifth-dimensional Earth. We have also referred to it as the Christ Consciousness Grid. It was anchored in 1987 as part of the Harmonic Convergence. This marked the start of a transition period referred to in the Mayan Calendar as the Time of No Time, or the time when time as we know it will be over. If this shows up in a profile, it is reason to celebrate, although adjusting to this grid may be stressful. Raise (right spin) the total adaptation to the grid for now and the future to 100 percent.

## Portals

Portals indicate some kind of dimensional doorway or rift. If approached consciously, they can be places of deep insight, the downloading of information, or even time and space travel. If you are unaware of their presence, however, you may experience disorientation or even fear-invoking experiences. It is best to be in this energy with your eyes wide open and fully grounded. Many sacred sites on the planet that were respected by the indigenous populations and used for ceremonies were not places people would ever live. The energies are just too volatile and unpredictable. Is there something we can learn from this?

## Lateral Flow

A lateral flow simply indicates an Earth energy line with a horizontal pathway. Ask for more detailed information.

## Quartz Fields

These can indicate a power place situated over an underground concentration of quartz crystal or granite, which has a high proportion of quartz. These can be very powerful healing places, as in the location of John of God in Brazil, where thousands come for miraculous healings every year. If you are living over one, it is another reason to celebrate, although the high energies can be taxing on your nervous system. Raise the adaptation level to 100 percent. If a quartz field shows up, ask if the client is being negatively affected by the field, or needs to seek someone out for healing.

## Conductive Energy Fields

These simply indicate the presence of highly conductive minerals or water in the area. Gold, iron, or copper veins may be close by. This may create a zone of electrical stimulation, which can be either beneficial or stressful. Use the Balance Chart to determine the overall effect and range. Ask your Guides or the Elementals if they can ground or insulate the energy flow if non-beneficial, or direct the energy to where it can be useful.

## Dome Energy Spirals

These are generally considered beneficial. They are the result of underwater springs radiating out from a natural vertical underground well that may not be noticeable on the surface. Check the Balance Chart for physical, mental, emotional, and spiritual effects. When effects are found to be negative and moving is out of the question, consider dowsing out (left spin) all ill effects and negative attractor fields in the people involved and raising (right spin) the adaptation level.

## Electromagnetic Vortices

These exhibit both inward and outward spins of energy—or "male" and "female" energies—as in a vortex within a vortex. They can be mentally and emotionally stimulating areas, and also places to ground and make a deeper connection with Mother Earth. They may be places that help imbalances in yin and yang energies.

## Electrical Vortices

These are right-spin spiraling energies from within the Earth with a male, or yang, polarity. As such, they tend to be stimulating and can exacerbate things like inflammation, infection, tumors, or other yang conditions. On the other hand, they can also stimulate creative ideas and visions. You will need to ground yourself after being in this kind of energy for very long.

## Distant Sources

The effect of distant sources either above or below ground can be either positive or negative. Use the Balance Chart to determine this. If they are negative, ask the elementals to divert the connection permanently to an area where they can do no harm.

## Ley Lines and Spirals

Black ley lines are the result of unhealthy radiation from minerals or polluted streams underground. They will concentrate as black spirals, which can be major causes of ill health, especially if a bed is situated over one. Spin them out (left spin) or divert them to where they are harmless. The healthy variety of these are white ley lines and spirals.

## Above-Ground Standing Stones

These stones indicate some kind of radiation from a standing stone at a distance. These are often granite structures. In Europe, they are found commonly associated with ley lines and sacred sites, and are known as dolmens or menhirs. Check for overall effects, and divert or amplify as needed.

## Clay

Clay is regarded as an unhealthy medium on which to build a home, and is associated with increased incidence of cancers. Perhaps this is because many clay sites are in river beds or deltas where moving water builds up an electrical charge. Unfortunately, many major towns and cities are built in just these kinds of sites. Remove the negative influence and raise the adaptation levels as needed.

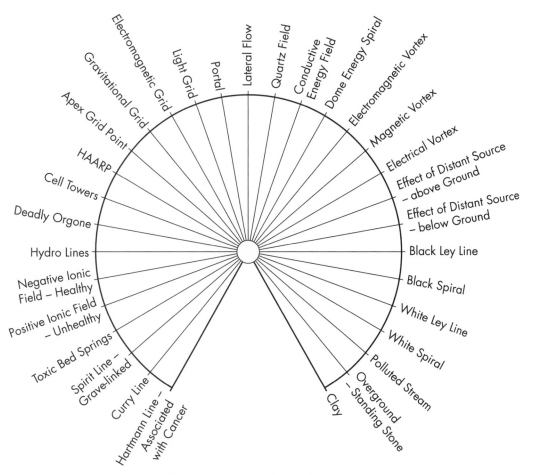

*Chart 28. Earth and Geopathic Energies*

## ON MAKING YOUR OWN CHARTS

As you can see, charts can reflect any number of different issues. Look to your daily life, your work, and your relationships for areas that can be charted. Start collecting your own set of personal charts. Find other dowsers with whom to start a chart library. There is tremendous freedom in knowing we no longer need to guess our way through life. It is likely that, someday, we won't need charts and other aids to live full and happy lives. But until that time, we heartily encourage you to use these tools to save time and reduce suffering.

# PART II

# Advanced
# Spiritual Dowsing

# INTRODUCTION

The purpose of this section is to awaken you to your natural state of joy, love, and freedom. This is a state of true self-empowerment. Dowsing is an ancient art that has been handed down through generations in many cultures to assist in communication between our conscious minds and the superconscious mind—in other words, to get answers to questions that are otherwise unattainable by us. Since we are all part of One Source, all answers are always available to every one of us at any time. Dowsing is a skill that is accessible to all that can be used for a seemingly infinite number of purposes.

We have been practicing the art of dowsing for a couple of decades and see dowsing as a way to "cut to the chase" in discovering and clearing energetic patterns that keep us blocked in our creativity and peace. As you clean unconscious limiting thought patterns from your field, you become more receptive (a feminine quality) to higher vibrational aspects of your consciousness. You become more aware of your true nature. Thus is the divine feminine awakened to bring inspiration and a creative flow (a divinely masculine essence) into all aspects of your life.

The divine feminine quality of receptivity is awakening in us all—men and women alike. For over 6000 years, we as humans have been using primarily masculine qualities to progress, move forward, and continuously expand in our evolutionary process. Expansion without contraction, expression without silence, movement without stillness—these create a great imbalance. We, as One Consciousness, are now becoming the balance. The sacred marriage of masculine and feminine brings us now to the zero point, or perfect space, allowing us to birth a new paradigm in which we will collectively transcend limitations, pain, and suffering. Through this perfect balance, we begin to get a glimpse of our infinite nature; we correct our limiting perceptions. This is how we may accelerate our awakening to our true essence as One Mind in God. Correcting limiting beliefs is the best we can do to move toward this remembering of Self. As *A Course in Miracles* tells us: "What is real cannot be threatened. What is unreal does not exist."

We are in the midst of what has been called the Shift of the Ages, or the Golden Age. This is a collective experience of coming to know ourselves as One Mind in perfect harmony. It is what we call awakening. In truth, we are perfect and could be no other way, as we are pure extensions of God's love.

There is nothing we need to attain or do. We simply need to remove the veils that obscure our experience or memory of this truth. We can simplify the process of awakening with these seven steps:

1. **Recognition:** Realize that there is something inherently wrong with life the way you have seen it, with its highs and lows.

2. **Desire:** Begin to desire more than anything to see things differently, to experience life with more constant peace and joy.

3. **Vigilance:** Commit to having a different experience of life. This attracts to you everything that will support your goal.

4. **Presence:** Practice being fully aware of what you are feeling and thinking in each moment. Become more "present."

5. **Acceptance and allowance:** Begin to see and accept the eternal truth about yourself and all others. Allow peace to replace the discomfort of old beliefs that sustain self-created walls of limitation and separation.

6. **Corrected perception:** Discover and clean all hidden beliefs that have kept you limited, incomplete, and feeling separate from the Creator and all others. Trade old limiting thought patterns for corrected perception simply by becoming more aware as discomforts arise, then choosing peace instead. Allow yourself to let go of the charge. As you see thought-energy patterns shifting so easily through your observation and intention (and dowsing), begin to understand that none of these patterns can be true. See that life as you have been living it is nothing more than illusion.

7. **Forgiveness:** Recognize that you, along with everyone else, have simply been playing out a game in which you have experienced yourself as separate from the Creator and one another. Begin to realize that there are no "sins." In truth, no one can do anything to you without your conscious or unconscious permission, nor can you do anything to others that they have not agreed to on some level.

Truth is unchangeable and without contradiction. You have been experiencing only relative truths based on past experiences and resulting perceptions. This is why dowsing works so well. On the level of your experience in this illusory world, or dream state, everything is energy, and patterns are easily shifted because they have no solid foundation. There is no hierarchy in level of difficulty in shifting these patterns, since they are all equally illusory. With dowsing, you reveal unconscious limiting patterns and neutralize the energetic charge through your clear intention and the spin of the pendulum.

Dowsing provides a focus and confirmation as you grow in understanding your limitless nature. The more you practice this and see positive results, the more confidence you gain. This results in more effective dowsing, since your growing trust allows you to bypass the conscious mind more readily and to access what yogi Sri Aurobindo called the "superconscious mind" where all thoughts are held. It is at this level that you can effectively re-create the foundation of your thought system. Here, you are free to choose what thoughts resonate with the truth of your being. By becoming more aware of your thoughts and becoming the conscious co-creator of your experiences, you see the world around you begin to change as well, because you are truly creating a new template for your life experience. "As without, so within." This prepares you for your inevitable homecoming to the state of Self-realization.

Each of us, as part of the collective mind, has been playing out every possible scenario to experience what it would be like to be individuated, to be separate. The truth about each of us as loving extensions of God's creative power makes us invulnerable. We are eternal Spirit having a brief encounter in individuated forms. True forgiveness recognizes the level of One Mind and realizes there is really nothing to forgive other than ourselves for the belief in separation.

We all always do the very best we can with the state of consciousness we are in at any given moment. We begin to access deeper peace and self-empowerment once we take full responsibility for the creation of all of our experiences. This takes us out of the victim role and takes the "charge" out of situations. We are free to choose peace consciously instead of continuing our default program of defensive reactivity. You could say that true forgiveness takes everyone "off the hook," thereby allowing for a shift that heals all relationships.

I recommend that, once issues or misperceptions have been revealed and neutralized through dowsing, the following act of personal responsibility may be taken in order truly to heal a situation. If you negate this final step, you are simply shifting energy patterns around—rearranging the deck chairs on the Titanic—and nothing significant really changes. Until you apply true forgiveness and recognize that the eternal nature encompasses us all, you will have similar situations recur in various forms, bringing your awareness to the same unhealed issues.

Since we are all One Mind, there is nothing that ever happens without the unconscious agreement of all concerned. The following prayer is a modified version of an ancient Hawaiian healing technique called *Ho'oponopono* that was recently made available worldwide through the work of Hew Len. For more information on his work, read (*Zero Limits*. by Joe Vitale and Hew Len Ihaleakala, John Wiley & Sons, Inc. 2007).

*You cannot solve a problem from the same level of consciousness that created it. (Albert Einstein)*

Hold in your mind the image of whatever person or situation seems to be disturbing your peace. You can choose to hold an image of yourself as well. Repeat the following words silently, until you feel peace enter your awareness:

*I love you.*
*I am sorry for any pain or suffering you have experienced.*
*Forgive me my misperceptions of you as I forgive myself.*
*I trust you to love me.*
*Thank you.*

Surrender the situation to the "highest good of all" and disengage attachment to the outcome. As you become more comfortable with the idea of joining minds on this level, it will suffice to simply say: "I love you. Thank you."

The second part of this book is specifically designed to assist you through your discovery process and help you learn what you have been using unconsciously to hold yourself back from becoming fully aware of your inherent nature as a pure creative extension of love. Enjoy the empowerment and freedom that come with discovering your true Self. All of the charts given here, as well as the technique noted above, are appropriate to use for yourself, other humans and animals, homes and properties, and in any other creative ways that you can discover in your imagination while you are still engaged in this illusory experience of time, space, and bodies—what we call life.

## DOWSING WITH GREATER AWARENESS

Please recognize that nothing exists outside of your mind. Although, when you are dowsing, it may appear that you are moving energies that are affecting you from "out there," the truth is that everything you discover is merely a projection from your unconscious imagination, which is also part of the collective mind. As you deepen your understanding of this, the very idea of being "victim" to anything becomes impossible. This reality becomes your key to liberation and peace. You unlock the door to true Self-empowerment.

The main purpose of dowsing is to release incoherent energetic stress patterns that are affecting your physical, mental, and emotional well-being. We unconsciously hold these patterns in a variety of forms. When you release them, you suddenly have greater clarity, peace, and confidence that, in turn, foster more expanded awareness and natural movement toward wholeness. You begin to realize that what can change is not real, so life as you have known it is illusory—a dream.

In quantum science, the "observer effect" implies that anything on which we focus our attention will change based on our observation and expectations. As we currently understand it, this happens on the level of photon light particles—in other words, on the level of unseen energy patterns. The foundation of our thoughts creates our life experiences. Thoughts actually originate from one of two sources: either from a feeling of individuation and separation, or from a feeling, or "knowingness," of wholeness and unity. We call this state of mind the Holy Spirit.

Our thoughts, when repeated, often become beliefs, which then create our experiences. Experiences trigger various feelings that have an electrical charge to them. These feelings then attract thought patterns that have a similar electrical charge. The cycle continues until we become conscious observers and release the energetic charge. By discovering your unconscious beliefs and neutralizing limiting energy patterns, you can move beyond your self-made constraints toward experiencing your unlimited reality. The process looks something like this:

Thought Source (ego or Spirit) leads to

Thoughts, which lead to

Beliefs, which lead to

Experiences, which lead to

Feelings, which attract

Thoughts, which lead to . . .

And so the cycle continues.

*Your task is not to seek for love,*
*but merely to seek and find all of the barriers within yourself that you*
*have built against it. (A Course in Miracles)*

Part II of this book contains eight chapters, each one focused on a specific topic and accompanied by relevant charts. The topic is discussed at the the beginning of each chapter, followed by sample dowsing phrases. These are only suggestions and, once you feel proficient in these dowsing methods, you can feel free to follow your intuition and expertise in creating your own statements as you cultivate deeper skills. We remind you that, when two or more minds are joined for the purpose of releasing obstacles to truth, divine support is always at hand. So be open to "blowing out all boundaries" and tapping into the quantum field of infinite potential!

# CHAPTER 7

# True Forgiveness

*To understand true forgiveness is to realize there is nothing to forgive. We're all in this together.*

DO YOU EVER WONDER WHY THE SAME ISSUES keep coming back up in your life? This happens because you believe that healing must occur layer by layer over the course of whatever time frame your unconscious mind has allotted for this particular issue to be resolved. This belief supports the continuity of the time/space/bodies matrix that was structured by the "split" mind to experience separation in every possible way. Under the illusory spell of individuated selves, we have elaborately constructed a holographic maze in which to get lost for a while, until all experiences of separation play out to extremes and we, as One Mind, are ready to awaken. Each of us is a creative collaborator in this and we are never alone in our creations. We couldn't be, since we are all equally expressions of One Mind. The choice to experience individuated selves is one of limitation.

Specific experiences arise within the One Mind as ideas to be played out—like thoughts of scarcity, loneliness, abandonment, and betrayal. These thoughts manifest repeatedly through us as experiences throughout lifetimes and multiple dimensions, until we clearly define what the experience is. In other words, we are seeking the remembrance of the original idea and the recognition that we chose to create all the experiences we have had playing it out. We do this in perfect collaboration with one another.

These ideas are held as unconscious beliefs that our minds project onto the screen of life. All those in my life who are seeking similar experiences, or resonating with the beliefs I am projecting, will show up in the right place and time to play out the situations with me because it is a joint desire. There are no victims here and never were! Life as we have known it has been a deliberate collective agreement to put on an elaborate play in which we, as part of One Mind, are simultaneously the playwright, producer, director, actors, audience—and clean-up crew! The play develops around the theme of separation and requires everyone involved to suffer a collective amnesia in order to portray isolation from infinite Wholeness convincingly. Like a dream that seems to last for hours but only spans a moment or two, this play, or illusion of separation, is just a momentary impulse of thought based on a tiny, mad idea: "I wonder what it would be like to experience something other than Wholeness—to be separate from God?"

## THE SIGNIFICANCE OF CONTENT VS. FORM

As you awaken from a dream, the characters and situations in your mind begin to fade, to become transparent, and you sometimes enter a lucid dreaming state. Since you are not caught up in the plot anymore, you may see a theme emerging. You may notice certain thoughts, feelings, and emotions arising that perhaps feel familiar to you. This is what I call the "content" of the dream, or your experience of it. The "form" of a dream, or of any experience you have in what we call your "awakened state," consists of the characters, the situation, the circumstances, and whatever actions transpire.

When you focus on the content of situations, you notice how you feel and what thoughts are arising. You become more conscious or "awakened," and step into what Timothy Freke calls "lucid living." This is also called becoming an observer or witness of your mind. Becoming the observer allows you to see life and lifetime themes. You begin to ask yourself: "What idea have I been fostering that has projected this experience?" The proverbial wheels start turning and you see that you have played out the same theme multiple times throughout your life, in different situations with different people, each time resulting in your feeling isolated, betrayed, or cheated. You begin to question whether the blame you have been putting on other people is perhaps sourced from your own misperceptions.

Then the lights go on and you begin to take personal responsibility for your experiences. You realize the obvious—*you* must have something to do with this. This is a huge step in liberation from suffering. Everyone in your life is always in alignment with your will or what you desire. Again, this is at the level of One Mind where we are all joined. So if you wish to experience anger, someone in your universe who wishes to play with the same frequencies will show up in perfect orchestration to gift both of you with what is desired. Let me repeat: No one is a victim, ever! Therefore, no one is a perpetrator and there is no need to rescue anyone! These are ego games. These three roles have held together a triangulation of ego-based relationships for eons. Guilt is the glue that holds it all together and forgiveness heals it *all*!

True forgiveness is the realization that there is nothing real to forgive. If we are all in collaboration at the level of One Mind (which we are), and if our joint purpose has been to experience separation and therefore limitation and suffering (which it has been), what is there to forgive but our own misperception of being separate from the Divine? Thoughts separate and experience unites. Let go of the stories by paying more attention to your emotions and how you feel—both your physical sensations and your over-all sense of well-being. For instance, if I am annoyed or angry, I may feel a tightness or constriction in my chest or solar plexus. I may feel a sense of expansion or lightness when I am happy. Realize that no one else has any power over how you choose to experience situations—ever. All you ever experience is yourself.

This awareness is really self-empowering. Knowing that you always choose what you want to be experiencing, you may choose again at any time and say, as we read in *A Course in Miracles*: "I choose Peace instead." Even if you don't feel more peaceful right in that moment, the more you practice this, the more it will become your "default" program and you will begin to see this choice reflected in your environment and your relationships.

The beliefs held in your subconscious mind and the thoughts they attract from the superconscious or collective Mind dictate the kind of experiences you have. Every thought you have drops into the pool of consciousness and sends out concentric waves that reach every other being and all universes and come back to you as manifested experiences of that thought. However, you are not a victim of your subconscious mind, since, even as those waves come back to you, you are free in each moment to choose how you will experience your creations. Your choices on how you will receive your creations determine what you will create in the next moment.

## FREEDOM FROM ENTANGLED RELATIONSHIP WEBS

Experiences are neutral, but our thoughts are not. Our thoughts are energetically polarized and it is these polarities that define duality. As you become mindful of what you are experiencing, the belief "charges" in your body/field literally begin to dissipate. Taking even a brief mental pause (perhaps with a deep breath in and out) to allow for the possibility of experiencing something in a new way rather than through your old default program of reactivity is all you need do to create huge shifts in your life. Eckhart Tolle calls this the "empowering breath."

Your thoughts about others literally keep both you and them stuck or imprisoned. Since all of your thoughts are limiting, even "keeping someone on a pedestal" restricts you both. The underlying premise here is that you believe that person is somehow more worthy than you or others in your life. Your thoughts about others define, not only them, but who you think you are. This is an ego game to maintain self-identity. You let everyone off the hook every time you notice and release your judgments.

Here's a favorite reminder that I use whenever I catch myself thinking that someone (like my grown children, partner, or clients) needs "fixing" or the benefit of my opinions:

> *I give you to the Holy Spirit as part of myself. I know that you will be released, unless I want to use you to imprison myself. In the name of my freedom I choose your release, because I recognize that we will be released together. (A Course in Miracles).*

Every time you let yourself or someone else "off the hook" by releasing judgments, you set us all free.

## SPIRITUAL DOWSING AND TRUE FORGIVENESS

Since the majority of limiting beliefs are held in the deepest recesses of our minds, we are often oblivious to judgments we are still carrying that are insidiously poisoning every aspect of our lives. The first three dowsing charts in this chapter are designed to be worked together in a way that reveals issues that still carry a charge in your field, relationships that are offering you an opportunity to heal these patterns at a core level, and specific areas in your body and field where you have been holding on to these energetic blockages. The fourth chart gives examples of corrected perceptions that may be dowsed back in with a right spin once the limiting patterns have first been released with a left spin.

You may choose to dowse in any words that seem suitable as a corrected perception. Recognizing that these patterns represent lessons you have chosen to learn allows you to release attachment to any stories around them and to forgive those involved. Remember, *you* are writing your script and others are joining in through mutual agreement. Even a little willingness to let go of these patterns goes a long way toward dissolving them. With this understanding, the dowsing session literally "collapses time" by saving you the need to keep re-experiencing these same ideas. You are able to go to the heart of the matter, the content of the issue, and let it go.

## FORGIVENESS LESSONS

Chart 29 allows you to uncover hidden issues that keep you limited and energetically attracting unhealthy relationships and circumstances in your life. This will continue until you recognize them, clear them, and forgive yourself for having used these beliefs to imprison both yourself and others.

Chart 32 shows the polar opposites, or corrected perceptions, of the forgiveness issues. Once you have uncovered hidden opportunities for forgiveness and released the patterns, you will be able to fill in voids with corrected perceptions that will lead you toward a healing on all levels of your being.

### Power

Imbalances in the area of power source directly back to our delusion that we are self-created and therefore have authority over our own lives. This is simply the ego seeking self-identity through various experiences of having more or less power over others and circumstances. This is always ego-driven and speaks of the belief that we usurped the power of God and were able to render lacking what was created in perfection—you, me, we are, as One Mind, perfect extensions of God's love. To be truly empowered is to align your will completely with Divine Will—which, in truth, are one and the same. This occurs when you silence your busy "monkey mind," ask Spirit for guidance, and allow for the experience of inspiration. What follows is a feeling of peace and an absolute knowing of what you need to think, say, and do next.

## Control and Domination

This is obviously entwined with power struggles and serves to perpetuate the essence of victimhood. You can see how this is played out in your own life and in every aspect of the world as you view it. Victimhood runs deep in the collective consciousness, since it is based on guilt perpetuated by believing in separation. You project on to others your internal strife, unconsciously making agreements to play out parts as victim, perpetrator, and rescuer repeatedly—until you realize that these concepts you have about who you are and who others are represent misperceptions of a mind that perceives itself to be incomplete and alone. The experiences you create validate this misperception. Simply uncover, release, and choose peace.

## Weakness

This is a symbol of judgment based on the illusory concepts of control and domination.

## Sexual Guilt

This guilt is held deep in the recesses of consciousness. It symbolizes your agreement to use gender and sexuality as a means of keeping the guilt game going through validating that the "body" is real and that it can have control over your true nature as perfect, lovable Spirit. Once you recognize the truth, your natural tendency will be to honor your body as a vehicle for awakening. When you choose sexual experiences that cultivate wholeness and union rather than guilt and further separation, this guilt will dissolve. If you want to be *free*, let the past go.

## Emotional Distance

Perhaps you have been in relationship with someone who never really seemed to "be there for you." Or maybe you were the one who couldn't let down the barriers to love. This is always fear-based.

## Judgment

Judgmental perceptions were introduced by the idea of separation from the Creator and are symbolized in the Christian tradition by the Tree of Knowledge. Once the idea to experience something other than Wholeness or completion occurred, perception became a weak substitute for knowledge. To perceive implies judgment. Even to judge something positively implies that there is a negative. When you clean this energy, you open your mind to more peace.

## Anger and Hate

This is always based on guilt and fear and is either directed at yourself or projected onto others. Since there are really no "others," it is always a debilitating blow to true Self. Understand that anger and hate are always a call for love.

## Betrayal

The question is: Who betrayed whom? If we are all of One Mind, it is irrelevant. Yet, like all of these other patterns, this can be a hidden ego-oriented hold-out from experiencing trust and unity. You are completely invulnerable as Spirit. No one and nothing can do you harm unless you agree to it on some level. These agreements are beyond your conscious understanding—why would we choose pain and suffering? The answer is that all of this is nothing more than various "flavors" of separation. And the truth is that no one is to blame. This dream is the result of a momentary curiosity to experience something entirely different. While dowsing out this pattern, bring the associated relationship into your inner vision and say:

> I see you as the Holy Spirit (or Spirit, Divine, whatever you are comfortable with) within myself. I know that you are free unless I use you to imprison myself. I release you and we are both free.

## Deceit

This is closely related to betrayal and is often entwined with this issue. Therefore, when dowsing, it may be appropriate to dowse out both issues.

## Non-acceptance

Lack of acceptance of self or others is a denial of Truth. Recognize that all of your relationships are mirrors of your relationship with your Self. The

Emotional Freedom Technique (EFT) that can be a great accompaniment to healing issues around self-love and self-acceptance. It is also an easy tool to use for Self-empowerment (see *www.emofree.com*). I like to have clients participate in their sessions as much as possible while I am dowsing or using other modalities. EFT works well for this.

## Dowsing Statements

Chart 29 shows the issues that are presenting as opportunities for forgiveness. Chart 30 shows the relationship that is presenting you with this lesson. Chart 31 shows which chakra or energy center is holding this pattern. Chart 32 shows the polar-opposite or healed aspect of each perceived forgiveness issue.

After achieving answers in the first three charts, ask your Spirit Guides (or connect at the level of Higher Self) to assist while you spin your pendulum. Left spin to release these patterns, while you say:

> *With the assistance of (this person's) Spirit Guides (Higher Self), I now release all patterns around the issue of (_____), in relationship with (_____), held in (person's) (_____) chakra for all dimensions and all time frames, healing this relationship and reversing all ill effects.*

# CHART 30: RELATIONSHIPS AND FORGIVENESS

All relationships are mirrors of your relation with your true Self. This chart will assist you in uncovering and healing issues that are holding both you and others in unconscious and conscious limitation.

True forgiveness is the only key to real awakening. This level of forgiveness sees that individuals are always doing the very best they can in each moment, based on the level of their conscious understanding at the time. You are not the thoughts you have; you are not the personality you think you are. All of this is simply a collection of concepts that you hold on to in creating what seems to be your individual identity.

This culmination of self-ideas is accumulated over lifetimes—from ancestral patterns, familial behaviors, societal influences, karma, responses to collective and personal traumas, etc. We expect ourselves and others to "be" a certain way based solely on our past experiences and conditioning. None of this is meaningful or loving in any way. As you can see, we have kept ourselves in such tight little boxes that it's a wonder we can laugh or love or find joy at all. You can choose freedom through seeing and shifting limited beliefs.

The true purpose of any relationship is to awaken to full awareness of yourself and others as one united, perfect, whole expression of Divine love. There are only two choices in how you or anyone else experiences the moment—in a state of love, or in a quest for love. Anger, resentment, frustration, sorrow, or any other painful expressions are simply unconscious calls for love. Whether someone is loving you or seemingly attacking you, the proper response is *always* love. When you find yourself thinking negative thoughts or behaving in a way that perpetuates separation and suffering, the only proper response is love. We are all in soulful agreement to assist each other in spiritual growth through shared experiences of love—and of what love is not.

How will you know if you are seeing your truth in another? Check your "internal peace meter" to see if you are feeling peace, joy, and comfort. It takes a desire to see things differently, to experience all of your relationships with new eyes each day, and to ask for divine assistance in this commitment each day in order to cultivate this True Vision expressed through relations.

A few specific relationships rate further explanation. The primary relationships in your life are with your initial maternal and paternal caregivers, whether they are your biological mother and father, adoptive parents, or other guardians. Your spiritual progress requires that these relations be healed and "wholey."

## Mother

This relationship is the foundation for the quality of all other relationships in your life and mirrors your relationship with the divine feminine aspect of Self. This essence is receptive, intuitive, and loving.

## Father

Your paternal relationship relates to your ability to function in the material world, including financial abundance and survival. This determines your success or failure in all areas of life and mirrors your relationship with the divine masculine, or the aspect of Self that is energetic, expressive, and creative.

## Romantic Partner

A companion on this level provides an opportunity for spiritual acceleration that can leave your head spinning! However, if you understand this as a benefit and learn how to create a holy, or "wholey," relationship, this level can save you eons of time in awakening. As a mirror that reflects your inner world so efficiently each day, your partner is a gift. It requires that you take full responsibility for your own happiness and you realize truly that you *only* experience yourself. In other words, only you are in control of how you experience anyone or anything.

## Authority Figures

Issues with authority figures all have a fundamental basis in our illusion that we are the identity figure that we have created—or ego. Ego is nothing more than a collection of thoughts you have accumulated to create a sense of self, to be the "you" that you think you are. On an unconscious level, this is the ego's attempt to be "creator." Attachment to beliefs about self-identity is really a denial that you are perfect as God created you, and that all of your creative ability is an extension of God's love. This false perception of self and forgetfulness of who created you sets the scene for internal conflict. The guilt that is perpetuated from this inner conflict is projected out by you to others. Thus, you may have issues with authority figures. You may also find specific past life connections to clear.

## Children

The majority of parenting is done unconsciously. Until we love ourselves unconditionally, we are unable to love someone else fully. Love equals freedom. When we come to a place of complete self-acceptance, we feel a deep peace and have a "knowing" about what we need to do and to be in each moment. In this state, we extend our peace, our love, and the confidence that comes with our knowledge into our parenting. The good news is that it doesn't matter how old you are, or how old your children are, when you achieve this. The healing will occur for all.

Once the pendulum has stopped, turn to Chart 32 and see what the healed perspective is for the issue you just dowsed. With a right spin, say:

*I now accept and fully integrate the corrected perception of (_____)*
*into (person's) relationship with (_____), filling all voids, including any*
*in the (_____) chakra.*

Here's a suggested option. While you are dowsing, have the client repeat this variation of the *Ho'oponopono* prayer:

*I love you.*
*I am sorry.*
*Please forgive me (for my belief in separation.)*
*Thank you.*

## A Note about Chakras

Our primary energy centers, the chakras, are portals between subtle energy fields and the physical body. These portals act as transducers of Light information, "stepping down" vibrational rates to a level acceptable to third-dimensional

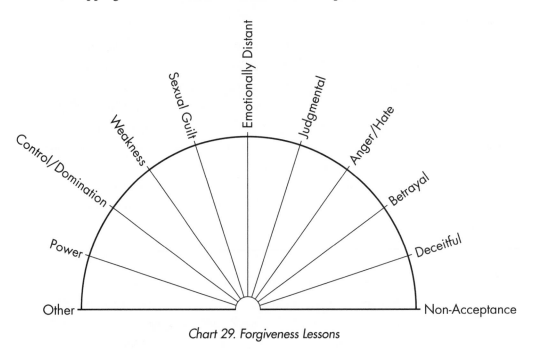

Chart 29. Forgiveness Lessons

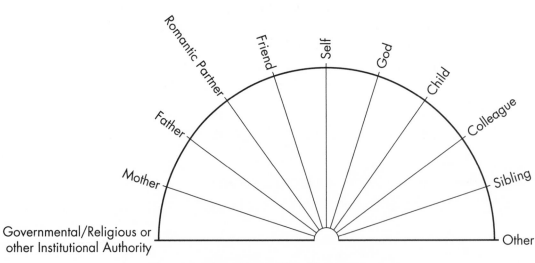

Chart 30. Relationships Offered for Forgiveness

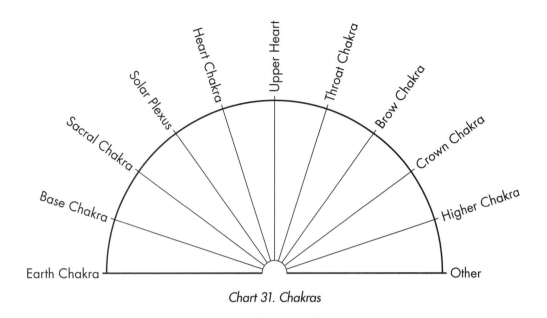

*Chart 31. Chakras*

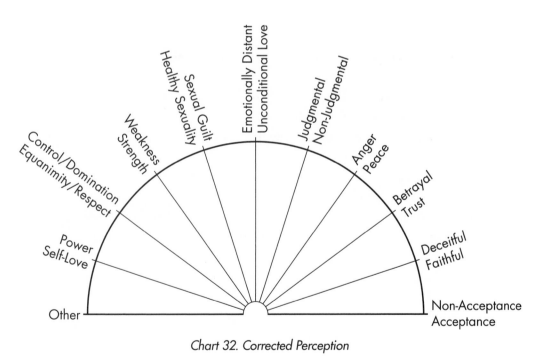

*Chart 32. Corrected Perception*

physical translation and use. Since there is a constant high volume of information processed in these centers, they must periodically be cleaned of congestion or things can get blocked up at times. Each chakra vibrates at a specific frequency that relates harmonically to certain colors, tones, emotions, physical organs, and other like patterns that are represented multi-dimensionally. A healthy chakra supports the physical well-being of all body organs and systems within that energy center's realm. The summary of the seven primary chakra centers (see below) details the seven main chakras and their relationship to physical and emotional health. You may find this list helpful in balancing specific issues associated with a particular chakra. You can also refer to Table 1. Be creative.

## THE CHAKRAS

Chakra energy flows through the front and back of each center.

- ✳ **Base chakra:** located at the root of the spine in back and the pubic bone in front.
- ✳ **Sacral chakra:** located at the lower region of the navel and the mid- to lower-lumbar spinal region.
- ✳ **Solar-plexus chakra:** located two to three inches above the navel and upper lumbar spinal area.
- ✳ **Heart chakra:** located mid-chest to the right of the physical heart and the mid-thoracic spinal region.
- ✳ **Throat chakra:** located near the larynx and mid-cervical vertebrae in the throat area.
- ✳ **Brow chakra:** located between the eyebrows and the occipital region in back of the skull.
- ✳ **Crown chakra:** located at the crown of the head and easily identified through a focal area of pronounced heat when open.

# CHAPTER 8

# Self-Empowerment

THERE'S SELF-EMPOWERMENT and then there's Self-empowerment. Only one of these is meaningful. The small self is concerned with having and doing, whereas Self is focused on Being. We are at a time like no other in our ability to let go of everything that keeps us attached to the small self. Self-empowerment occurs through embracing Self-knowledge, Self-responsibility, and Self-love. What do you feel you need to be Self-empowered?

You are an extension of God's love—an aspect of the eternal flow of divine creativity. As such, you are always creating. There can be no other way. You can, however, miscreate. Whenever you are in the state of forgetfulness of your divine Self, you are simply choosing the experience of separation, which, by definition, implies the qualities of incompletion, disconnection, scarcity, and lack. When you associate with this belief, your creations mirror this back to you and you will always experience a sense of lack in your "reality." You will see a world that holds pain and suffering.

This is projection, not creation, since the foundation comes from a sense of lack and the need to fill a void. You cannot create anything solid or real based on an unstable structure. The key to the transcendence of all suffering lies in this realization. Whenever you know your Self in truth, you will see the beauty of that wholeness and perfection in every relationship and every experience. Understanding this is key to Self-empowerment.

When you are fully realized, you extend God's nature and your essence creates a world that reflects this love. This is true Creation. And this is the only way that you can experience Self-empowerment. How do you know whether you are projecting or creating? What is your experience in the moment? We *only* experience ourselves. The key is to discover where you have been choosing to disempower yourself, to release those limitations, and to choose consciously to own and express your truth.

It is your choice. You can choose unconscious attachment to "small self," which creates projection that fosters false perceptions and resulting experiences noted by limitation, scarcity, lack, and incompleteness. Or you can choose to create from Self-love, which exends Itself as knowledge. In this case the experience reflects Grace through feelings of empowerment, peace, completion, and unlimited potential.

Self-empowerment never relies on "doing." It is based on how you are experiencing any given moment. Just practice being the witness or observer of how you feel in each situation.

The issues listed for Charts 33 and 34 are pretty self-explanatory. Use Chart 33 to see what area of your life is calling you to a new level of Self-empowerment. With a right spin, bring in the acceptance of Self-empowerment in that area. Chart 34 will help you see what belief you have been using to create energy blockages in your expression of Self.

## OPPORTUNITIES FOR SELF-EMPOWERMENT

What area of your life is presenting you with the best opportunity in this moment to become consciously more Self-empowered? When you shift how you experience one aspect of your life, every other area must reflect this as well. Chart 33 reveals what area of your life calls your attention; Chart 34 presents the essence of what needs to be released in order for you to embody true Self-empowerment. Examples of dowsing statements for both of these charts are given below Chart 34.

Here are some clarifying questions to help you determine where you are disempowering yourself:

What distraction am I using to keep peace away?

How am I limiting myself?

Do I choose to be right (in this situation) or do I choose peace?

Am I projecting or extending love through my creations?

What habits have I been using to keep myself limited?

What relationships have I used to keep myself and that person imprisoned?

Have I been using addictive behaviors to keep myself in guilt, shame, and fear?

## Relationships

Have you been using a specific relationship to keep yourself stuck in the separation and suffering game? Some ideal relationships for this are between parent and child, with a romantic partner, or with friends and colleagues. Remember that any time you feel anything less than peace and joy, it means that *you* are unaware of wholeness in that moment. As a perfect expression of God's infinite, divine essence, you are invulnerable and free to create infinitely. This is why we are all free to experience whatever we wish, including the sense of individuated selves. It is your own choice to experience whatever you want. The only thing over which you have no control is your own Being. You cannot change what was already created perfect and whole.

## Career, Hobbies, Creative Expression

Is it time for you to spread your wings and find joy in expressing your innate gifts? Don't forget that it is your natural inheritance to be infinitely creative.

## Healthy Body and Mind, New Location, Abundance

Wherever you feel stress in your life—whether this is due to illness, a worn-out stay in a certain location, or poverty consciousness—make no mistake that this simply reflects lack of true Self-awareness in the moment. Consider the benefits of making outer changes to reflect and reinforce an inner decision to grow.

## Spiritual Connection

Let's get down to nitty-gritty. A spiritual disconnect on any level, after all, constitutes the foundation for all other suffering.

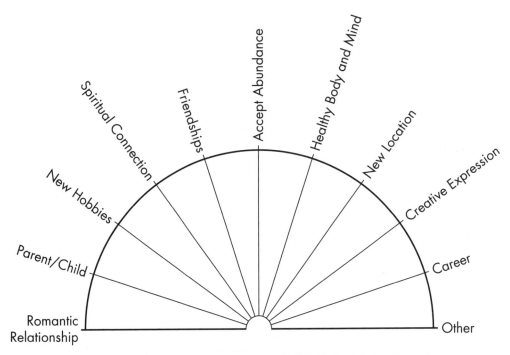

*Chart 33. Opportunities for Self-Empowerment*

## BLOCKAGES TO SELF-EMPOWERMENT

Your natural state is one of pure creative energy as an extension of the infinite stream of divine love. In your experience of life, everything is founded on energy—from electromagnetic fields to the smallest perceived measurement of energy in contemporary scientific studies, the photon.

We are Light Beings. So, here's an energy that surpasses in potential and magnitude anything you can imagine. We each possess the power to do and create anything we can imagine, and beyond. We just don't know it. It's kind of like an elephant in the circus that is held captive by a relatively thin tether from the time it is a baby. Despite an adult elephant's size and strength, there is never a need to secure the creature's leg with anything more substantial, because this wonderful but naïve being is conditioned into believing it is trapped and that any attempt to escape will be futile. There is a lesson in this for us. We imprison ourselves with beliefs that keep us small and boxed-in. This need not be so.

What we call blockages are simply little "hiccups" in the flow of awareness that are calling for our non-judgmental attention. Here are the steps to dissolve those blockages:

Be receptive to any physical, mental, or emotional sensation that feels stuck, constricted, painful, flat, or static.

Let go all judgment or urgency to change, stop, or fix anything.

Observe and be kind; always allow for the presence of self-love and acceptance, regardless of how you are feeling in the moment. To deny our emotions is ineffective. However, we can choose to add a little love to any of our experiences.

Allow any associated patterns or trends to come to the surface—for instance, a situation or person may pop into your attention suddenly.

Release the patterns through dowsing and forgiving the experience.

Allow yourself to accept an altered view or belief that serves to expand your awareness and bring you a sense of gratitude and joy.

## Dowsing Statements

For Chart 33, right spin and say:

*(Person) accepts Self-empowerment with joy, confidence, and gratitude in the life area of (_____), flowing through (him/her) in pure infinite creative expression. Thank you.*

For Chart 34, left spin and say:

*(Person) releases all patterns of resistance and limiting beliefs around (not being heard, fear of failure, trust, etc.) on all levels of (his/her) Being, for all time frames and dimensions. I reverse all ill effects and heal all relationships that are implied by these patterns.*

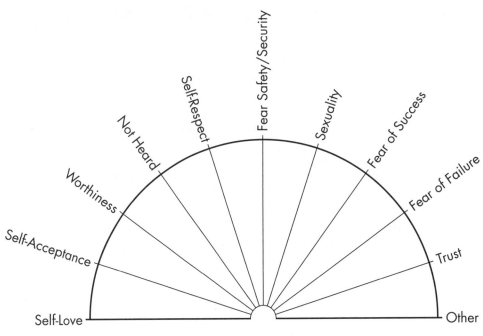

Chart 34. Blockages to Self-Empowerment

## CHART 35: LIMITING ARCHETYPES

Archetypes are images representing stereotypical personalities held in the collective consciousness. They have also been seen as "personality overlays" that resonate with parallel lives. When you have unconscious attachments to these patterns through "owning" them as part of your identity or projecting them onto others, you impose limitations. Although there may be some benefit in calling on particular aspects of consciousness to serve you in the moment—for instance, if you are learning piano, you may wish to call on the essence of a great pianist to assist you in a musical piece—to become attached to anything ultimately serves as a self-limiting step. Chart 35 focuses on releasing any unconscious attachments to specific archetypes, which are often discovered as hidden barriers to an individual's spiritual growth and recognition of greater Self.

Once you have discovered which archetype serves as a potential limiting factor in your life, use Chart 36 to determine what realm would best serve to release this pattern completely at this time.

## Victim, Persecutor, Rescuer

Humanity has been directing the duality dance between these three bedfellows for eons. The roles are equal in their abilities to keep you stuck in a never-ending cycle that perpetuates illusion. You see, they all hold the idea of "me and the other" neatly in place. When you are rescuing or "fixing" someone else, you are avoiding the real work within you; at the same time, you disempower that individual.

## King/Queen, Master/Slave

This presents polar opposites in issues around domination, control, victimhood, etc. Perhaps someone who has had an experience of being cruel in a regal position in one incarnation will hold unconscious guilt that may manifest in a chronic fear of stepping into their power in this lifetime. The slave mentality runs deep in the collective consciousness, with guilt, anger, fear, and resentment secretly passed down from generation to generation until someone "gets it" and clears the pattern.

## Priest/Priestess

This pattern can serve to hold you in a place of feeling "special" by giving you some underlying sense of positioning yourself above others in an imaginary hierarchy. Conversely, you may hold some sense of guilt and remorse if your position as priest or priestess in some other incarnate experience led you to abuse your position. There may also be a strong religious-oriented conflict within.

## Warrior/Martyr

Again, this speaks of guilt, victimhood, persecution, mistrust, and attachment to the limitation of identification with the physical body.

## Seducer

In this archetype, the dark side of trust issues, of intimacy, and the illusion of vulnerability are perpetuated. This pattern involves manipulation and therefore, separation. True intimacy cannot co-exist with this archetype lurking.

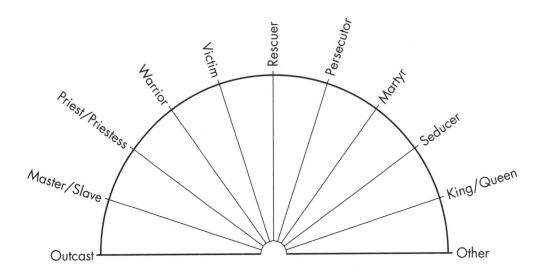

*Chart 35. Limiting Archetypes*

## CHART 36: REALMS TO RELEASE ARCHETYPES

Miracles are happening all the time; we just don't notice them. When we get out of the way, miracles will appear at whatever level the mind will accept them in the moment. There is nothing other than this moment in truth. The past is just a memory and the future is an anticipated event. We experience all of these ideas right here, right now, in our minds. We present opportunities to ourselves with one experience after another, lifetime after lifetime, in multidimensional expressions as we learn certain lessons.

The truth is that all experiences ultimately serve but one purpose—to spark the memory within each of us of our own Divinity. While dancing through the death and rebirth cycle of life, we unconsciously create situations that have the same or resonant frequencies as our original experience. Basically, they provide us with the essence of the same lesson served up in different forms, until we neutralize the charge of that lesson. We do this by becoming observant of our feelings and thoughts in each situation, releasing any judgment that comes up, forgiving this world of illusion, and loving and accepting ourselves without reservation.

Healing occurs at whatever level your mind can accept. This acceptance must be congruent on a conscious and unconscious level. So, if you consciously believe that a particular therapy is most effective for a certain condition, but your unconscious belief does not hold this to be true, the therapy will have varying degrees of effectiveness—all directly correlated to the degree of incongruence in belief between your conscious and unconscious mind. On an unconscious level, you may be ready to release a traumatic memory that occurred in another incarnation, but unable to heal that same pattern as it reappears in this lifetime in the form of a current crisis in your life. Your mind is ready, for whatever reason, to release the pattern in the context of a specific time and event. This is why dowsing for specific time frames, dimensions, and other areas like the Akashic Records may prove to be quite effective in a session.

Chart 36 partners nicely with Chart 35, although any of these charts may be used independently. As you progress in your work, you will see that each of these charts presents endless possibilities in your work.

Chart 35 helps you uncover unhealthy attachment to specific archetypal patterns; Chart 36 allows you to find the area that best serves in this moment to release this pattern. Your mind will direct you to the most appropriate place in the time/space continuum to do the work. The good news is that, once the pattern is released, it clears for all time frames and dimensions.

## Preconception, Conception, Gestation, Birth

You are being called to go to whichever of these specific time frames comes up through dowsing to release the archetypal imprint (from Chart 35) from the initial time you accepted it into your belief system and became "attached" to the pattern. In this case, it would have been during the active process of journeying into this incarnation. You are able to go back and rewrite the script.

## Past, Present, Future Incarnation

Again, you are being called to go to a specific time frame to release the pattern. First, ask where you need to go to release the pattern for the most effective results. The past? The present? The future? See which one gets a yes response. Then follow the steps listed under Vows, Agreements, and Contracts (below) to assess the year you need to go to.

## Other Dimensions

There is a need to access an other-dimensional aspect of your consciousness. Dimensions are a way that we categorize levels of awareness as experienced in specific rates of vibration. Everything in the cosmos is vibrational. The faster the vibration, the higher the dimension. The slower the vibration, the lower the dimension. For instance, the fourth dimension is the realm of thoughts, emotions, auric fields, the astral plane, and collective consciousness. We cannot physically see these things, because their vibrational level is higher than that of our physical bodies here in the third dimension. When we are in an altered state of consciousness—in an alpha or delta state—we are vibrating at a faster pace and may be able to see auras or beings in higher dimensions.

We subscribe to Barbara Clow's nine dimensional model. There are other models. Know which model you are using and your results will reflect your intent.

## Ancestral Patterns

This realm suggests that you need to release non-beneficial archetypal patterns that have been passed down through the lineage. In general, our ancestors are often part of our soul family. We, as a soul group, have specific lessons that we are working on in order ultimately to heal all sense of separation. We come around again and again in incarnations, working out the same issues with each other. You may have been your mother's father or sister in another lifetime. We give each other opportunities to heal our belief in the illusion of separation. When one person in the lineage heals a pattern, it clears this for all ancestors as well, particularly if that is clearly the intention while dowsing. Trust that all is in perfect timing.

## Karma

The energetic signature of each of us is compiled of various frequencies, each specific to all the thoughts, feelings, and deeds we ever experienced. There is no right or wrong attached to karma. We simply continue creating events that resonate with these frequencies until a time when we no longer hold them—when we have learned whatever lesson we were working on and are ready to move on.

## The Akashic Records

This is a record of every circumstance, every thought, and every thing that ever has been or ever will be part of consciousness. All of your lessons, all of your relationships, and all of the circumstances of your life are held in the Akashic Records. When this comes up through dowsing, your mind wants to take a trip to the Hall of Records to bring completion to some part of your history. You can search deeper with questions, but often you do not need to know the specifics about what you are completing. (See the exercise given with Chart 52.)

## Dowsing Statements

For Chart 35, left spin while saying:

> *I release the archetypal pattern of (_____) and associated issues from all aspects of (person's) being. I release attachment, reverse ill effects, and heal relationships implied by this pattern for all time frames and dimensions.*

For Charts 35 and 36 combined, left spin while saying:

> *I go to (past/present/future, ninth dimension, Akashic Records, etc.) and release the archetypal pattern of (_____) and associated issues from all aspects of (person's) being. I release attachment, reverse ill effects, and heal relationships implied by this pattern for all time frames and dimensions.*

You can use Chart 36 alone to find what realm best addresses anything you are clearing. Left spin while saying:

> *I go to the area of (_____) and release the pattern of (_____) from all aspects of (person's) being. I release attachment, reverse ill effects, and heal relationships implied by this pattern for all time frames and dimensions.*

## Vows, Contracts, and Agreements

This implies the need to render all vows, contracts, and agreements that are no longer beneficial null and void. We are our "word" and must take responsibility for all thoughts, words, and actions that we produce. In most cases, it is unnecessary to know details when this issue surfaces. Simply ask if it is necessary or beneficial to find out more information in order to release yourself from these vows, contracts, or agreements. If the answer is yes, ask if a specific time frame in necessary. Left spin and say:

> *I now release (person and all those who are involved) from any vows, contracts, or agreements made in the year (_____) that no longer*

*serve the highest good, rendering these agreements null and void for all time frames and dimensions. I reverse ill effects and heal all relationships implied. I release all (_____) archetypal patterns from (person's) being that are associated with these agreements.*

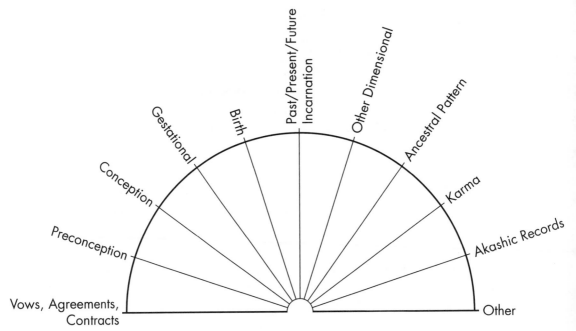

Chart 36. Realms to Release Archetypes

## CHART 37: POSITIVE ARCHETYPES

Now that you have cleared limiting thoughts and personality attachments from your body/mind field, you may wish to call back those aspects of your consciousness that represent qualities that support a new level of Self-empowerment in your life. Let's face it, our experiences have pearls in them as well, as we have all accumulated insights, skills, and traits that can serve us well. These patterns assist our souls in progressing toward full awareness of Oneness. It is always the purpose that we give to any of our experiences that either directs us toward awakening or lulls us into staying asleep within the illusion a bit longer. It's all about where you place your focus.

Advanced Spiritual Dowsing

Calling these positive archetypal patterns in is one way in which we can experience soul retrieval, as we pull together all the scattered aspects of our selves into one experience. For instance, tapping into a positive archetype may also help you gain clarity and confidence toward a new career or accelerate your ability to excel in a new passion like music or art. In general, the meaning behind these archetypes is the one you give them. What potentially helpful or positive attributes come to mind when you think about any one of these that come up for you? Your insights will reveal to you those qualities that you are ready to have surface in your life. Go for it! I will give a few general interpretations here, but many of the potential qualities in these archetypes are subjectively understood.

For instance, Teacher and Healer are perhaps egging you onward to share your own insights and wisdom in whatever areas captivate your heart, as well as igniting the passion and direction necessary in your life to best help others to heal themselves. We are drawn to give that which is most cherished by us, as giving and receiving are the same flow.

The Farmer archetype is deeply rooted in the earth and involves a passion to join with Nature in cultivating life-sustaining produce. You may feel called to help structure innovative ways to feed humanity.

Planetary Seeder indicates a soul whose purpose involves birthing life forms on various planets throughout the galaxies. This archetype, when spun in, may enhance your appreciation of the universal diversity in life forms and the sacred thread that links us all together.

Spiritual Guide comes in to align you with your greater wisdom and Higher Self as a Guide, perhaps for many others in a parallel dimension. Listen to your Inner Guide for inspiration. Begin by asking how many archetypes apply to your current situation, then identify them one by one.

## Dowsing Statements

With a right spin, say:

*(Person) accepts the positive influence, knowledge, and experiences of the positive archetype of _____ into (his/her) present-day awareness. I now direct these energies into projects, relationships, or situations that may benefit from them.*

Or, with a right spin, say:

> *I now call to (person's) present self and experience of time all discon-*
> *nected parts of (him/her) entrapped in alternate time frames. I call upon*
> *all skills, talents, knowledge, and abilities from these aspects of (his/her)*
> *being in the form of positive personality archetype(s) of _____ to be*
> *applied to this present life in service to the Light and to (his/her) highest*
> *purpose at this time.*

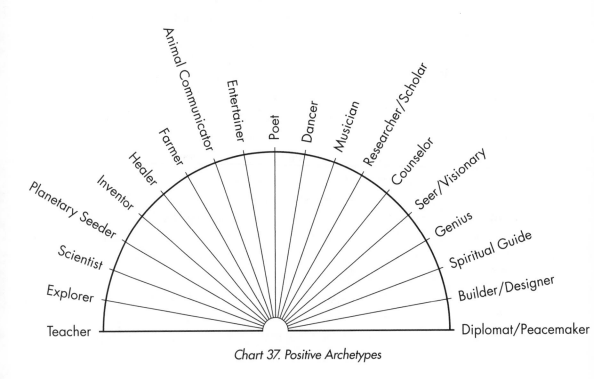

*Chart 37. Positive Archetypes*

# CHAPTER 9

# Releasing Core Fear-Based Issues

ABANDONMENT, TRUST, AND SELF-WORTH ARE ISSUES that go hand in hand. Our first memory of change occurred at the moment of separation—the illusion of the "fall." This is why the fear of change or separation is foundational for all forms of fear. We unconsciously feel abandoned and also guilty, because we feel that we are responsible for the suffering that has ensued since the idea to experience separation was birthed. Because this is our foundation in unconscious memory, we are always in a state of conflict. Thus, duality persists.

Since the separation never occurred, we can regain our essence of trust, wholeness, joy, and peace through correcting this misperception. Opportunities arise for this correction when we have a "charge," or when an emotional reaction to a trigger of some kind emerges. These energetic imprints of past traumas are held in our field until they are recognized and healed. A charge gets stronger (more polarized) each time it surfaces and triggers a reactive response. These hidden charges ensure that we draw situations and relationships into our experience that resonate with these specific frequencies.

This is how manifestation occurs. The stronger the charge (emotion, feeling), the more powerful and instantaneous the manifestation in our experience.

## THOUGHT + EMOTION + FEELING = MANIFESTATION

Instead of being victims to this sequence, we must recognize it, undo it, and use the formula to our benefit instead. Whenever you choose conscious manifestation, it works with the same principle. Our relationships are what

Greg Braden calls our "temples of initiation," since it is through them that we are able to see ourselves clearly—with healed and unhealed aspects equally revealed. In *Walking Between the Worlds*, Braden speaks of the three foundational fears noted below.

So, how do we know if we have unhealed issues around trust, abandonment, and self-worth? We become witnesses to our thoughts, emotions, and feelings. Does a specific situation or relationship trigger a feeling of tightness in your chest, neck, or stomach area? Do you notice that the same thoughts surface repeatedly? Does a slight irritation arise in you whenever someone speaks to you in a certain tone of voice? Be mindful of your experience. Our mindfulness shows us where we have healed issues and the progress we are making by the amount of peace we notice in ourselves. Perhaps things that used to push you through the ceiling a year ago don't phase you anymore. You won't know unless you notice.

Abandonment may be an issue for you if:

⁂ You notice a trend of failed relationships in your life that left either yourself or another in the wake of devastation.

⁂ You have fostered a fear of "being left behind," which proves true in many of your experiences.

⁂ You run in the other direction when a good relationship shows up so that you do not get hurt.

Issues around not feeling worthy are evident when:

⁂ Issues that trigger low self-esteem repeatedly emerge in your life.

⁂ You continue creating relationships of career, friendship, and romance that match your experience of not being "good enough."

⁂ You typically judge yourself to be better than or in awe of others, maintaining a self-serving hierarchy to secure a limited self-identity.

Issues around surrender and trust may need healing if you notice:

⁂ An inability to surrender to your experience.

⁂ Relationships that frequently mirror your expectations of this world as being unsafe and unworthy of your trust capture your attention.

⁂ A feeling of being safe in your body is lacking. (Illness is a sign, not a cause, of this.)

* A frequent feeling of being ungrounded, confused, or "stuck" in life.
* A fear of change and a resistance to opening yourself to new experiences in life.

Since these issues are closely related, it stands to reason that it would be a good idea to release them together. Chart 38 provides you with various choice points in time and space in which to best release these patterns. Your unconscious mind will choose when and where it is ready to recognize and clear these issues.

## RELEASING CORE BELIEFS

The importance is always on the content or essence of an experience, rather than the form. Again, since you will not need to repeat a particular lesson once healed, you will have literally collapsed time in that instant. Your purpose is always to recognize yourself as love. We offer ourselves multiple opportunities in which to discover this truth.

The concept of an ancient mind goes back to the moment that the idea of separation was conceived. All of the experiences that seem to us to encompass eons occurred in one single impulse. Because time was made up 'after the fact' as part of the illusion of separation, this is the point of origin of fear.

### Ancestral Fears

This reading implies the need to focus on the ancestral lineage to heal these core issues. Specify whether you need to focus on the father's or mother's lineage.

### Third- and Other-Dimensional Fears

Perhaps these issues are rooted in a specific dimensional experience. If Other Dimension comes up, access the number of that dimension on your Chart of Ten.

### Other Planet, Star, Galaxy, or Universe

These beliefs are related to a specific time/space focal point. You can create your own charts listing individual planets, stars, galaxies, etc. to explore this further. It may be useful to connect with an aspect of yourself that recognizes association with another planet, star system, or dimension. This may invoke an initial realization that your experiences reach far beyond what you had previously acknowledged. This potentially expansive experience is, however, only a small stepping-stone to realizing that all experiences in all dimensions are still just part of a dream we have created, and even the most grandiose expression of your self is only a glimmer of your true Self.

## Point of Conception

At this point you merge the patterns you are bringing into this incarnation with those from your parents that will best serve your learning purposes in this lifetime.

## Dowsing Statements

With a left spin, say:

> *I now release all unhealed patterns around abandonment, trust, and self-worth (at the time of . . . , in the area of . . . ) from all aspects of (person's) being, (reversing all ill effects, releasing attachment to these fear-based patterns, and healing relationships implied for all time frames and dimensions.*

# BASE CHAKRA

The first three chakras pertain to your physical, mental, and emotional well-being in relationship to your experiences here in physical form. These are very important centers and your overall physical and mental health is dependent on the functioning capacity of these energy centers. All of your chakras need to be aligned with one another, optimally open, and spinning in a healthy manner in order for you to access and process information and experiences from higher vibrational aspects of consciousness effectively.

The base chakra is associated with survival, the ability to provide life's necessities, family and group safety and security, the ability to stand up for yourself, and the ability to stay grounded, structured, and safe in the physical body. This chakra may hold ancient fear patterns dealing with galactic catastrophes, planetary traumas like the abrupt demise of civilizations, persecutions, etc. Here are a few specific areas.

## Catastrophobia

This is the title of a book by Barbara Hand Clow that describes fear patterns held in the collective DNA memory and human morphogenetic field that have origins in major catastrophes experienced by Earth and humans, like the deluge and the demise of Atlantis.

## Ancestral Miasms

These are energetic patterns passed down through either ancestral lineage or collective consciousness that can lead to physical, mental, and emotional illness. You can clear these patterns, not only for yourself, but for the whole ancestral lineage.

## Disconnection from Mother Earth

When you hold fear-based patterns in your lower chakras, particularly the base chakra, you have a difficult time feeling a sense of belonging and safety here on Earth. This pattern may also imply a disconnection in your relationship with the divine feminine.

## Dowsing Statements

With a left spin, say:

> *I release all patterns associated with (_____) from (person's) base chakra, releasing attachment, reversing ill effects, and healing all relationships implied. I bring the base chakra into optimal spin, function, openness, and alignment with all other chakras.*

You may wish to have your client add:

> *I love, honor, and respect Mother Earth and connect myself with a column of Light extending from my base chakra to Earth's core. This Light column keeps me centered and grounded, extending through all chakras in and around my body and all the way to the galactic center. I am always safe, secure, and supported.*

# SACRAL CHAKRA

The sacral chakra is the seat of relationships and creativity. It is the energetic womb for both men and women. Any blockages and incoherent energy patterns held here will certainly have an impact on your ability to express yourself creatively, to have healthy relationships, and to experience these abundantly. Three ways we express ourselves in life that are strongly interwoven with this chakra are sexuality, financial abundance, and creativity. If you feel blocked in any one of these areas, you can be sure that, on some level, the other two areas are also affected. See Table 1 for more information. Here are a few areas with which you may identify.

## Creative Expression

You are by nature pure creative expression. The only thing standing between you and the continuous joyful expression of your creative essence is the conditioned beliefs that you hold that keep you limited and unaware of your amazing potential. Place your attention on the area of your belly and imagine three points connecting your hips and your navel in a triangular shape. Close your eyes and feel this area for energetic flow. Does this area feel tight, constricted, or energetically flat? Can you imagine or feel energy swirling around this area? Do you feel open here and are your hips relaxed?

Simply placing your attention on particular areas of the body without judgment or the intention to force any change will often effectively open and release energy to a healthy level of flow. Dowsing to open this chakra can be quite life-changing, in the sense that you may release unconscious resistance to healthy relationships and abundance in every aspect of your life.

## Parenting

This implies an opportunity to heal relationships between parent and child. This healing will occur in all of your primary relationships, including those with your parents and with your children, as well as your internal relationship with those aspects of yourself. (See chapter 7 for more information on Mother and Father archetypes.)

## Psychic Cords

Energetic cords are created between you and others through your unconscious intention and attention toward one another. Non-beneficial cords are essentially fear-based energy waves that carry patterns like resentment, lust, envy, and the victim-rescuer paradigm. They create unhealthy bonds between family members and lovers based on ego-based entanglement that seeks to validate self-identity. Psychic cords drain your energy and keep you in a fragmented ego-oriented state of being. Clearing cords from the past allows for a healthy relationship to develop.

## Dowsing Statements

With left spin, say:

> *I release all unhealthy patterns around (_____) from (person's) sacral chakra, releasing attachment, reversing ill effects, and healing all relationships implied by these patterns. (Person) allows relationships in all aspects of (his/her) life to flow with trust, respect, love, and creativity.*

# SOLAR PLEXUS

The solar plexus is the core of our relationship with power. When we are in our true power, we are in alignment with Divine Will. Actually, a primary lesson in our incarnations is to get to a point of complete surrender in our need to control anything in our lives. We arrive at a place where we realize how futile all of our attempts have been to avoid change and to control everything and everyone in our lives. Domination, persecution, and victimhood are all blatant examples of power struggles. Addiction as unconscious habitual behavior (addiction to anything, including our thoughts) is perhaps the most common self-perpetuated power game, which ultimately leaves us disempowered.

This area also serves as a gateway between the upper and lower chakras. Keeping it clear of blockages will enhance the function and flow of all other energy centers. Restriction in this area is evident, especially in Western cultures, in the typical trend toward shallow breathing. Practices like yoga, which involve conscious breathing techniques, are very beneficial in opening and maintaining the flow of energy here.

## Attachment to Drama and Judgment

The unconscious creation of dramatic situations in your life serves to keep you powerless. Addiction to drama and judgment guarantee perpetual conflict.

Taking steps to remove yourself from drama-oriented situations and becoming observant of any judgment as it arises in your awareness will result in greater peace. Suffering is eliminated when we practice what Byron Katie calls "investigating our thoughts." Her simple, yet profound, method, called The Work, is based on four simple questions, which are outlined in her book *Loving What Is*.

## Energetic Weapons

Like cords, energetic weapons are symbolic of unhealed relationships. Angry words and thoughts, as well as consciously directed curses and attacks on an individual, may be energetically attached, as in the form of a knife, gunshot wound, etc. In most cases, knowing the exact form of a weapon is not necessary. In some cases, long-standing physical pains resolve when that body area is cleared of a weapon. As noted earlier in this book, psychic weapons may also reflect residue from actual physical events in a person's history through various lifetimes.

## Dowsing Statements

With a left spin, say:

> *I release all unhealed issues around (_____), particularly from my solar plexus, to the Light, releasing attachment, reversing ill effects, and healing all relationships implied by these patterns in all time and dimensions..*

With a right spin, say:

> *I align myself with Divine Will. (This is always appropriate to add to any dowsing statements.)*

With a left spin, say:

> *I release all psychic cords and weapons, cleansing them of fear-based patterns and sending them back to their source with love, forgiveness, and gratitude.*

With a right spin, say:

> *As I align myself with Divine Will, I love and accept myself completely.*

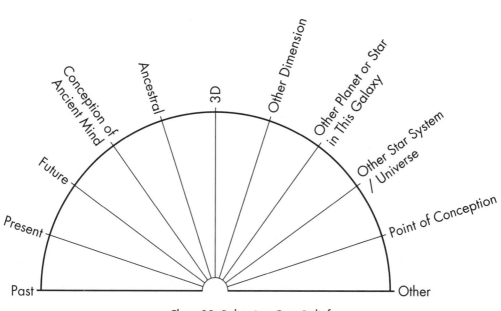

Chart 38. Releasing Core Beliefs

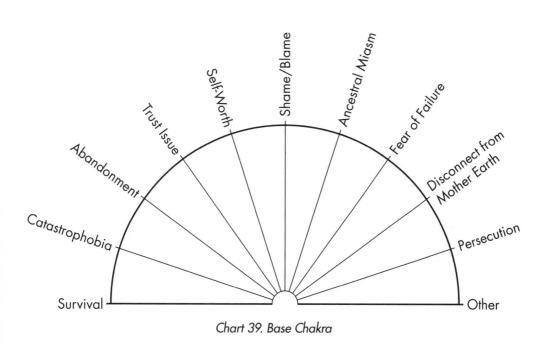

Chart 39. Base Chakra

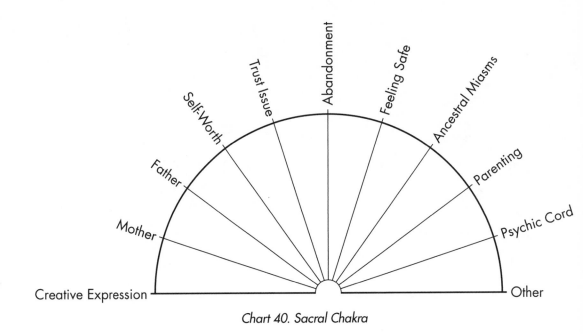

*Chart 40. Sacral Chakra*

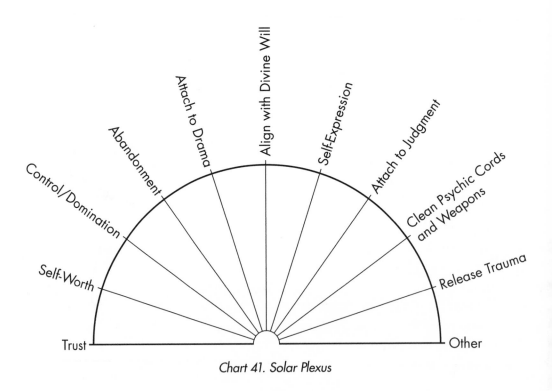

*Chart 41. Solar Plexus*

# CHAPTER 10

# Cleaning the Upper Chakras

OUR CHAKRAS VARY IN VIBRATIONAL RATES. These rates correlate to specific frequencies of energetic information processed through each chakra. The higher the chakra's vertical alignment with the physical body, the higher the vibrational rate of the chakra. This accounts for the association of specific colors with each chakra. Those who are able to see auric fields and chakras physically report that the colors generally range from the lower end of the visible color spectrum—red in the area of the base chakra, all the way to violet at the crown chakra. (See Table 1 for more information on individual chakra properties.)

Each chakra resonates with frequencies that are associated with specific colors, tones, emotional patterns, and physical attributes. This is why we often find positive changes in physical and mental/emotional balance when we remove energetic blockages in a specific chakra. For instance, someone who has a history of stomach-related issues (influenced by the solar plexus) may also have adverse reactions to hearing the note E played on a piano. In this case, the individual may be deficient in that particular tone and may have related energetic blockages in the solar plexus. It is possible that the person's stomach issues could resolve through the clearing of blockages and through dowsing in the E note and all of its benefits to balance that chakra and to bring it into harmony with all other chakras. This is just one example of how powerful the connection is between multi-dimensional resonant energetic patterns.

Just as the lower chakras are very much correlated to our denser vibrational experiences in physical incarnations, the upper chakras process the higher vibrational aspects of our consciousness like information coming through angelic realms, Spirit Guides, and other cosmic channels. Alignment with your higher purpose, connection with your soul mate, accessing your inner vision, and expression of your divine creativity are a few of the areas that are associated with balanced higher chakras.

## HEART CHAKRA

The heart chakra is often considered the center of the chakra system, although for the purposes of this manual, it is added to this chapter on the upper chakras. The heart chakra acts as a gateway to experiencing yourself as whole Spirit in the physical body. The heart vibration resonates with the essence of love, which is our experience of Oneness, of being a perfect aspect of Creation, of flowing from and always being a part of God. To know this is beyond what words can convey.

To connect with and strengthen this center, close your eyes for a moment and place your awareness in the center of your chest. Breathe deeply and rhythmically with the in-breath and the out-breath equally honored by your attention.

The heart and brow chakras assist in generating powerful scalar waves that communicate your essence to the world and allow you to "see" everything and everyone with True Vision. The vision you experience through your heart wave is felt rather than seen, as it is through your physical eyes. Although words cannot really describe this feeling, there is a "knowingness"; with it, you find yourself experiencing a sense of completion, of sameness with your environment and the situations and people around you. The boundaries of your inner and outer worlds dissolve and you have a glimpse of your Self, your Oneness.

The wave emitted from the heart extends exponentially farther than that which is generated from the brow chakra. We are collectively emerging at this time as heart-centered Beings. With this, we are coming to know ourselves as part of One Divine Song. Here are a few statements to help you see what hidden beliefs may be keeping you from this level of heart-centeredness. Create your own statements as well.

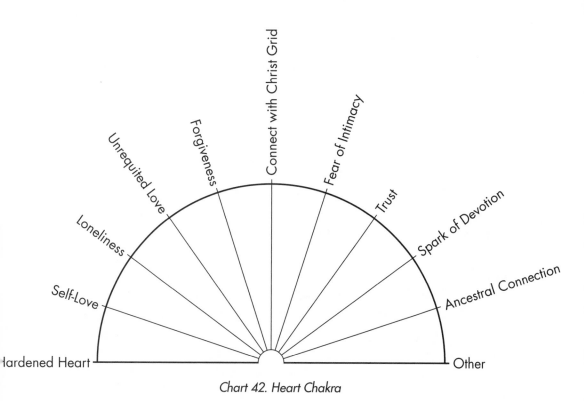

Chart 42. Heart Chakra

## Dowsing Statements

With a left spin, say:

*I release all limiting beliefs around (self-love, loneliness, unrequited love, fear of intimacy, trust, ancestral connection, etc.) held in my heart chakra, transmuting these patterns to Light and healing all relationships implied. I open this center to give and receive love freely.*

With a right spin, say:

*I forgive myself and all others for the belief in separation. In the name of the Divine, I love and accept myself deeply and completely.*

With a left spin, say:

*I release all limiting beliefs that have contributed to a hardened heart, transmuting these patterns to Light, and I open this center to give and receive love freely.*

With a right spin, say:

*I open my heart to connect fully with the (Christ Consciousness Grid, my spark of devotion, etc.), allowing myself to receive and give only love, and to see with True Vision.*

## THROAT CHAKRA

Just as the heart chakra allows you to experience your true essence, the throat chakra is about expressing your divine nature. This chakra rules the cervical vertebrae in the neck (which involve ancestral patterning), and the thyroid and parathyroid (which regulate metabolism, pH balance, and many other functions in the maintenance of physical homeostasis). For instance, if someone is challenged with an acidic physical state, dowsing out blockages in this area can bring pH balance and proper metabolism back. This chakra is also associated with your upper back and shoulders, the lower occipital area of your brain (housing the limbic system, which is a processing center for emotions and the reptilian brain), and your jaw. When working with TMJ pain, you may wish to evaluate this chakra for clearing.

The throat chakra represents your ability to express creatively, to speak and to be your Truth, and to embody true Self-empowerment. Suppression of these traits, which is linked with the constriction of feminine energy, has held this chakra in great imbalance for thousands of years. It is no wonder that many people today have thyroid malfunctions, TMJ pain, and cervical disc disease. Currently, thyroid imbalances are all too common among women. This represents a surfacing of old beliefs long held in this area that must be recognized and released to the Light as a symbol of our return to love.

This return is simply a change in your perceptions. Since giving and receiving are the same, your ability to express yourself creatively is dependent on your ability to give others total freedom to express themselves in their unique creative ways. True Vision allows us to recognize the sameness of us all in Divinity, while appreciating each others' unique expressions as sons and daughters of God. After accessing whatever patterns need to be resolved you may choose from the following sample statements or create your own.

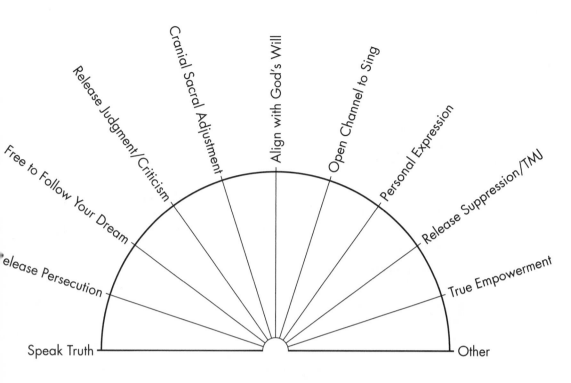

*Chart 43. Throat Chakra*

## Dowsing Statements

With a left spin, say:

> *I release all beliefs held in my throat chakra that have limited me in (speaking truth, releasing persecution, being free to follow my dreams, releasing judgment and criticism, aligning with God's will, opening channels to sing/speak, personal expression, releasing suppression and TMJ, true empowerment, etc.), transmuting these patterns to pure Light in all aspects of myself, for all dimensions and time frames, and healing all relationships implied.*

With a right spin, say:

> *In alignment with Divine Will, I now and forever freely and fully express my creative nature as I release all others from judgment and allow them to express their divine nature fully.*

With a right spin, say:

*I now receive a full cranial-sacral adjustment and all of the benefits this brings.*

## THIRD EYE/BROW CHAKRA

The third eye, or brow chakra, is your portal to alignment with True Vision through corrected perception. While you are here in this experience of duality, you can choose to "be in this world, but not of it." The brow chakra helps you to heal the split mind. It represents your ability to recognize the power of mind, to realize that all of your experiences are reflections of what's in your mind, and to make conscious choices that will change your experience of the illusion.

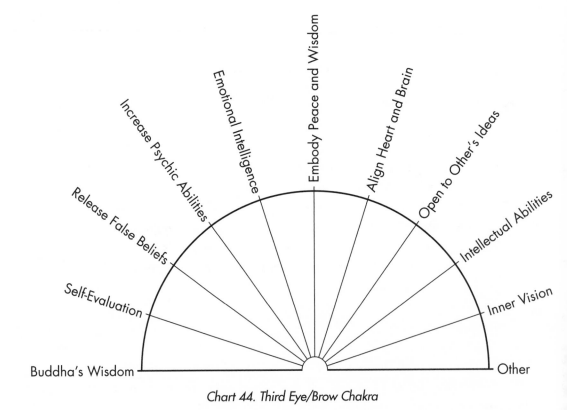

*Chart 44. Third Eye/Brow Chakra*

Advanced Spiritual Dowsing

Mastery of *Maya* (the world of illusion, according to Hindus) occurs through devoting yourself to becoming wholly connected heart, soul, and mind. The Third Eye, or brow chakra, opens your awareness to knowing yourself as a multi-dimensional being within the dream, thus experiencing life in a more expanded way. Ultimately this leads you to recognizing yourself in the state of Oneness. This chakra can best serve you when it is clear of limiting beliefs. You access your inner vision through silence. Meditation, yoga, chanting, conscious breathing, and extended time in Nature are a few practices that can successfully cultivate your ability to silence the mind.

Your sensory experiences of sight, smell, taste, hearing, and feeling through touch are affected by the function of your brow chakra. Brain functions, the pineal and pituitary glands, and the nervous system are associated with this center. Issues in any of these areas—seizures, brain tumors, mental/emotional imbalances, hormonal regulation, and nervous system/sensory problems—can be supported through working with this chakra. (See Table 1 for more information on this chakra.) Here are some sample dowsing statements.

## Dowsing Statements

With a left spin, say:

> *I release all limiting beliefs held in my brow chakra that prevent me in any way from (accessing Buddha's wisdom, releasing false beliefs, true self-evaluation, increasing psychic abilities, accessing emotional intelligence, embodying peace and wisdom, aligning heart and brain, opening to other's ideas, accessing intellectual abilities, knowing true inner vision, etc.) on all levels of my being. I transmute these patterns to pure Light energy in the most appropriate structure to use for my highest purpose. (Note: it is OK to "piggyback" a "removal" intention, which is usually a left spin function, on top of a a right spin statement. The "dowsing system" knows your intent and will work with your particular approach or style.)*

With a right spin, say:

> *I devote myself to seeing with True Vision, to harmonizing my heart/brain connection, and to assisting others in recognizing their Light as they are touched by the radiance of my own recognition.*

# CROWN CHAKRA

The meeting of Heaven and Earth is experienced through the crown chakra. Inspiration, access to higher states of awareness, connection with those aspects of consciousness that we call angels, Ascended Masters, and our Spirit Guides are associated with this chakra. Accessing higher dimensional aspects of Self is available through focusing on bringing in Light through the crown chakra. As you connect with a broader experience of Self (without judging or attaching to the experience), you begin to have a sense of how limitless your nature is.

It is said that our souls are connected to our bodies via a silver cord that comes into the body through the crown chakra. This cord extends downward through the entire body and all chakras, keeping the soul grounded in the third dimension. If the soul chooses to travel outside the body (called astral travel) during sleep or deep meditation, the silver cord provides a pathway back to the body when the journey is finished. Children especially may sometimes have a difficult time reuniting with the body after this type of travel. Perhaps this is because they are still young in their current incarnations and may need their memories jogged to recall the intricacies of balancing their physical and etheric-realm experiences.

A note on this: If a sleeping infant or child suddenly demonstrates a fitful or fearful state and cannot seem to awaken fully, you may want to assess this possibility. Simply ask if the child is stuck in another dimension. If so, bring them back into the body. Here are some statements that may help.

## Dowsing Statements

With a right spin, say:

> With the assistance of Archangel Michael, I now bring (name) fully back into his/her body with the silver cord through the crown chakra, brow chakra, throat chakra, heart chakra, solar plexus, sacral chakra, and base chakra, and securely ground and connect him/her with the Earth chakras and Gaia. I release all fear-based patterns and energetic attachments from (name's) entire being and the silver cord. (Name) is now a fully connected soul in body, and is centered and surrounded by a field of pure white Light that allows only love-sourced vibrational patterns to flow in and out.

This statement will help clear the crown chakra. With a left spin, say:

*I release all limiting beliefs held in my crown chakra that prevent me from (balancing sensitivities, experiencing faith and courage, experiencing divine Self, releasing fear-based patterns, integrating spirit and matter, accepting golden light, aligning all chakras to my master chakra, releasing depression and anxiety, opening to inspiration, devotion, and trust, etc.) and open to full realization of Self.*

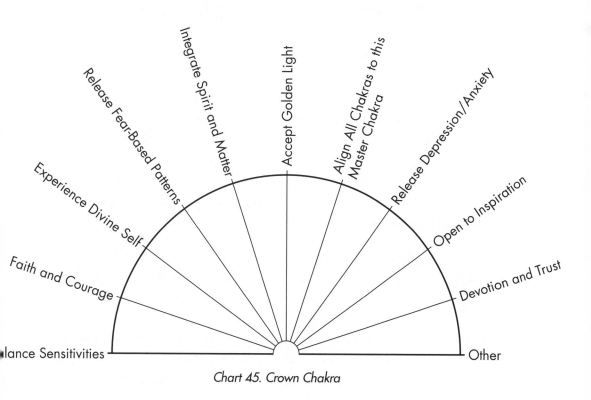

*Chart 45. Crown Chakra*

# CHAPTER 11

# Dissolving the Illusion

THERE IS A SOURCE OF ALL THAT is that some variously call God, the Divine, Creator, etc. The name you use is irrelevant. In fact, our very use of words supports the illusion that we are somehow separate from each other and from that Source.

Our collective experience of life has been based on what *A Course in Miracles* calls "a tiny mad idea" or a momentary impulse within the Mind of God in which the question "What would it be like to experience individuation?" arose.

As an aspect of God's Creation, we, as One Mind, created the experience of separation. To truly pull this off, we needed to momentarily "forget" that we are part of the Whole. We, as a creative extension of God's love, constructed a masterful plan to experience individuation in all possible ways that we could conceive. This "dream" was orchestrated through the aspect of Mind that chose to shut down its awareness of Truth. This is what we call the "split" Mind. We chose momentary amnesia, forgetting that we are inseparable from God. Our forgetfulness does not in any way change the truth of our Oneness and is in no way "sin." It is simply one possible creative experience from an infinite Source of creativity.

The ego is nothing more than a collection of thoughts that is compiled to project an image of a separate self. You see, in truth, there is no ego. It's just a bunch of meaningless thoughts that perpetuate a façade in this game we play.

All that we call energy, time, space, and bodies (including all aspects of these) are simply part of this imagined or dreamed state. "Stress" is a point of resistance in the creative energy flow. There is always an internal conflict in our maintenance of the lie that we are separate. Thus we are in continuous states of stress due to this self-perpetuated resistance to remembering our Oneness with God. *It's time to awaken!*

## TIME, SPACE, AND BODIES

The good news is that, to awaken from this dream of limitation, all it takes on your part is 1 percent willingness to want to see with True Vision. Your physical eyes will still see this world, but your perception or experience of everything will be different. As you go about debunking the illusion, you begin to feel more whole and unified with others. Peace and "causeless joy" emerge within you and radiate outward. These qualities are then reflected back to you in your relationships and environment. Change your inner world first to see changes in your outer world.

My friends, the war is over. You can let down your guard and simply allow resistance to experiencing life fully in each moment to dissolve. Since you created the ideas of time, space, and bodies, you can shift patterns around your experience of them to serve the highest good. Release attachment to old fixed patterns and ideas and allow yourself to flow passionately in the stream of life. Here are a few sample dowsing statements.

### Dowsing Statements

Refer to Chart 46 for specifics. Begin by saying:

> *I release all patterns around (ego attachment, attachment to the past, belief in limitation, resistance in my conscious and unconscious awareness to this devotion to corrected perception and increased awareness of infinity, etc.). I choose to see things differently and forgive my belief in separation, with associated benefits on all levels of my being. I choose to learn all lessons through love.*

With a right spin, say:

> *I broadcast into my conscious and unconscious awareness this devotion to corrected perception (increased awareness of infinity, I choose*

*to see things differently, I forgive our belief in separation) with all the associated benefits on all levels of my being. I choose to learn all lessons through awareness of love.*

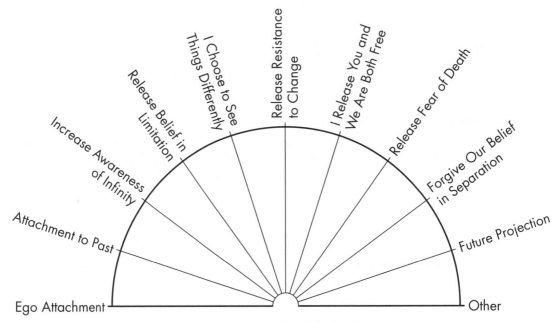

Chart 46. Time, Space, and Bodies

## RELEASING ILLNESS

All illness is reflective of a split mind. There is no judgment in this; it is simply part of the collective agreement to experience separation. Nothing is personal here. Do not get caught in the trap of blaming yourself for any experience you are having. Being ill or not has no relevance to your level of spiritual awakening. As long as we are in these bodies, we are working for the whole in creating a variety of lessons that ultimately lead us back to Truth.

Your nighttime sleep state is symbolic of the collective dream we have created. When you fall asleep in the evening, you know you will awaken at some point. In the same way, it is destined that we will collectively awaken from illusion. Imagine a morning when you flow seductively in and out of a dream state before fully awakening. You wouldn't beat yourself up over taking your time awakening or for any of the things that happened in your dreams, would you?

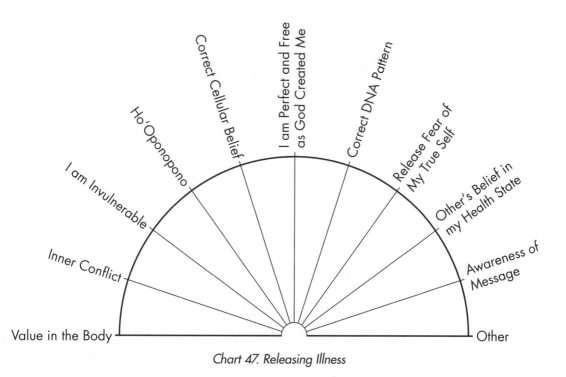

*Chart 47. Releasing Illness*

Sometimes, we have lucid dreams in which we realize that we are dreaming while in the dream state. At this point, we are able to change the parameters of the dream as we like. The key here is to learn to *live lucidly*. (Check out a great little book called *Lucid Living*, Hay House 2005, by Timothy Freke.) Once you understand that you are in the driver's seat, you can change the direction of your route if it is no longer desirable.

Here are a few descriptions of the ideas in Table 2 to help you better understand the intricate web you weave that may be part of holding you "stuck" in the experience of illness. Dowsing this chart may completely release the patterns of illness, or may provide a great adjunct to any other treatment you are using. Use whatever tools you have to release stress in your life.

## Value in the Body

We keep our focus limited to the body. Let's face it, illness is a great distraction that will keep you stuck on trying to "fix" yourself, not offering you much time for silence and peace.

## I am Invulnerable

There is nothing and no one who can change the truth of who you are. You are never a victim. This reading reminds you of what is always so.

## Ho'oponopono

This reading is a suggestion to practice this powerful technique in your healing process. Imagine that you are face to face with yourself. Repeat the phrases noted earlier in this book until you feel a sense of peace arise. It may be advantageous to incorporate this technique in your daily activities until you have reclaimed your health, or have found peace in your current situation.

## Dowsing Statements

Consult Chart 47. With a left spin, say:

> *I release all patterns associated with (value in the body, inner conflict, fear of my true Self, other's beliefs in my health state) on all levels of my being for all time frames and dimensions. I correct DNA and cellular memory to now hold only healthful, loving light vibrations.*

With a right spin, say:

> *I broadcast into my awareness on all levels (I am invulnerable, I am perfect and free as God created me, etc.), and I am open and ready to receive the message of this illness so that I may let it go.*

# ADDICTIONS

In general, we think about addictions in terms of substance abuse, eating disorders, and other destructive behavioral traits. We all are addicted to one thing or another, however. And as a whole, we are addicted to the illusion. The form of addiction is basically irrelevant. This does not mean that taking other measures to change the addictive behavior is not appropriate. In the case of unhealthy relationships with drugs, alcohol, and food, for instance, it may serve the individual well to follow some proven beneficial standards like a 12-step program's basic advice to remove yourself from people, places, and events that trigger the addictive behavior.

The primary cause of addiction is always associated with the internal conflict between ego and the recognition of your true identity, regardless of whether it is an ancestral hand-me-down behavior like alcoholism or some other pattern. Beliefs create biochemical changes in the body and cause negative DNA mutations. (Read Bruce Lipton's *Biology of Belief*.) Ancestral patterns can be changed through changing your beliefs at the level of the unconscious mind.

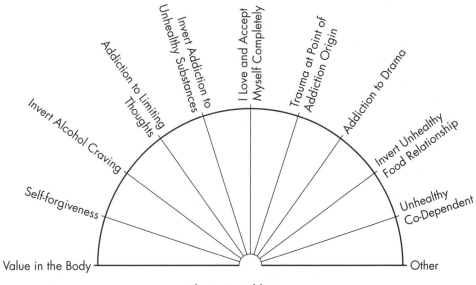

*Chart 48. Addictions*

## Dowsing Statements

With a left spin, say:

> *I now release all limiting patterns associated with (value in the body, self-forgiveness, addiction to limiting thoughts, trauma at point of addiction origin, addiction to drama, unhealthy co-dependency, etc.) on all levels of my being. I release attachment, reversing ill effects and healing all relationships implied by these patterns.*

With a right spin, say:

> *I now (invert alcohol craving, invert addiction to unhealthy substance, love and accept myself completely, invert unhealthy food relationships,*

*etc.) on all levels of my being and accept all benefits therein, accepting this as corrected perception. I transmute all previously limiting beliefs in this area to love.*

## LIMITING BELIEFS HELD IN THE BODY

We literally hold traumatic memories and limiting beliefs as energetic patterns throughout the physical body and in other areas of our energy fields. Until you recognize and release this built-up energy, it acts as an attractor field, bringing resonant experiences to you that trigger the same emotions and feelings. It is not the form of a situation that is important in these repetitive life challenges, but the content. It is always the underlying emotionally charged feelings that play the same record continuously in our lives.

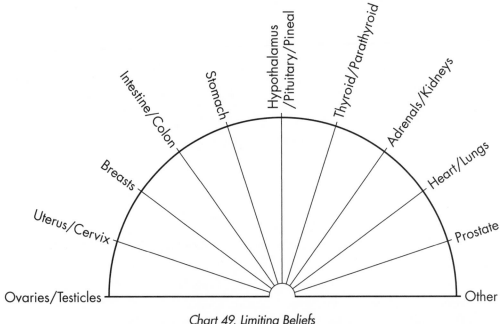

*Chart 49. Limiting Beliefs*

For instance, perhaps you have had a sequence of partners throughout your life that appeared to be completely different from one another initially. However, as each relationship matured, you found that the same problems seemed to surface. Your partners are simply providing you with perfect mirrors to see what lies unhealed within you. This works both ways. To clarify the content provided by these reflections, observe what emotions and feelings arise when familiar problems repeat.

As you commit yourself more and more to taking complete responsibility for *all* of your experiences, you gradually heal these hidden issues. Then, you see the "right" relationship come into your life. This happens, of course, as a result of creating the "right" relationship with your Self and then seeing it mirrored back to you through your partner. In other words, looking for a thread of similar patterns throughout your life can lead you to discover whatever hidden unhealed emotional patterns and limiting beliefs have been attracting the "same old, same old" into your reality.

## Hidden Beliefs Held within the Body

This chart offers ten possible areas in the body where you may be storing limiting beliefs. I encourage you to create your own charts as well, with areas of the body and energetic fields represented. Take, for instance, the spine.

We store a lot of memories along the spine and at the base of the occipital skull area. Along the spine, you may find correlations like these:

Ancestral patterns are often linked with the cervical vertebrae in the neck.

The area where the lower thoracic and upper lumbar regions meet (near the diaphragm) often holds on to old traumas.

The mid-thoracic region (upper back and chest area) can be associated with unresolved grief and lost love.

Lower spinal pain and weakness may be related to how supported and safe you feel and how able you are to maintain a flexible yet strong life structure.

The tailbone may hold in various fear-based memories from personal and collective catastrophes accumulated through eons.

You can find more information about emotions stored in the body in Caroline Myss's and Louise Hay's many published books on this topic.

Certain organs are also associated with, but not limited to, specific patterns. Here are a few examples:

Ovaries/testes relate to creativity and fertility in all areas of life.

Uterus/cervix relate to cultivation of the creative nature, nurturance, and the birthing processes.

Breasts relate to self-love and acceptance, and bonding.

Intestines/colon relate to relationship with the mother.

Stomach relates to the ability to accept and process life experiences.

Hypothalamus/pituitary/pineal glands relate to higher levels of understanding, cosmic and Higher-Self connection, and inner vision.

Thyroid/parathyroid relate to being and speaking in divine alignment, and the expression of your creative nature.

Adrenals/kidneys relate to life force and primal fear patterns.

Heart/lungs relate to love, trust, and unresolved grief.

Prostate relates to self-expression, integrity, strength, and courage.

When one of these choices comes up during a dowsing session, you may choose to access more information by asking concise questions regarding the nature of a limiting pattern.

## Dowsing Statements

Using the heart and lungs as a dowsed choice, you may want to ask a few additional yes or no questions: Is the pattern held in the heart? Is it held in the lungs? In both the heart and lungs? Next, ascertain whether the pattern involves beliefs around love, trust, and/or unresolved grief. Now, see if there is a core point in time which, if accessed, may help in releasing the pattern—some specific date in past, present, or future life. Use time travel to access the exact date that will best release the pattern.

With a left spin, say:

*I go back to (date) and bring all traumas and patterns associated with the limiting beliefs that I have been holding in (body area) to zero point, transmuting these patterns now to the most appropriate energy structure that will support my highest good. I reverse all ill effects and heal all relationships implied.*

With a right spin, say:

*I now realign myself with life-enhancing acceptance of my true nature as an invulnerable, perfect creation of God's love. My body now heals itself with ease and grace.*

Note: It is often not necessary to access additional information (as we did here) in order to clear a belief pattern. It is a personal preference. You may simply go right to the left-spin statement above and leave out the date while releasing the pattern.

# CHAPTER 12

# Multi-Dimensionality

THE WAY WE EXPERIENCE SOMETHING or how we choose to perceive things either leads us to awareness of our wholeness or perpetuates the dream for us. You expand your awareness when you let go of fixed ideas and attachment to what you have created as your identity. The more you dissolve self-imposed limitations, the greater your ability to entertain the possibility that perhaps the truth of you is beyond your wildest dreams.

When we talk about multi-dimensionality, we push our awareness outside the three-dimensional box. Dimensions categorize aspects of consciousness through the specific vibrational rate they hold. Consciousness includes all of what we call matter and everything else. Scientifically, we know that everything is energy and therefore vibrates.

To simplify this idea of dimensions, let's look at this example. Take a block of ice. It has a certain density and weight—you wouldn't want to drop it on your foot. Once you take the ice and melt it in a pan, it becomes water—it is less dense and less heavy. As the heat continues, the water evaporates. The heat speeds up the vibrational movement of the water molecules and atoms. As this occurs, the ice changes to water and then evaporates. You could say that the transformation of ice into evaporated water is similar to a dimensional shift.

⚹ The faster the vibration, the higher the dimension.

⚹ The slower the vibration the lower the dimension.

We are not limited by the bodies we see or the thoughts and emotions we experience. When you are in a deep state of meditation, for instance, you actually vibrate at a faster rate, thus accessing a higher dimensional aspect of experience. On some level, we are all experiencing every aspect of consciousness, every dimension, at all times. We are just not always aware of this.

Through dowsing these charts, you can explore these other areas of your consciousness to see where you are ready to make a change or to create a shift. Energy patterns that are "stuck," on whatever level, create density and slow your overall vibration. This applies even if the pattern is at, let's say, a sixth-dimensional aspect of your being. When you release these patterns and allow the movement of energy to resume in a natural flow, you often feel "lighter."

## NINE-DIMENSIONAL ALCHEMY

This chart is based on Barbara Hand Clow's book, *Alchemy of Nine Dimensions,* *(Hampton Road, 2010),* which provides an interesting dimensional model. It allows you to connect with whatever vibrational aspect of consciousness holds a key for you in this moment. As with all of the charts in this book, you are encouraged to use them creatively. Here are two ways you can work with this chart:

✳ You can use this as a stand-alone chart to discover what dimensional aspect of your self calls for more awareness of it. See the descriptions below to get a sense about the essence of each one so that, as you are broadcasting a specific dimensional frequency into your awareness, you can ponder the attributes of that dimension.

✳ When you are working with any issue, you can ask if there is a specific dimension listed in the chart that offers the best opportunity to access a release of the situation.

Although the dimensions seem to have distinct vibrational rates and attributes, there is an orchestration of all dimensions and all time frames playing in resonance all the time. It may help to imagine a vertical column of light moving seamlessly through all of these dimensions, from the first to the ninth. Accessing more awareness in any of the dimensions expands your experience of all of them. Here are a few attributes of each dimension.

### First Dimension

This dimension encompasses the crystalline core of the Earth. It acts as a conduit to anchor in the light all the way from the center of the galaxy. We are transmuting from carbon-based to more silicon-based beings, becoming more crystalline in our structure. Earth really is our Mother in many ways, and connection to the first dimension reinforces our relationship with her.

## Second Dimension

This dimension is represented by Earth's mantle. This dimension provides the biosphere for elementals (fairies, gnomes, elves, etc.) and primordial life forms. Organisms like bacteria and viruses have their origin here. Whenever you are dowsing an illness related to these life forms, it's helpful to thank them for whatever message they have brought you and to send them back to the second dimension. This dimension is also home to the mineral kingdom.

## Third Dimension

This is where the physical and non-physical worlds intersect. The third dimension is linear by nature. However, our experience in physical bodies is expanding to one that will be non-linear. We are experiencing what may be called a "descension" of expanded consciousness into physical form, or becoming Light beings.

## Fourth Dimension

Thoughts, emotions, collective consciousness, and the astral plane are sourced in this dimension. This is where information from higher vibrational dimensions is "stepped down" in frequency to dualistic concepts. To become more aware of your thoughts and emotions and their interaction with your body in the form of feelings greatly increases your ability to experience multi-dimensionality. Being absolutely present in the moment is key to accessing awareness of multi-vibrational states concurrently. Conscious breathing is also of primary importance.

## Fifth Dimension

The vibration of love—the Christ Consciousness Grid—is accessible here. This dimension is assigned to an extraterrestrial race called the Pleiadians, who resonate at this vibrational level and who will assist you to access this state when asked. This is the natural vibrational state of the heart. As we become more heart-centered, we are moving toward a fifth-dimensional state of being.

## Sixth Dimension

This is the dimension of sacred geometry. Here, higher vibrations of sound and light begin to create matter through geometrical form. We see repeated patterns throughout Nature that show us the pureness of these original structures, like those seen in the base of pinecones and in crystalline frozen-water patterns. Yoga is one way to use your physical structures to access this dimension. Choose a position and focus your attention on the space around you. Allow your physical boundaries to dissolve in your awareness. You will be able to have a sense of connecting with this dimensional vibration.

## Seventh Dimension

Light waves from the eighth dimension are slowed down in vibration here, creating sound waves. Vocal toning and chanting, sacred singing, and using musical instruments put you in touch with this aspect of your being. Powerful physical, mental, and emotional shifts occur with the conscious use of sound and light.

## Eighth Dimension

Light is structured at this level and moves through all other dimensions, creating endless forms. Your physical structure is based on an invisible light grid and your meridians are points of intersection on this grid. Your chakras work as light-information channels. The primary function of your DNA is to receive and transmit light information throughout the body.

## Ninth Dimension

The center of the galaxy pulses time waves outward, projecting what consciousness has created as a time/space experience. Our solar system is currently aligning with the center and will be in full alignment in the future. At that time, it is predicted that reality as we have known it will shift to an entirely different experience.

## Dowsing Statements

With a right spin, say:

*I broadcast the vibration of (dimension) and all the benefits associated with this dimension into all aspects of my awareness. I fully integrate this awareness and use it for the highest good of all.*

With a left spin, say:

*I release all patterns associated with the issue of (\_\_\_\_\_) from all aspects of my being in (dimension), releasing resonant patterns from all other dimensions and time frames, reversing ill effects, and healing all relationships implied.*

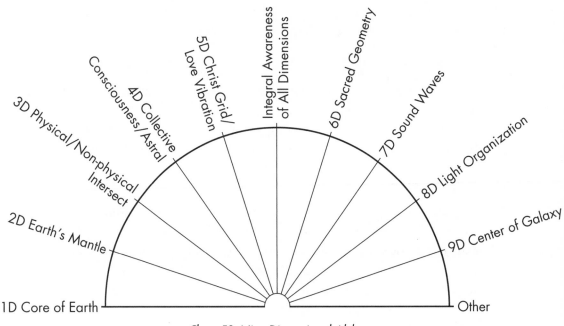

*Chart 50. Nine-Dimensional Alchemy*

## MULTI-DIMENSIONALITY

It is our perception that determines how large or how small we are living. As you allow yourself to break free from the self-limiting confines that you have established, you are free to live life truer to your natural state as an unlimited creative being. Based on measured gravitational field parameters, scientists agree that we are aware of only ten percent of the matter in our universe. Interestingly, this is the same percentage associated with the degree of conscious awareness utilized in our minds—at best, only ten percent.

Could there be a correlation? You betcha! When we talk about becoming more multi-dimensional, we refer to the inevitable expansion of what we experience through our senses and our minds. The more we open our minds to other possibilities, the quicker we activate more of our potential. Even as you read this book, there has been an exponential increase (which has been going on since at least 1999) in people awakening their extrasensory perceptions through clairaudience, clairvoyance, and other paranormal means. Prior to this time, these skills were accessed by a rare few. This is a reflection of our emerging collective awareness of multiple dimensions. This chart offers you various keys to expanding your consciousness to tap into the 90 percent of your potential that you haven't realized yet. Imagine that! Here are some of the choices that warrant further discussion.

## Allowance

Miracles are natural and happen all the time when we *allow* for them. Just get out of the way! Saying yes to your life experiences and releasing resistance opens you to infinite possibilities. When you limit yourself through the values you hold about what you think life should look like in order to be happy, you are surviving rather than thriving. Let yourself break free and see what happens!

## Heart-to-Brain Connection

In a healthy state, there is a bi-directional energy flow between the heart and the brain. Both generate powerful scalar waves that create portals for multidimensional communication. A scalar wave holds a field of pure potentiality that provides a powerful carrier wave once clear intention is applied. Conditioning based on traumas and other variables can form an energetic blockage that needs to be cleared in this connection. When your heart-to-brain connection is open, you generate an enormous coherent energy field around you.

## Enhance DNA Light Communication

Your DNA serves as a powerful light receiver and transmitter. Mutations resulting from suppressed emotions and toxic beliefs "dirty" this capability. Clean them up! Scientists have proven the relationship between emotions, thoughts, and our DNA. As we become more conscious of the choices we are making with our thoughts and associated emotions, our DNA is able to release old patterns and create new ones.

## Surrender Beliefs

This is the ultimate tool. We surrender our beliefs to the Divine, realizing the meaninglessness of thoughts that are based on past conditioning. When you surrender beliefs, you state your desire and willingness to correct these misperceptions of Self.

## Increase Vibrational Resonance

The higher your vibration, the more expanded your awareness.

## Silence the Mind

Your ego default program is designed to keep your mind busy with chatter in order to continue the façade of a small limited self. We call this the "monkey" mind. It is a problem-maker by nature and is relentlessly active. Creating a daily practice to silence your mind for at least twenty minutes twice a day (and as often as possible) is essential to attaining peace in your life. You can dowse up your desire, passion, and ability to do so.

## Activate Kundalini

This "twin-serpent" energy moves up your spine, activating and aligning your chakras and awakening you to superconscious awareness. Cosmic energy descending into your crown chakra meets with this Earthly energy to create a vessel for the divine marriage of Spirit in matter.

## Dowsing Statements

With a right spin, say:

*I now enhance and increase (allowance, heart-to-brain connection) in all aspects of my being, expanding my awareness of multi-dimensionality and my spiritual growth.*

With a right spin, say:

*I now (all other choices), accepting all benefits therein as I intentionally enhance and increase my awareness of multi-dimensional states, which leads me toward ultimate knowledge of infinite Self.*

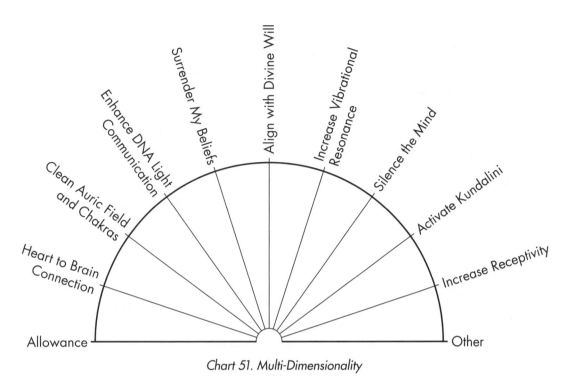

Chart 51. Multi-Dimensionality

## THE AKASHIC RECORDS

The Akashic Records are the comprehensive story of consciousness. They hold all information of everything that ever was, is, or will be experienced within the dream. Every relationship you have or will ever have, all of your karma—all ancestral patterns, agreements, vows, and contracts—are held within these records. Therefore, when you are ready to release old patterns, release some karma, or heal and complete a relationship, you may want to access these records and clean them up here and there.

It is the fear-based patterns that change. You can bring them to completion and literally change the path or direction of your life in this way. Since everything is your own creation at the level of mind, all you have to do is change your mind to rewrite the script. Why not live a happy dream while in it? Why not create peace in your life so that you can see beyond the dream? The greatest gift in this is that you are able to prove to yourself again how easily changes can be made, thus showing the illusory quality of what you have been calling reality.

This directs you toward true knowledge beyond the understanding of this world. What you are doing on an energetic level is accessing a certain point of information in the time/space continuum. Quantum science shows that, once we observe something, it changes. Using your conscious intention combined with the pendulum spin, you interfere with that wave (accessed information) and create another reality. It's really simple and effective. Here are explanations for some of these chart choices.

## Psychic Cords

As noted in Chart 40, these are fear-based energetic cords that hold unhealthy attachments in relationships. Releasing them allows the relationship to heal, regardless of what form it takes.

## Reprogram Current Incarnation

We make agreements and structure our life paths based on chosen lessons that provide us with forgiveness opportunities to help in our awakening. You can, at any time, change your mind and rewrite the script.

## Etheric Implants

These are energetic devices that hold some kind of programming in place. They can be implanted in the physical or etheric bodies. At some level, you have agreed to these implants somewhere along your chosen life paths. This reading implies that the implants no longer serve your highest good. It is now appropriate to remove them.

## Release Attachment to Separate Lifetimes

If you are still holding on to any unfinished business from other lifetimes, you may be limiting yourself in the current one. Since form never matters and we are always offered repeated opportunities in various forms to resolve the same old patterns (the content or unhealed theme), letting go of other lifetime issues doesn't negate your ability to heal the core issue. You will get another chance. On the other hand, releasing perceived unfinished business may be all you need do to resolve whatever issues you were working on. None hold importance.

## Disconnect from Soul Family

We are each part of what is called a soul group or soul family. Even as we are all equally part of One Creator, we do have what seems to be a unique essence or energetic signature. We resonate with others who have a similar signature and whose chosen lessons and contributions to the whole are aligned closely with our own. You are part of a group or family in this way. Often, your ancestors and family members are part of this soul family as well.

For various reasons, you may become disconnected from your soul family, which results in a sense of discordance and fragmentation. Reconnecting with the family can make a difference in your sense of belonging and feeling supported.

## Unfulfilled Life Purpose

We all hold an internal desire to complete whatever lessons and accomplishments we came into each incarnation to achieve. Ultimately, they are all designed to assist us in awakening to full Self-realization. We accomplish this through the function of forgiveness and the extension of love. Wherever you hold guilt over what you did or didn't do, you are keeping yourself from fulfilling your true purpose of returning to the awareness of yourself as Love.

## Fragmented Soul

In the plan to experience individuation, we forget that we are part of the whole and believe ourselves to be separate. We play out various roles in what seem to be different lifetimes. Yet this is all within the same dream. You may choose to incarnate into separate forms in what appears to be the same time frame in order to offer yourself an accelerated spiritual growth opportunity. As you project more division, you may come to experience yourself as more fragmented. Although this is not true in reality, within the dream, it becomes yet another veil over your awareness. You can bring these fragmented soul aspects together to experience yourself as more whole and unified.

## Guided Visualization

Add a guided visualization to the dowsing set-up for this chart if it feels right to you. Once you have accessed the issue at hand, imagine yourself walking up a path and through a door into the Hall of Akashic Records. Now ask the Record Keeper to bring to you whatever book holds the history of this issue for you. Open to the appropriate page/pages and, while dowsing the issue, see the Record Keeper stamping those pages "complete." This liberates you and all relationships that have ever or will ever be affected by this issue.

Albert Einstein noted that our imagination is far more powerful than our intellect. Why not put it to good use?

## Dowsing Statements

With a left spin, say:

> *With gratitude, I assist as the Record Keeper stamps "complete" on every page that holds the history around this issue of (___). I willingly let go of attachment to this, releasing myself and all others affected by this belief pattern. All associated contracts, vows, and agreements are completed.*

With a right spin, say:

> *Through Divine Grace and forgiveness, all relationships involved are healed and unified. I now create love-based lessons and experiences that fulfill my ultimate purpose for the highest good of all.*

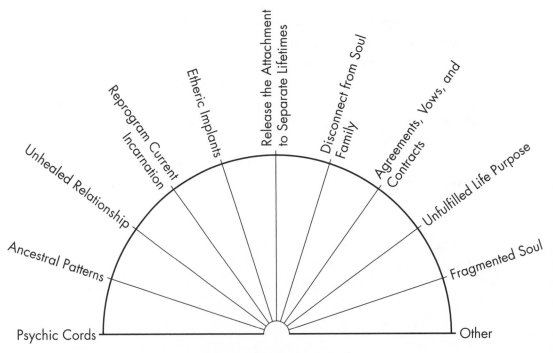

*Chart 52. The Akashic Records*

# INDIVIDUATED EXPERIENCE

Can you recall an earlier time and place in your life when you felt most at home? This memory may invoke a sense of belonging and the recollection that you were comfortable with yourself at that time. Perhaps it seems that that time in life was simpler or less chaotic. You may not have a memory from this life that satisfies those feelings, but you may have found that certain places, people, and situations give you a sense of familiarity—of being "at home." Within this dream, it seems that the more we fragment something, the greater the sense of chaos and disorder that arises.

We all seek stability and comfort. The more major life changes we have in a short period of time, the less secure we are apt to feel. This may also be true in the unconscious memories of various parallel lifetimes. It is likely that you are drawn by some sort of resonant longing to a place of comfort—perhaps the first or primary point of your experience as an individuated soul, or the first recalled incarnation of imagined separation. You may have an associated sense of being closer to God at that point. This is, of course, illusory, since the separation never occurred.

If you are drawn to work with this chart in a session, it implies that there may be something gained from discovering a primal point of connection within the dream. This discovery may open for you a reconnection with some family members you didn't know you had. Once you discover the primary point of origin, you can choose to go further on your own through intentionally connecting with other beings from that realm. It may serve you well to ask if there are any of these family members who can assist you as Spirit Guides.

So much has been written in New Age literature on the specific locations noted in this chart that I feel individual explanations are not necessary. Please explore further on the Internet or in New Age books if you feel called to. I will mention that there is no hierarchy of importance here—no one location or realm is more important than another. If you get Other Dimensional as a reading, you can go further and access the specific dimension. If you get Other Universe or Other Star System, use your creativity by asking more questions to attain more information if you desire.

## Dowsing Statements

With a right spin, say:

*I increase my receptivity to connection with (____) in all ways that would serve the highest good of all, bringing any memories that would best serve me to surface in my conscious mind. I open myself to communication with other divinely aligned beings from this realm. I activate the positive aspects of myself that this realm represents.*

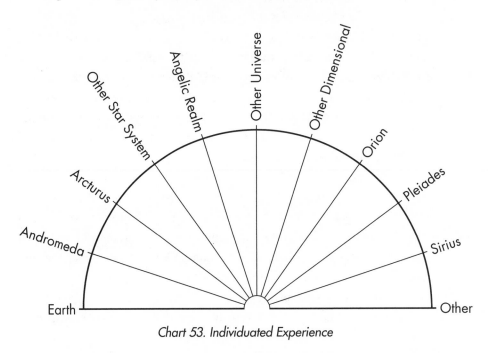

*Chart 53. Individuated Experience*

# CHAPTER 13

# Unconditional Love

WE ARE MOVING INTO THE "HEART" OF THE MATTER now. This is it, folks—all we are ever seeking is unconditional love. The game as we have been playing it has been set up actually to prevent us from this goal. We have created the dream to experience separation, right? So, in the ego mind, the point has never been to realize that our very nature is unconditional love, because that would interfere with our experience of individuation. We have set up the illusion that love is something we need to attain, a goal that we need aspire to reach. Our focus has been on seeking this outside of ourselves through relationships. The truth is that there is nothing outside of yourself that you need to attain and nothing you need achieve. There is *nothing* outside of yourself.

To "have" and to "be" are one and the same. If you wish to experience unconditional love in your life, just find out where you have not allowed yourself the experience. What and who have you been using as scapegoats to keep you from discovering the truth about yourself? It all comes down to how much Self-love you are ready to accept. Your ego—remember, it is nothing more than a compilation of thoughts you have used to make a self-image—is supported through your relationships. Within the dream, this is also how we co-create together. It would be more accurate to say "co-project" together. Remember the play in which you are writer, director, producer, actors, and audience? You develop characters through their relationships with one another. Through the use of archetypal behaviors, the characters develop into various identities. There are good guys and bad guys, victims, perpetrators and rescuers, whores and Madonnas—the list goes on.

This is what we create for one another. We project onto others whatever we unconsciously want them to be for us, all in an effort to solidify our self-identities. For instance, you may (unconsciously) project neediness onto your partners, children, and clients to establish your sense of importance. This projection comes from your illusory sense of a separate self, so you are always projecting partial, lacking qualities that are mirrored back to you through your relationships. You see, this always reinforces your belief that the world (and you) are lacking, suffering, incomplete. It serves to perpetuate the ego's never-ending game of pretending to seek love.

All you need to do is realize the game you have been playing, forgive yourself and everyone else for making it up to begin with, and live more lucidly. There is only one question and one answer. The question is: What am I? The answer is always: Love. Whether you or someone else seems to be in a state of love or seeking love in the moment, the appropriate response is always the same—just *love*. That's what makes it unconditional. These charts will help direct you to whatever you have been using to hide love.

## BLOCKAGES TO SELF-RELATIONSHIP

There is an endless stream of possibilities in what we unconsciously create as distractions that keep us from knowing our Selves. How do you know when you are using something or someone to block your relationship with your Self? Check your internal peace meter and be honest with yourself. Imagine a meter placed in your body somewhere with a gauge that measures from zero to 10. Create a habit of checking in on the reading frequently. A number that represents your level of peace in a given moment will appear in your mind. Know that, if it is anything less than 10, you are not truly at peace. Rather than trying to force a change, all you need do is ask yourself what it would be like if your peace meter read 10 right now. Your observation and curiosity will create a phase shift and you will most likely see a change. Your mind is a powerful tool. Your willingness to use your mind and make new choices is 'you' at your most powerful expression.

### Addictions

Addictions are a perfect distraction to keep you from peace, to keep your ego intact, and to ensure that you not love yourself. Actually, the guilt that usually accompanies addictive patterns is what holds the unconscious behavior in place. It doesn't matter if you are the one who is addicted to something, or if you are using someone else's addictions to keep yourself from peace. And the form of addiction doesn't really matter, since the underlying purpose is the same. Either way, you are using the energetic pattern of addiction to keep yourself distracted from truth.

## Unhealthy Romantic, Workaholic, Punishing the Body, Worry about Others

These are all specialized areas of addiction. Simply assess whether you are thinking and acting in a truly loving manner in each of these areas.

## Eternal Busyness

It's very easy to justify why you are so busy all the time. It may be your children, work, social commitments, a sick mother, etc. We are all 100 percent responsible for how we are experiencing life and we create what we want to in our lives. We are not victims of *any* circumstances. In order to become Self-realized or have a loving peaceful relationship with Self, you need times of silence in every day. Make no mistake about it—if you are not creating the space for some silence, it is because your ego nature is resisting your awakening.

## Self Righteousness

Being firm in your convictions is another way to say that you are being judgmental, and this is an energy blockage.

## Over-Intellectualization

Another way to say this is that you are over-analyzing. This is born of the ego and sustains its identity. An old saying comes to mind: "Analysis is paralysis." Practice allowing yourself to have experiences without quantifying or qualifying them.

## Punishing the Body

The body, like anything else in the dream, can be used as a tool for either ego or for Spirit. When you are doing things that are detrimental to your body through action or inaction, it's ego-based.

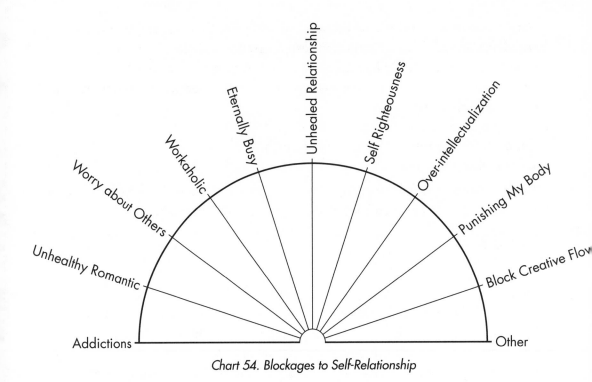

*Chart 54. Blockages to Self-Relationship*

## Dowsing Statements

With a left spin, say:

*I release all patterns associated with (___) from all aspects of my being, releasing attachment and reversing ill effects in all time frames and dimensions, healing all relationships implied. I joyfully give and receive love.*

With a right spin, say:

*I transmute this energy to pure radiant love, triggering full awareness of my true nature..*

## PROJECTING THE UNHEALED SELF

We, as extensions of God's love, must always create. It is what we do. When we are coming from a blocked awareness of this truth, our creations are called projections. When we are in full awareness of our Oneness with God, we create or extend love. Our creations (in other words, everything and everyone we see) always mirror back to us what we are giving. To give and to receive are one and the same thing.

Your projections always mirror back to you your internal sense of scarcity. This comes in the form of seeing a world that is suffering and perpetuating separation. When you extend love, you see mirrored back to you an internal peace or essence of God that you feel rather than see with your physical eyes. You are able to perceive, beyond physical appearance, an individual's true nature. This experience is beyond what words can convey.

This chart is designed simply to assist you in uncovering what relationship you are using to project unhealed Self-relationship issues. A clue to this is found in any judgment (regardless of how large or small it may seem) you have toward any individual or group. Again, the form that is being mirrored back is unimportant. It is the content that offers you a look within. For instance, you may have anger toward a religious organization for what seem to you to be misleading and controlling standards in their dogma. This doesn't necessarily mean that you are doing the exact same thing or have done it in previous lifetimes. It does mean that the feelings and emotions that are triggered in you are based on unhealed thoughts and issues within. See what feelings come up for you around this to see where you have not forgiven yourself or others for anything that evoked a similar reaction. Be open to letting go of the old beliefs that hold you prisoner.

## Spirit Guides and Angels

This seems to be the only category here that warrants explanation. You can become dependent on angels and other guides in the same way that you can become dependent on a partner for your happiness. Don't give your power away to anyone. Respect for anyone who has achieved higher understanding of truth is appropriate. Awe is not appropriate for any being other than our Creator. It implies hierarchical structures, which foster the belief in separation.

## Dowsing Statements

With a left spin, say:

> *I acknowledge and release (_____) from all projections of unhealed rela-*
> *tionship issues with my Self, healing this for both of us on every level of*
> *awareness for all time frames and dimensions.*

With a right spin, say:

*I see you as the Holy Spirit within myself. I know that you are free unless
I use you to imprison myself. In the name of the Holy Spirit, I release you
and we are both free.*

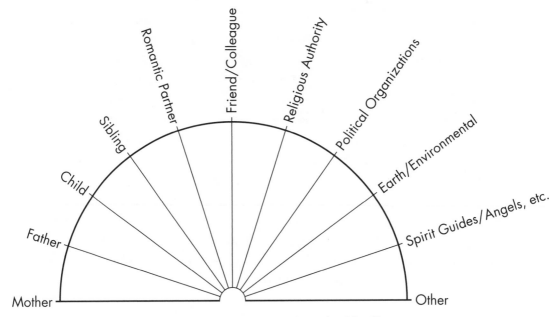

Chart 55. Projecting the Unheald Self

## VEILS OBSCURING OUR TRUE NATURE

This chart further explores unconscious distractions that blind us to our true
nature of love. Here we see core levels of fear, such as fear of the true Self. It
matters not where your mind chooses to release unhealthy patterns, since any
distractions are equal in their ability to hold you in the illusion. I will address
a few of these further.

### Fear of Scarcity

This stems from the fundamental lack that, in turn, stems from a mind that
believes itself to be separate. If you only address issues around abundance in

specific areas, you are missing the boat and your results will be partial. All of your fears around scarcity are founded in the belief that you are something other than your Truth. "Seek ye first the Kingdom of Heaven and all else will be given you." Your mind and your creations are one and the same. What have you created? How you choose to experience your creations in this moment determines what you create in the next.

## Past/Future Orientation

Whenever you are thinking about the past or worried about the future, you are, of course, not present. This type of orientation has become the human default program. Become more aware of *now* by paying attention to your thoughts, feelings, and emotions as often as you can. It takes practice

## Attachment to Time, Space, and Bodies

These are the enduring and pernicious of all illusions. Begin to pay more attention to how you are experiencing life. Your feelings and emotions are keys to detaching from a focus on form. This puts you in greater awareness of your Self, which leads you in the direction of awakening

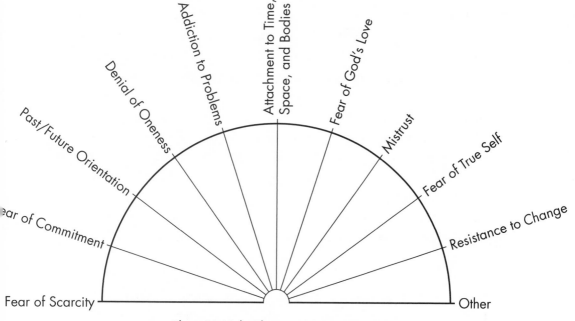

*Chart 56. Veils Obscuring Our True Nature*

### Fear of Divine Love

Once you remember fully the love of Creator through experience, the ego is history. Your conditioned mind is gravely afraid of disappearing and will throw in whatever it takes to keep you distracted from awareness of God's Love.

### Dowsing Statements

With a left spin, say:

> *I release the veils of (_____) that obscure my inherent nature of love, transmuting this energy to pure joy and freedom. I release all attachment I have to avoiding my true nature and forgive myself on all levels.*

With a right spin, say:

> *I awaken fully to my inherent nature of love, knowing that I am perfect, as God created me. I am eternally grateful for this truth.*

## EXPERIENCING THE SELF AS UNCONDITIONAL LOVE

This chart provides keys to accessing full awareness of Self-knowledge. Through imprinting corrected perceptions in your field, personal growth through Self-love is enhanced. You have conditioned yourself through the repetition of limiting feelings and thoughts. So it is through the repetition of corrected perceptions that you can change these beliefs. In truth, it takes but one instant when you are ready for it to know your Self fully. Correcting your misperceptions prepares you for this holy instant.

Each of the ideas on this chart is a high-vibrational statement that may ignite a greater sense of awareness in you. Although some of the statements seem very close in meaning, your mind will choose the words that represent exactly what is needed in the moment. Use this chart to help you move beyond limitation. Here are explanations for a few of the ideas.

### Giving is Receiving

In this case, "giving" refers to the act of creating and "receiving" refers to that which is mirrored back to you through your creations. You are always creating, since it is your very nature. You can, however, miscreate when you are coming from a place of perceived separation. Since everything is a mirror of your Self-relationship, your miscreations or projections will show you a world of lack and suffering. On the other hand, when you are coming from a place of One-Mindedness, everything you create will mirror back to you the love you are extending. Enhancing this understanding heightens True Vision and dissolves the illusion.

## I See You as the Divine Within Me

This statement acknowledges Oneness.

## True Forgiveness

This is always achieved through the assistance of the Holy Spirit within and focuses on the only level of cause, which is the belief in separation. In truth, there is nothing to forgive. Letting go of the importance we have placed on our judgments and values is an active practice of true forgiveness. (Refer to chapter 7 for more information on this.)

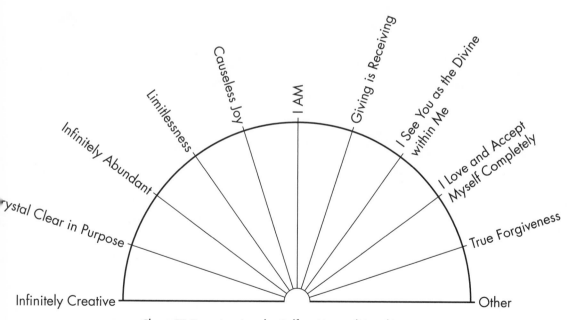

*Chart 57. Experiencing the Self as Unconditional Love*

## Dowsing Statements

With a right spin, say:

*I accept this corrected perception of (___) into all aspects of my being, expanding my awareness and allowing me to experience myself as unconditional love. Thank you.*

# CHAPTER 14

# Alignment with Highest Purpose

OUR HIGHEST PURPOSE IS ALWAYS TO AWAKEN to complete knowledge of our Oneness with Creator and all else. This is not an action, but a state of Being. When you say "I Am," you acknowledge this. There is no need to say anything else. Your highest function is true forgiveness, since this is what leads you to fulfilling your highest purpose.

Often when people speak of their "highest purpose," they are referring to a specific action that they are called to fulfill in this lifetime. We could call this action a "secondary purpose" in order to clearly distinguish it from the person's true highest purpose and function. This action (which may be in the form of a career choice, social contribution, or life passion) will often provide opportunities for us to practice our highest function and to align with our highest purpose.

Another way of looking at this is that we can often discover our greatest gifts through observing our greatest challenges in life. The mastery you develop in transcending difficulties throughout your lifetime enables you to forgo judgment and assist others through similar challenges. Ultimately, it is not what you are doing, but the purpose behind your doing it that counts. If you aspire primarily to know your Self and practice forgiveness where appropriate, there will be no confusion around what you need to "do" in life. You will know.

This chapter focuses on aligning with your highest purpose (state of Being) and allowing it to guide you in your secondary purpose (action) in life. As you embrace your unity with others, you naturally become more conscious of the highest good for all in your endeavors. The more you practice this level of thinking and interject gratitude into your daily life, the greater the gifts you will receive.

The final two charts in this book offer transformative statements designed to assist you in experiencing yourself as whole and perfect—as you were created. Corrected thoughts can lead you to the Truth. To know the Truth is to experience it.

## BLOCKAGES TO YOUR HIGHEST PURPOSE

As noted, we can say that the highest purpose for each of us is to recognize ourselves fully as One. Our highest function is the practice of true forgiveness, which fulfills our highest purpose. Our secondary purpose is the focused story or action we take in life to serve our spiritual growth and the highest good for all. This chart, as well as all others in this chapter, will help to release any blockages and to enhance the synchronistic flow of these three aspects of your spiritual awakening. Chart 59 is designed to release blockages.

Here are a few explanations of issues not mentioned in previous charts.

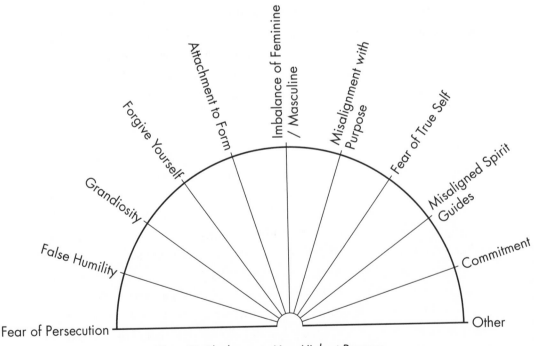

*Chart 58. Blockages to Your Highest Purpose*

Advanced Spiritual Dowsing

## Attachment to Form

This refers to misdirected priorities. If you snag your attention on what you are supposed to be "doing here," rather than placing your primary focus on your state of Being, you will be incongruent in your purpose and your efforts will bear unstable results. Creating the right foundation is always the determining factor in a strong structure.

## Fear of True Self

This is the same as a fear of God's love. Make no mistake about it; this is the core of all fear.

## Imbalanced Feminine/Masculine

When your feminine aspect is imbalanced, so is your masculine aspect. Your ability to be inspired and then creatively express the inspiration relies on this balance. The feminine/masculine relationship is moving into the perfect state of balance or marriage in every aspect of Creation now. The illusion is holographic and, as all patterns are repeated endlessly, even the smallest aspect of Creation carries the whole of these patterns within it. As each of us comes into a state of perfect marriage within ourselves, we see this pattern represented as well in the progressing alignment of our Sun (masculine) with the center of our galaxy (feminine).

The preparation for this new birthing of unity consciousness is already in progress. This collective awakening will allow the fulfillment of the sacred marriage of masculine and feminine. This shift in consciousness will birth us into the Golden Age, where we will express ourselves as One Mind in God's creation. Ultimately, this awakening within the dream will lead us finally home to God, which is beyond form.

## Dowsing Statements

With a left spin, say:

*I release all patterns around (____) from every aspect of my being, releasing attachment and reversing ill effects in all time frames and dimensions. Through the Holy Spirit, all relationships implied by these patterns are healed with forgiveness. I align myself with love as my highest purpose.*

# GATEWAY TO YOUR HIGHER PURPOSE

We go through gateways to move from one location to another. So it is with the choices on this chart. They are options to assist you in your movement into full alignment with all aspects of your higher purpose and function in this lifetime. Use the following descriptions to help you understand, while using your own insights to guide you.

## Hear the Voice of God Within

This is similar to being receptive to divine guidance. This choice is calling you to allow for silence, for stillness of mind, so that you are able to hear the loving voice inside that is what we call the Holy Spirit. When you feel a sense of deep peace growing within and you have a "knowing" without any question in your mind of what to do next, you are hearing God's voice within.

## Align with the Planet/Star System of Origin

This connection may offer you a sense of support and belonging (see Chart 52). Aspects of your experiences within the dream can serve as tools to help you

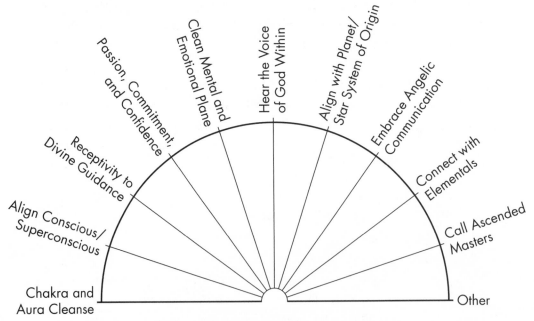

Chart 59. Gateway to Your Highest Purpose

awaken if they assist you in feeling more whole and connected. The key, again, is not to get caught up in or attached to any experience. Allow experiences to direct you toward unification—the feeling of peace is a good clue that you are moving in the right direction. Flow through the experience and do not place importance on the form.

## Call Ascended Masters

This choice is bringing to your attention the benefit of connecting with certain Ascended Masters. One good source of further information on these beings who have achieved full awakening within their lifetimes is Doreen Virtue's card deck *Ascended Masters*, Hay House 2007. She also has extensive published information in books and cards on beings in other realms of consciousness, like our angelic friends.

## Clean Chakras and Aura; Clean Mental and Emotional Planes

Either of these choices is calling for a clearing of energetic patterns on these levels.

## Dowsing Statements

With a left spin, say:

> *I clean my (chakras and aura, mental and emotional planes) of all limiting beliefs and non-beneficial patterns that are creating blockages to my full alignment with higher purpose. I transmute these patterns to pure love energy and use them to open, optimize, and balance these aspects of myself.*

With a right spin, say:

> *I broadcast into all aspects of my being the vibration of (_____), accepting all benefits of this integration and enhancing my receptivity to divine inspiration. I align myself completely to my highest purpose.*

# KNOWING YOUR SELF AS INFINITE LOVE

These charts are composed of ideas from *A Course in Miracles*. Some of them are lessons from the *Course's* workbook. All of them are designed to assist you in experiencing yourself as love, which is your eternal nature.

Much of the material covered in this dowsing book is based on *A Course in Miracles*, which is a non-dualistic teaching for the Western world. It is by no means the only non-dualistic teaching out there, but it is a very effective path for those who are drawn to it. It is a self-study program and there are no parameters on how long it should take each student. David and I have worked with the *Course* for a good number of years now, and we both agree that this teaching has changed our lives profoundly by altering the way we experience life.

You can measure how well a particular path is serving you by noticing how much peace grows within you. When following the right path, you begin to see the world differently. Ultimately, you find that nothing and no one in this world needs to change. It is only your perception of the world that needs correction. Once this occurs, you will notice the miracles that are happening all the time, and you will see the world and those around you through loving eyes. It is this corrected vision that allows others to become the love that is their truth. Make a choice to release yourself and all others from the imprisonment of your perception. Choose love; choose peace with daily diligence. Savor the miracle of each moment and practice forgiveness when love is not apparent to you.

Dowsing, like everything else we do in this world, is called "magic" in *A Course in Miracles*. There are no varying levels of illusion. You are either experiencing Oneness or you are entertaining illusory thoughts. Whether you are doing energy work or psychotherapy, practicing medicine, or whatever else in the moment, any shifts or changes that occur are simply moving energy around or changing your experience at that time. This, in itself, is not truly healing or awakening. A miracle is a change in perception from experiencing yourself as separate to knowing your true Self.

So why do we bother dowsing or doing anything else to relieve suffering? Do not get caught up in "level confusion." We are still in bodies living in the illusion of time and space. Everything we do in this world is part of the dream of separation. However, while we are here, we can use all of the tools we have for the purpose of the Holy Spirit and to prepare us for our homecoming. When we assist one another in achieving more peace and less stress, we are able to share glimpses of what our true nature is—One Mind in God's creative flow.

Any time you join another in a purpose that leads you to unity, you are correcting your misperceptions about separation. Although this does not take you "all the way home," it leads you in the right direction. Healing only occurs with a change in perception and through the application of true forgiveness. Since you are not capable of forgiving at this level with your conscious mind, you must surrender the final outcome to the Holy Spirit, which is the Divine Messenger; the Voice of God within you.

So help in whatever way is most appropriate at the time to relieve suffering and stress. But don't stop there. In order for miracles to occur, you must always take the final step. How do you take this final step in resolving a situation?

Know that there is only one problem, which is the ego—in other words, the belief in separation. All suffering stems from this fear-based foundation. There is only one solution, which is the Truth and divine love of the Creator.

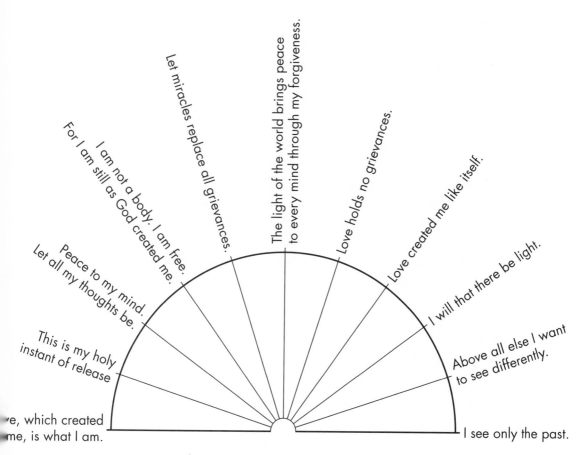

*Chart 60. Awakening to the Love Within*

First, realize that your thoughts (all of them) are meaningless, since they are based on the past and your belief in separation. Consciousness can be seen as the collective mind that initiated the dream, and thoughts are all projected from this one mind, which believes itself to be separate from God. Therefore, no thoughts are neutral.

Recognize that you need not rescue, save, or change anyone. Whenever you feel the need to do this, it is your ego making the illusion real. Become more aware of your interactions. Listen to others by putting aside your own opinions and thoughts as they arise, thus allowing you to be more fully present. When you really listen to someone, you allow them the space in which to unfold the answers to their problems. Each of us has all the answers we ever need. Often, you simply need to join with another to unfold your story and let go of it.

Always ask for guidance from the Holy Spirit, which represents that part of your mind that holds Truth within it, and that sees the Truth that truly forgives. Simply say: "I choose the peace of God."

> *As you do that and let go, the Holy Spirit shall bring you, truly, a new perception, a true perception; the vision of your brother (or sister) which is the Vision of Christ . . . You will first perceive, then believe, then experience in one great moment of joy and ecstasy, the truth of what your brother (or sister) is—which is the perfect, untarnished, joyful, free and Beloved Son (and Daughter) of God . . . In that same instance shall come welling up within your being the awareness and the experience that that, in all its beauty, is exactly what you are, and what you have ALWAYS been . . . " (Brent Haskell, The Other Voice)*

## Dowsing Statements

With a right spin, say:

> *I receive the vibration of this statement, (_____), on all levels of my being for the highest good of all. I joyfully awaken to the truth of our Oneness. As I surrender the outcome of this session to the Holy Spirit, I allow for miracles to flow freely in my life and the lives of all others. Thank you.*

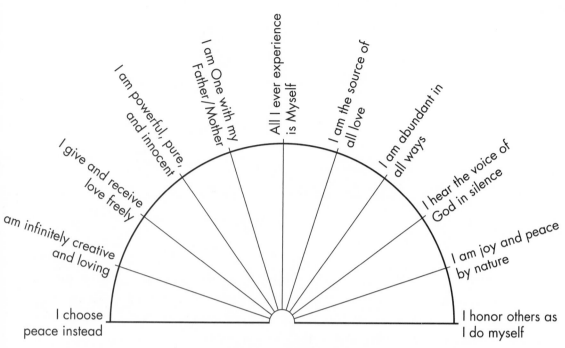

Chart 61. Knowing Your Self as Infinite Love.

# APPENDIX

# Making Your Own Charts

BY NOW, YOU HAVE HAD A TASTE of the wide variety of topics that can be charted and dowsed. Our intent is for you take this method and make it your own—run with it and see where it can take you! One way you can personalize your dowsing practice is to start making your own charts. Blanks are provided for you below. Any topic or subject that can be itemized is a candidate for a new chart. Simplify the things and decisions you do every day by charting them. As you collect your personal set of charts, you may even evolve them into a book. That's what we did!

When we are faced with a whole list of tasks and only one day to get them done, we reduce stress considerably by making a quick chart of the day's options, asking how many are truly priorities for that day, and dowsing to identify them. Usually, a list of a dozen demands becomes two or three tasks that are easily done in the time available. Of course, the use of your hand chart gives you a readily available Chart of Ten or Balance Chart to address practically any situation as it arises.

Whenever you are embarking on a new venture, business idea, relationship, or other involvement with people or groups, it is always a good idea to dowse the overall integrity, business integrity, honesty, or truthfulness of the person or situation. This can save a lot of grief down the road.

The charts below are copyrighted. You may, however, copy and use them for your own personal use or study. We simply ask that you do not reproduce them for profit.

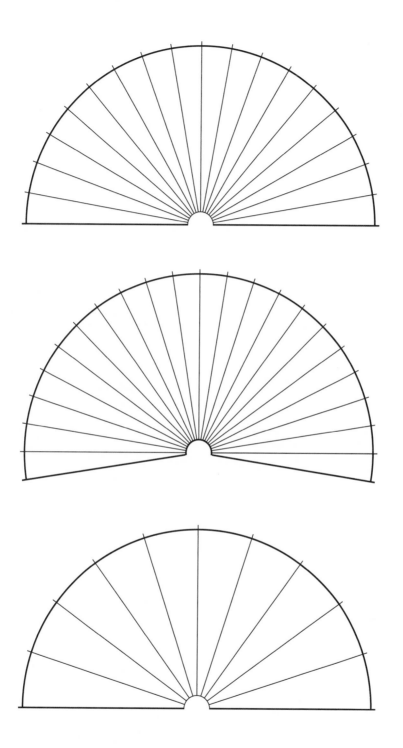

Making Your Own Charts

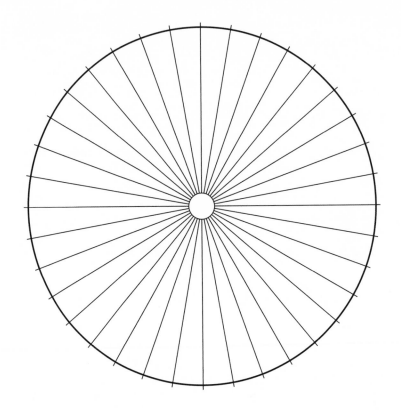

Making Your Own Charts

# ABOUT THE AUTHORS

**David Ian Cowan** is a licensed Spiritual Health Coach who lives in Boulder, Colorado with his wife and co-author for this book, **Erina Cowan**. Dave has morphed from a professional musician, counselor, alternative health practitioner, and biofeedback trainer into an author of and speaker on modern Spirituality. Erina's career path led from years practicing as a P.A. in Functional Medicine to working in Energy Medicine and Quantum Biofeedback. Eventually she became an international trainer and educator in this area.

Together, the Cowans created *Blue Sun Energetics* in order to share some of the things you have read here, and in Dave's book *Navigating the Collapse of Time*, through classes, webinars, and other publications, and to introduce cutting edge futuristic technologies. Currently, they offer classes in Spiritual Communication and Relationship Healing, and a certification program in Spiritual Dowsing. Their courses are designed to empower, enliven and enrich lives. Our teachings are founded on the non-dualistic principles presented in "A Course in Miracles."

David and Erina invite your questions and comments, and also invite you to sign up for the newsletter on the website to stay updated on events, products, and other writings on topics of timely esoteric interest.

For more information or to email the author, please contact him at *info@bluesunenergetics.net* or visit the website at *www.bluesunenergetics.net*.

# TO OUR READERS

Weiser Books, an imprint of Red Wheel/Weiser, publishes books across the entire spectrum of occult, esoteric, speculative, and New Age subjects. Our mission is to publish quality books that will make a difference in people's lives without advocating any one particular path or field of study. We value the integrity, originality, and depth of knowledge of our authors.

Our readers are our most important resource, and we appreciate your input, suggestions, and ideas about what you would like to see published.

Visit our website *www.redwheelweiser.com*, where you can learn about our upcoming books and free downloads, and be sure to go to *www.redwheelweiser .com/newsletter/* to sign up for newsletters and exclusive offers.

You can also contact us at info@redwheelweiser.com or at

Red Wheel/Weiser, LLC
665 Third Street, Suite 400
San Francisco, CA 94107